T0368344

Thought of the Day

A One Year Devotional

MARTY PRESSEY

WESTBOW
PRESS®
A DIVISION OF THOMAS NELSON
& ZONDERVAN

WestBow Press books may be ordered through booksellers or by contacting:

WestBow Press
A Division of Thomas Nelson & Zondervan
1663 Liberty Drive
Bloomington, IN 47403
www.westbowpress.com
1 (866) 928-1240

Scripture quotations taken from The Holy Bible, New International Version® NIV® Copyright © 1973 1978 1984 2011 by Biblica, Inc. TM. Used by permission. All rights reserved worldwide.

ISBN: 978-1-9736-8181-6 (sc)
ISBN: 978-1-9736-8183-0 (hc)
ISBN: 978-1-9736-8182-3 (e)

Library of Congress Control Number: 2019920196

Print information available on the last page.

WestBow Press rev. date: 12/13/2019

Dedicated to my Mom, who taught me about God
and took me to church when I was young.

Introduction

This devotional is designed to provide you, the reader, with a thought to ponder as you go through your day. You will find various topics in random order as it is my belief that we do not simply encounter the same topic or issue just once, but we wrestle with the same issue at various times throughout the year. Therefore, it is good to have the same topic referenced at various times.

You will find that each days' thought contains a Scripture reference, includes questions, typically a reference to how the world thinks, and how we should think based on the Scripture. This style helps each of us relate to the thought and put it into action.

It is my hope that you read the days' devotional in the morning so you start your day with a Scripture reading and a thought you can take with you. As you ponder the thought for each day, it is hoped that you will find your life change for the better. The accumulation of change over the course of a year can be enormous. Make it a positive change.

May God bless each one of you.

January

January 1

"I am the Alpha and the Omega," says the Lord
God, "who is, and who was, and who is to come, the
Almighty."

— Revelation 1:8

How many people do you run into each day that either believe God
is dead or simply choose to ignore Him? I know many of us may
primarily interact with other Christians. However, there are many
of us who are out in the work force, in schools, or out amongst the
community and encounter several people each day that would fall into
one of these two categories.

Perhaps you believe God is non-existent, or you ignore Him.
Perhaps you just wish He would go away. I'm here to proclaim to you
that He is not going away, He is not dead, but He is very much alive
and active in this world. You can ignore Him. Or you can accept the
truth.

I'm sure many of you would be in absolute fear of standing before a
judge in a courtroom. I'm sure most of you would be fearful if you were
sentenced to a maximum-security prison with the worst of murderers,
rapists, child molesters, thieves, and so on. So why would you not have
a healthy fear of the Ultimate Judge, God, who will decide where you
will spend eternity?

Sometimes we need to be scared straight, as the old saying goes.
Sometimes we need to see arms opened wide when we return home.
We should look at God with both of these images in mind. His arms
are opened wide, waiting for you to return home.

January 2

As Jesus went on from there, two blind men followed him, calling out, "Have mercy on us, Son of David!" When he had gone indoors, the blind men came to him, and he asked them, "Do you believe that I am able to do this?"

"Yes, Lord," they replied.

Then he touched their eyes and said, "According to your faith let it be done to you"; and their sight was restored.

— Matthew 9:27–30a

Do we believe God will help us? I'm sure some, perhaps many, of us will remember the saying "God helps those who help themselves." There is truth in the statement that God will help us when we are helping ourselves. Of course that doesn't mean He deserts us when we fall flat and are ready to give up.

Here's the real crux of the issue ... it's not really a question of whether God will help us, it's a question of our belief. Do we really believe He will? Do we have faith in Him? Or are we trying to do it all on our own and failing miserably? Are we ignoring God altogether and just flailing, living in chaos with no direction in our lives?

Won't you reach out to God? Won't you decide to put your belief, your full faith, in Him? That doesn't mean you stop doing things yourself, but it does mean you seek His guidance and His direction and His help in your life. I pray we all make the positive decision to put our faith in God and reach out to Him for our help.

January 3

I can do all this through him who gives me strength.
— Philippians 4:13

Are you feeling overwhelmed? Do you wonder if you will ever get your head above water again? Are you currently in a situation that you can't see a way of getting over, around, or through? How is your faith? Do you have full confidence that God will get you through it?

It's when we are at the end of our rope that we recognize we need God. It's not that we don't need Him every moment of every day, but we just don't admit it. We believe we are in control until things fall apart. If we don't have at least some bit of faith before we fall into the pit, we likely won't find it there. Why? Without some inkling of faith, we don't even know to look up. Can God provide for us anyway? Absolutely!

The point is, we need to build our trust in God and increase our faith throughout our lives. In doing so, we will be stronger, meaning we will lean more heavily on God when the storms hit. Some will incorrectly interpret today's Scripture to mean you can be or do anything *you* want as long as you ask God. It doesn't. It means that in any situation God will carry you through it to accomplish His plan for you.

So trust in God, lean on Him daily, learn about Him daily, and know that He has a plan for you. Commit yourself to His plan and you will achieve more than you can imagine and do things you can't even dream of today.

January 4

"This is my command: Love each other."

— John 15:17

Do you show your Christian love? I'm sure most, if not all, of us have had someone say, "I love you" and not really mean it. Perhaps it was a smirky remark from a classmate or co-worker. Perhaps it was an ugly remark from someone in a long line of people or while in traffic. Maybe you've even said it yourself.

But we are called to show our Christian love to the world. This is not merely saying "I love you" to someone. It means showing love through actions. For you English majors, it's an action verb, not a noun, that labels something. You must act, you must demonstrate, you must be a positive, loving example to others.

Jesus commanded us to love one another. He didn't say to do so when it was convenient. He didn't say to do so when you felt like it. He didn't say to speak the words but not do anything. His life was the perfect example of love for us. We are to emulate Him—be a person who loves others and who demonstrates it through our actions.

I pray we all obey His command and take on the actions of demonstrating love to one another. We have a responsibility to love as Jesus did. Will you take up the challenge and responsibility to obey Jesus and become a loving person, someone who shows His love to the world?

January 5

It is for freedom that Christ has set us free. Stand
firm, then, and do not let yourselves be burdened
again by a yoke of slavery.

— Galatians 5:1

Are you guilty? Are you guilty of living in the freedom provided for
you through Christ? Not the freedom to do whatever you want, but
the freedom to do what is right. It is the freedom to be the light to
others. What does this freedom look like?

When we demonstrate our freedom in Christ, we show compassion,
mercy, love, caring, joy, responsibility, peace, humbleness, courage,
patience, gentleness, kindness, and the light of Christ. In other words,
we are the positive examples to those we encounter rather than being
negative.

Our freedom in Christ frees us from the fear and anxiety of this
world. It frees us from the worries so many are entangled in. Does that
mean we don't have needs? No! We have needs and we have wants.
However, our freedom means we believe God will provide for our
needs. He will deliver what we need, and sometimes, that will come
at exactly the moment we need it.

I invite you to experience your freedom in Christ. I invite you to
have the faith that He will provide. I invite you to lose your fears and
gain your freedom from slavery. Christ is the answer! I know this from
first-hand experience. I pray you will accept it and experience it too.

January 6

And we know that in all things God works for the good of those who love him, who have been called according to his purpose. For those God foreknew he also predestined to be conformed to the image of his Son, that he might be the firstborn among many brothers and sisters. And those he predestined, he also called; those he called, he also justified; those he justified, he also glorified.

— Romans 8:28–30

Are you answering the call? Do you know God is calling you each and every day? He has put a task on your to-do list. His plan is to strengthen you, build you up, and prepare you for a future task. He has a plan for you.

Each of us has a purpose. Each of us has a task to perform. Each one of us are a part of God's larger plan. That plan is to redeem the world. What part are you to play? God puts a task in front of us each day. We simply need to listen, look, and recognize the task to accomplish it.

We may not know how to take on that task or how we might accomplish it. That's okay. That is when we need to ask God for His guidance. When we are weak, God reveals His strength in us. When we are at a loss as to how to complete the task, God steps in and helps us. That is Him teaching us to rely on Him.

Are you answering the call? I pray each of us answers His call each and every day. That is how we grow and how we have a positive impact on this world.

January 7

So in Christ Jesus you are all children of God through
faith, for all of you who were baptized into Christ
have clothed yourselves with Christ. There is neither
Jew nor Gentile, neither slave nor free, nor is there
male and female, for you are all one in Christ Jesus.
If you belong to Christ, then you are Abraham's seed,
and heirs according to the promise.

— Galatians 3:26–29

Are you accepting? Will you accept those who are different into your
worship? Or will you be judgmental and shun them? Will you be like
Christ, or will you be like the world?

Many of us fool ourselves into thinking we are accepting of
others. Unfortunately, when that prostitute or drug addict or thief
or murderer shows up, we turn our heads away and ignore them. We
hope they leave and don't come back. We don't want to be in the same
building as them—let alone associate with and welcome them.

We aren't faced with those types of situations at every worship
service, but we do worship with people of differing views. Don't you
think that there were differing views among the apostles? They were
fishermen, a tax collector, a treasurer, and a thief and betrayer. Paul
was a Pharisee, torturer of Christ followers, law follower, extremely
well educated yet deceived, but ultimately, he was changed by Jesus.

I pray we are accepting of those who are different. Jesus accepted
people of all walks of life. Let's decide to follow His example!

January 8

Make every effort to keep the unity of the Spirit through the bond of peace. There is one body and one Spirit, just as you were called to one hope when you were called; one Lord, one faith, one baptism; one God and Father of all, who is over all and through all and in all.

— Ephesians 4:3–6

Unity. Unity? Unity! Do you pursue unity, or do you allow the divisiveness of this world to influence you? Do you understand what unity is? Jesus says we are to be perfected in unity (John 17:23), meaning of one mind and one spirit. We need unity, not division.

Christ commanded us to love God and love others. If we demonstrate through thought and actions that we love each other in Christ, we will be unified. Unfortunately, I've seen divisions over the insignificant personal preferences, causing us to deny the love of God.

We are to be unified in the Spirit. We are to be unified by the love of Christ. When we are unified in Christ, truly unified, we can withstand anything. Since Satan prowls around like a roaring lion (1 Peter 5:8), we need to be unified to withstand his attacks. If we are not unified, Satan will pick us off one by one.

I pray we all will decide to love each other in Christ and pursue unity of Spirit. Pray that Christ fills us with His Spirit. Pray that we demonstrate His love to each other. Pray that we are all unified in Him.

January 9

You were taught, with regard to your former way of
life, to put off your old self, which is being corrupted
by its deceitful desires; to be made new in the attitude
of your minds; and to put on the new self, created to
be like God in true righteousness and holiness.
— Ephesians 4:22–24

Do you need a redo? Perhaps you've taken a look in the mirror and
decided you are not very accepting of others. Perhaps you've railed
against other people. If these or other mirror reflections have caused
you to decide you need to start over, then restart today.

Each of us has the option every morning to follow Christ and
pursue becoming more like Him, or follow the world and be corrupted.
Will we be perfect in our pursuit? No. Can we decide each day to
continue the pursuit? Yes. We are damaged goods, every one of us.

God has forgiven us through Christ. We are now free to follow
Him in all that we do. We are free to renew our minds (Rom. 12:2) in
Christ. We can leave the worldly ways behind and pursue the spiritual
ways. We live in this world but we aren't of this world (John 15:19). We
are followers of Christ and free to rise above the dirtiness, nastiness,
hatefulness, vengefulness, and sinfulness of this world.

I pray each of us determine to renew our commitment to Christ.
You just might be the brightness a brother or sister needs today to
continue their pursuit of perfection. Be there for each other.

January 10

Do not conform to the pattern of this world, but be transformed by the renewing of your mind. Then you will be able to test and approve what God's will is—his good, pleasing and perfect will.

— Romans 12:2

Are you taking care of yourself? The real question is, are you taking care of your relationship with God? Are you searching out His will for your life? Are you studying His word? Are you praying at least daily? Are you earnestly seeking to know Christ even better than you know your brother or sister?

We need to take care of ourselves in this manner. Too often we are distracted by worldly wants and desires. We have a list of TV shows we want to watch that is longer than our arm. We want to go out to a party, the movies, shopping, and so much more. None of these are bad in and of themselves.

Folks, if we are so busy that we can't or won't take time to read and study God's word, can we really blame God if He isn't answering our prayers the way we want? I'm not saying God will give us what we want so long as we do what He wants. What I am saying is, put yourself in God's position. Will you reward someone who isn't doing what they should? Why do you expect God to?

I pray each of us decides to spend quiet time with God and pursue a close relationship with Him through reading and studying His word. Make that decision today.

January 11

Each of you should use whatever gift you have
received to serve others, as faithful stewards of God's
grace in its various forms.

—1 Peter 4:10

Are you a servant? Do you serve others? When we are in a good relationship with Christ we become a servant, just as He was. We recognize the needs of others and provide for them. Can we serve all? No. Can we serve those around us? Yes. Does this mean we give them everything they want? No.

The servant Christ wants us to be is one who provides for the needs of others. Provide for their physical needs, such as food, water, shelter, and clothing. Provide for their emotional needs, such as love, appreciation, acceptance, joy, and peace. Provide for their spiritual needs, such as teaching the Word of God, proclaiming Christ, helping them to understand the meaning of Scripture, and providing them guidance in their walk with Christ.

Physical, emotional, and spiritual needs. We all have them. We all need them filled. We are to serve one another. If we desire to become like Christ, to have a deep relationship with Him, we must determine to become servants.

I pray each of us decide we will be servants and provide for the needs of others. Decide to serve today.

January 12

Then Jesus came to them and said, "All authority in heaven and on earth has been given to me. Therefore go and make disciples of all nations, baptizing them in the name of the Father and of the Son and of the Holy Spirit, and teaching them to obey everything I have commanded you. And surely I am with you always, to the very end of the age."

— Matthew 28:18–20

Servant leadership. We hear this term a lot in our churches and, now, even in our workplaces. Some who are less experienced may not have heard this expression. Some may have heard it and not understood it. Servant leadership is extremely relevant in our Christian walk and is also key to our working careers.

Servant leadership is not the same as leading by example. Being a servant leader is an attitude demonstrated through actions. This attitude puts others ahead of self. It means really deep-down caring for people and demonstrating it through our actions.

Do you consider Jesus a servant leader? I would argue He was the perfect servant leader. As He states in Matthew 20:28, He came to serve, not be served. He is our perfect model. He taught His disciples the true meaning of God's Word.

I pray each of us would study the servant leadership of Jesus and follow His example. Doing so will not only better other people's lives, but each of us will see improvement in our own lives.

Marty Pressey

January 13

Now this is eternal life: that they know you, the only
true God, and Jesus Christ, whom you have sent.

— John 17:3

Will you rise up? Will you rise up to heaven and spend eternity with
God. Will you? Do you know? We should all be assured of our eternal
home.

I dedicate todays thought to my neighbor, friend, and classmate
from high school, Rusty. He battled stage 4 liver cancer. Thinking of
him this morning caused me to think of a question so many ask. Rusty,
your acceptance of Jesus Christ as your Savior guarantees that you
and I will see each other for eternity. How wonderful is that?!

For all of us, we really should be assured of where we will spend
eternity. There are only two places to choose from. And here's the
kicker, we get to choose! If we choose to accept Jesus as our Lord
and Savior, we get to spend eternity with Him and everyone else who
has followed Him. I want to caution you, though. Jesus demands we
follow Him. That means continuing to study, learn, grow, and follow
in His footsteps.

I pray we live each day worshiping God, being kind to one another,
serving one another, and growing in Jesus. I pray each of us examine
ourselves, commit to following Jesus every day, and be confident in
knowing we have an eternal home with Him. Commit to Jesus today.

January 14

Answer me quickly, LORD;
my spirit fails.
Do not hide your face from me
or I will be like those who go down to the pit.
Let the morning bring me word of your unfailing
love,
for I have put my trust in you.
Show me the way I should go,
for to you I entrust my life.

— Psalm 143:7–8

What do you do on cloudy days? What do you do when you are down in the dumps? What do you do when things don't go your way? What do you do when it seems the world is against you?

When we are having a cloudy day we need to reach out to God. We need to pray. We need to tell God what we are wrestling with. We need to ask Him to give us strength, courage, understanding, and comfort. We need to believe, have faith, and trust in God to deliver.

So many of us try to rely on our own strength or our own wisdom. When we do that, we fall prey to Satan and his evil desires. He doesn't want us to reach out to God. Yet we need to for ourselves and for those we love. When we try to do it all on our own, we not only hurt our self, but we hurt those around us as well.

I pray each of us reach out to God not only on cloudy days, but every day. We need Him far more than we are willing to admit. When we start relying on Him, we will notice things get better. Reach out to God today.

January 15

I tell you that in the same way there will be more
rejoicing in heaven over one sinner who repents than
over ninety-nine righteous persons who do not need
to repent.

— Luke 15:7

Do you hear the bells ringing? It has been said that every time a bell
rings an angel gets its wings. I don't believe there are angels without
wings.

All of heaven rejoices when a sinner comes to Christ. Yes, all
people are God's children, but not all are followers of Christ. Imagine
your own children. What if one goes off to a life of crime? What if that
child repents? Repenting means to not only confessing, but turning
away from the wrongdoing. Now that your child has turned away
from a life of crime and becomes a productive person again, would
you not rejoice?

All of heaven rejoices when a wayward soul comes home. You see
it in the parable of the prodigal son (Luke 15:11–32). God forgives
our sins. He allows us to return to a right relationship with Him. He
welcomes us with open arms. Why? Because each of us is His child,
whether we obey Him or not. But He requires obedience, submission
to Him, and a change of heart to be rewarded with eternal life in
heaven.

I pray each of us will fill our hearts with Christ. I pray each of
us rejoice along with heaven when a sinner returns home. After all,
heaven rejoiced for each of us when we returned to our true calling
to follow Christ.

January 16

"I have told you these things, so that in me you may have peace. In this world you will have trouble. But take heart! I have overcome the world."

—John 16:33

Do you have a safe place to go? No, I'm not talking about tornadoes, hurricanes, or earthquakes. I'm talking about those times of personal struggle or troubles such as financial struggles, relationship issues, getting fired from your job, or health problems. We all need a safe harbor when those storms roll in.

We need a place where we will be comforted, strengthened, and find peace in the middle of the storm. We need to find this place before the storm comes. All good sailors know the routes they sail. They look at the map, find the places of safe harbor in the event a storm brew's up. They track their course and know where the nearest safe harbor is. We need to apply that to our lives.

So go, find a safe harbor. Perhaps it's an inner room for prayer (Matthew 6:6). Perhaps it's sitting on your back porch. Perhaps it's down by the lake. Wherever it is, we all need a quiet place to spend time with God. While we are in that quiet place, we need to tell God our troubles and listen for Him to guide us.

I pray each of us finds that safe place, safe harbor to spend time with God. It will become a special place for us, a place where we are covered with the peace of God.

January 17

"My prayer is not for them alone. I pray also for those who will believe in me through their message, that all of them may be one, Father, just as you are in me and I am in you. May they also be in us so that the world may believe that you have sent me."

— John 17:20–21

Where do you live? I'm not asking for your home address. The question is about your mental and spiritual life. Do you live in this world's fears, worries, and desires? Or do you live in Christ? We all have the choice to live in Christ or live as the world does.

The world would have us worry about so many different things; buying new clothes, a new car, a new house, going out to eat, to the movies, to concerts, and so much more. The world would also have us be in fear; of murderers, of kidnappers, of car accidents. We don't have to fall prey to those.

When we live in Christ, our faith keeps us from worrying about those things, it keeps us from living in fear. So what if we don't get the new car? So what if we are killed? What!?! If we are in Christ, we know where we will be in the next moment. Only joy, peace, love, and glory. I'm not advocating looking for death, but we should not fear it either.

I pray each of us come to live in Christ. It is the only place we can live and have the joy, peace, love, and abundant life He promised us. When we live in Him, He lives in us. What a wonderful thing!

January 18

"How can you say to your brother, 'Let me take the speck out of your eye,' when all the time there is a plank in your own eye? You hypocrite, first take the plank out of your own eye, and then you will see clearly to remove the speck from your brother's eye."
— Matthew 7:3–5

Are you a hypocrite? I'm sure some of you are offended by that question. I think it's a fair question that each of us should ask ourselves each and every day. "Am I being a hypocrite today?"

Maybe some are unsure what the meaning of hypocrite is. It originates from the Greek word that described a stage actor. In other words, it means one who play acts at being something different than they really are. Do we ever pretend we are something we are not? I'm sure we all have at some point in our lives.

Should we be hypocrites? No. What we should do is pursue true positive change in our lives. Be the one who says no to drugs. Be the one who says no to doing something illegal or immoral. Be the one who stands up for what's right. But it needs to be who we are from the inside out. Don't be the person who fakes being nice and proper. Be the person who *is* nice and proper.

I pray each of us will pursue Christ genuinely, with our whole heart. If we do, we will be changed for the better, for all time. We will see Him move in our lives in ways we could never imagine.

Marty Pressey

January 19

See to it, brothers and sisters, that none of you has
a sinful, unbelieving heart that turns away from the
living God. But encourage one another daily, as long
as it is called "Today," so that none of you may be
hardened by sin's deceitfulness.

— Hebrews 3:12–13

What do you do when you stumble? We all stumble in our lives.
None of us are perfect by our own actions. We all need the mercy
and grace of God to be made perfect. Since we are all in the same
situation, should we not help each other become better through love
and encouragement?

If we were perfect, we would not need Jesus Christ. If we were
perfect, we could earn our way into heaven. If we were perfect, we
would do no wrong, doing everything perfectly in accordance with
God's will. Unfortunately, we are not perfect.

We are all made perfect in Christ. This is not something to be
proud of, but something that should humble us. We show our gratitude
for Christ's sacrifice by living in Him. We demonstrate Christ through
our love toward others, being kind, patient, gracious, encouraging,
supportive, and teaching them about our wonderful Savior.

I pray each of us realize that we are perfect in Christ, not of our
own doing. The most we can say is that we made the right choice.
Praise be to God that we did! Commit to helping others make the
right choice, too.

January 20

As soon as all the people saw Jesus, they were
overwhelmed with wonder and ran to greet him.
— Mark 9:15

Are you in awe? Many of us are amazed when we see celebrities,
whether they be actors, sports stars, or politicians. There is something
in us that is surprised, overwhelmed, joyous, and sometimes weak in
our knees when we meet someone famous. But are we in awe of God?

There is nothing inherently wrong in being excited when we meet
famous people. There is something very wrong when we are more
excited to meet them than to meet God. It becomes idol worship.
What can that idol do for you? Can they save you for all eternity? Are
they going to give you a million dollars? Are they even going to notice
that you are there?

These can be harsh truths, especially to those who are young.
Yet we all need to learn to make the best choices based on our faith in
Christ. He will grant us eternal life in heaven. He will grant us love,
joy, and peace here on this earth. He will be with us through all those
tough times. He will never leave us. Isn't that someone we want to be
with and should be in awe of?

I pray we are all in awe of God. He is so much bigger and more
amazing than we think. Come to Christ in amazement and accept
His wonderful gift.

January 21

Do not be anxious about anything, but in every
situation, by prayer and petition, with thanksgiving,
present your requests to God. And the peace of God,
which transcends all understanding, will guard your
hearts and your minds in Christ Jesus.

— Philippians 4:6–7

What do you do when you are anxious? So many of us are anxious
about so many things. It could be we don't like being alone. We might
be anxious about paying the bills. Maybe we're anxious or worried
about a sick loved one. We are anxious about far too many things.

First, I will not pretend it is easy to reduce or eliminate our
anxiousness. I know it is hard and it takes a lot of trust in God. If we
brush off our anxious feelings without God, we are foolish. God is the
One who can fully remove our anxiousness.

To start down this path, we first must trust God in small things. As
we experience His grace, we will see Him removing our anxiousness
about the small things we've trusted Him with. As we experience this,
we can then trust Him with bigger things. Eventually, we get to the
point of trusting Him in all situations and all our worries and anxious
moments. When this happens, we experience the true peace of God.

I pray we all start trusting God more and more. If you don't trust
Him, start by trusting Him with the small things. Experience Him
taking control. Then trust Him with it all.

January 22

"I have told you these things, so that in me you may have peace. In this world you will have trouble. But take heart! I have overcome the world."

—John 16:33

Are you overcoming the obstacles, mountains, and valleys in your life? Some may be earning a degree while going to school at night. Some may be looking for a better job. Some may be battling one or more illnesses. Doesn't it just seem like the world is against you sometimes? Well, it is. So, how do you overcome it?

The world is filled with the ugliness of bad decisions made by mankind. There are atrocities, accidents, illnesses, lies, and self-centeredness. We can become overwhelmed and ready to give up. But don't you dare! Gain new strength and courage in God.

Accept Christ into your life, wholeheartedly! This no intellectual exercise. It is a heart exercise. It is what we believe in our inner most being. Fully accept Christ, make the changes He wants us to make, lean on Him for all things, and we will find the peace we need. Will we become rich? Maybe, maybe not, if we are talking about money. We will absolutely become rich, if we are talking about peace, love, and joy.

I pray each of us will bring Christ into our inner most being. Accept that He is living inside you and lean on Him. Accept the peace of Christ and overcome this world with Him.

Marty Pressey

January 23

Who shall separate us from the love of Christ? Shall trouble or hardship or persecution or famine or nakedness or danger or sword?

— Romans 8:35

Do you know you are loved? Unfortunately, there are many people in this world who don't. Perhaps their parents abandoned them or just won't tell them or are on drugs and don't even know who/where they are. Perhaps these people have tried to find love in others and made many mistakes along the way.

Are you a person who isn't convinced you are loved? Do you really believe you are loved? If you do, it changes the way you act, doesn't it? When we know we are loved and we love back, the world becomes a glorious place with beautiful colors, wonderful experiences, and we feel like we are on top of the world. When we know our parents love us and are proud of us, we have a confidence others don't have.

Regardless of our background, race, ethnicity, or national origin, we are loved by God. Christ came to save the entire world, not just Israel. Christ came to demonstrate God's perfect love for us all, forever.

I pray each of us come to know deep in our heart the love God has for us. Accept Christ as your Savior. Love God and obey Him. You will be blessed beyond your wildest dreams.

January 24

Even youths grow tired and weary, and young men
stumble and fall; but those who hope in the Lord will
renew their strength. They will soar on wings like
eagles; they will run and not grow weary, they will
walk and not be faint.

— Isaiah 40:30–31

What do you do when you are faced with challenges? Do you determine
to do it on your own and gut your way thorough it? Perhaps you ask
others for help. Maybe you give up, try to hide from it, and hope it goes
away. What should we do?

It's easy to say what we should do. Sometimes it's hard to put
it into practice. It may take as much discipline to trust in what we
should do as it does to gut our way through it. However, there is a big
difference between the two. If we gut it out, we may get through it this
time, but there will be a time when we fail.

What should we do? We should lean on God, lifting up our
challenge to Him, laying it at His feet, and trusting He will guide us
through it. When we do this and He guides us through our challenge,
it increases our faith. We will then continue to trust Him in all
situations, and He will never fail us.

I pray each of us makes the decision to trust God, laying all our
challenges at His feet. Let's admit we are weak and allow God to lift
us up. He will provide us with His strength and courage, increasing
our faith.

January 25

Each one should use whatever gift he has received to serve others, faithfully administering God's grace in its various forms.

—1 Peter 4:10

What are you doing? What are you doing as a part of Christ's body? The convenience store clerk you were snooty to this morning is dealing with a brother who is continuously stealing money from him for drugs. You didn't notice your fellow worker's eyes were pink around the edge and her nose was running from crying. You don't know that she found out she's pregnant and her fiancé decided to break off their relationship.

Are you seeing, I mean truly seeing, the people you meet every day? Are you looking at them and noticing they are struggling with various issues? If each of us sees each other struggling and helps each other, will not our struggles be taken care of?

Here's the issue, we need to put others ahead of ourselves. When we do, we are blessed beyond belief. When we decide to be a servant, we are served. If we continue to be self-centered, we will continue to struggle on our own. We all need to be a part of a community of servants so that each of us is served.

I pray each of us will decide to be servants. If not because you want to serve others, decide to do it for yourself. In the end, you will be changed and serve others for them rather than you.

January 26

The thief comes only to steal and kill and destroy;
I have come that they may have life, and have it to
the full.

—John 10:10

Are you noticing what's going on around you? We might commonly
refer to this as situational awareness or SA. In human terms we mean
noticing traffic, movement, sales, intentions, opportunities, and any
number of other things. But what does it mean in spiritual terms?

We see in 3D from the time we are born. We have to learn to see in
4D, the 4th dimension being the spiritual dimension. What is included
in the 4th dimension? Seeing the spirit working in this world. Seeing
new life in the spring. Seeing God changing people from the inside
out. Seeing the spirit moving in our lives. And also seeing the spiritual
warfare going on every day.

God has won the war. Satan can only win the small skirmishes. But
Satan continues to take pleasure in winning those small skirmishes
and drawing each of us away from God. Our situations change as we
go through our lives. We must see in 4D to get the whole picture. We
can learn to see in 4D, we just need to make the decision to do so.

I pray each of us will make the decision to learn to see in 4D. See
the Spirit moving in your life. Come alive again, wake up to God's
wonderful view.

January 27

"Love the Lord your God with all your heart and with all your soul and with all your mind and with all your strength.' The second is this: 'Love your neighbor as yourself.' There is no commandment greater than these."

— Mark 12:30-31

What do you believe? Do you believe you will be paid for the work you do for your employer? Do you believe you have many years left on this earth? Do you act on your beliefs? We do act on our beliefs.

If we didn't believe our employer would pay us, we wouldn't work there very long, would we? If we didn't believe we had many years left on this earth, we wouldn't save money for vacation, new vehicles, or retirement, would we? So, do we believe Jesus is the Son of God?

If we truly believe Jesus is the Son of God, that He walked this earth, was crucified for our sins, and rose again to be our living Savior, why don't we act like it? He gave us two simple commands and said all the law and prophets were contained within them. When asked who our neighbor is, He told the parable of the good Samaritan (Luke 10:25–37). So, do we really believe He is who He says He is?

I pray each of us will act on our belief that Jesus Christ is our Savior and do as He commanded. Let's all decide to demonstrate love rather than hate or indifference. Pray that the Spirit guide you in *all* you do.

January 28

But God demonstrates his own love for us in this:
While we were still sinners, Christ died for us.

— Romans 5:8

Do you know how much you are loved? So often we equate love to someone buying us jewels, clothes, cars, or any number of gifts. We often hear the rote repeating of "I love you" without any real meaning behind it. There are many who never hear those words. There are some who can be told they are loved and never believe it. Why is that?

Love can only come from one place. We will say it has to come from the heart. That is true, but it can't come from the heart if our heart is not filled with God. God shows us and fills us with the one true love. Without Him, it is just a human emotion that can fade as quickly as it came upon us.

God loves each of us far more than we can comprehend. He has shown us His love. We simply have to believe it. Why don't we believe it? We judge ourselves and believe instead that we are not worthy of love. Don't fool yourself, don't allow Satan to steal your love, don't continue to stand on the outside of the circle of God's love. Believe He loves you in a very deep, personal way and have confidence in that love.

I pray we all come to understand just how much God loves each of us. I pray we return our love to Him and show it to others. Have the heart of God.

Marty Pressey

January 29

But you are a chosen people, a royal priesthood, a
holy nation, God's special possession, that you may
declare the praises of him who called you out of
darkness into his wonderful light.

—1 Peter 2:9

Are you a priest? Most of us would say we are not. In fact, we might
even laugh if we were asked that question. But are you sure? Perhaps
you are not looking at it from the correct perspective.

We often have an image in our mind of a priest being someone in
flowing robes and sashes. A person who has been judged by man to be
worthy of honor. A person to be respected. Someone who has studied
extensively about the Bible and the history contained within it, as well
as being led by the Spirit.

However, from God's perspective, we are priests. We are called
into His kingdom. We are called to lead others to Christ. We are
justified, honored, and exalted in Christ. We are to know the gospel
story and tell it to others. We are brothers and sisters in and with
Christ. Should we not know our brother?

I pray we each determine to know Christ and become a true
brother or sister. Be the priest God says you are. Be a person who
shares the gospel.

January 30

Do you not know that your bodies are temples of the
Holy Spirit, who is in you, whom you have received
from God? You are not your own; you were bought
at a price. Therefore honor God with your bodies.

—1 Corinthians 6:19–20

Are you taking care of God's temple? You may think of that as
a cathedral or church building or even a temple. All of these are
buildings. However, we are told that God cannot be contained in a
building. So, what am I talking about?

So many people think of the church as a building. Too many times
they also think that is the only time God is present with them. Both
of these thoughts could not be further from the truth. The church is
not a building and God is always present.

God lives inside of us as well as throughout the entire universe
and all that is created. He is not contained in us anymore than He is
contained in a building, but He is in each of us. We are God's temple.
So, are you taking care of God's temple?

I pray we all take care of ourselves. Remember that you were
created by God and for God. He lives in you.

Marty Pressey

January 31

"In the last days, God says,
I will pour out my Spirit on all people.
Your sons and daughters will prophesy,
your young men will see visions,
your old men will dream dreams."

— Acts 2:17

What are your dreams? Are you pursuing your dreams? We often have big dreams. For instance, as a child I wanted to play baseball for the St. Louis Cardinals. In every imaginary game I played in the yard, I was playing for them. But, do we dream the wrong dreams?

Dreams of success in this life are fleeting. When we realize we won't reach the dream, we dream a smaller dream. As we go through life, we continue to reduce our dreams until our dreams are more in line with reality. For some of us, we may stop dreaming entirely.

What if we could dream a dream that is guaranteed to be true? We can! We can dream of being in heaven with our brother Jesus Christ. This dream has been purchased for us by the One who loves us more than anyone else. Are you willing to dream that dream?

I pray each of us dream to be with Christ for eternity. I pray each of us pursue it with all our heart. Choose to dream the perfect dream.

February

February 1

Do not forget to show hospitality to strangers, for
by so doing some people have shown hospitality to
angels without knowing it.

— Hebrews 13:2

Do you entertain angels? You might scoff at the thought. How would
any of us entertain angels?! Surely angels would not stoop so low as
to be with us mere mortals. Even if they did, wouldn't they look a bit
odd in our world with their wings?

We are so blind we can't see what is right in front of our face. We
look through dirty lenses. We don't even recognize our brother and
sister in Christ has the Holy Spirit living in them. We don't see the
light shining through them. Why? We don't look into their eyes, which
are the pathway to their soul.

When we are kind to others and show them hospitality, we just
may be entertaining angels. We are told to be hospitable to strangers.
Do we think an angel would appear to us looking like someone
we already knew? Think about that. Wouldn't an angel appear as
someone we didn't know? They may appear as a stranger next to us in
a restaurant or a person crying on the curb or someone that sees us in
need and gives us a few bucks to get us through.

I pray each of us will be hospitable to strangers in need. I pray we
all approach them as if they were an angel. You just might meet one!

February 2

It does not, therefore, depend on human desire or effort, but on God's mercy.

— Romans 9:16

Do you depend on God? I'm sure many of us do depend on God for many things. On the other hand, I'm also sure many of us depend largely on ourselves. We often depend on ourselves far more than we depend God. When will we learn that we don't really control much of anything and decide to depend on God for everything?

It doesn't matter what our circumstances are. We may be poor, or we may be rich. We may have everything going our way or we may feel the entire world is against us. We may be young and strong, or we may be old and frail. No matter the circumstances, each of us need to depend on God for everything in this life.

Why is it important to depend on God? Depending on God will give us peace. We will know that He is in charge. This isn't easy to do at first, but it becomes easier the more we depend on Him. We will see Him at work and our peace will increase. When our peace increases, we worry less. When we worry less, our health is better. Does it mean we will never have physical ailments? No. It does mean they will be less concerning to us.

I pray we all decide to depend on God in all circumstances. When it comes right down to it, depending on God is part of accepting He is in control and we are not. This is not indifference but is deference. Depend on God.

February 3

So the men were sent off and went down to Antioch, where they gathered the church together and delivered the letter. The people read it and were glad for its encouraging message.

— Acts 15:30–31

Do you gather? That might seem like a strange question, but it is something we should do as Christians. We should gather so that we may encourage and uplift one another. In the early church, just a few years following Christ's death and resurrection, the church would gather on a near daily basis.

I'm sure some of us would say there is no way we would go to church on a daily basis. If our idea of going to church is to go into a building, we're probably right. However, that is not what the early church did. They gathered to eat meals together, heal the sick, take care of the widows, and educate their children.

We need to gather more often as Christians taking care of each other and rely less on this world. It is often believed that family takes care of its own. Well, the most important family of all is the family of God. It's through our gathering that we find joy, peace, and love in Christ.

I pray we all decide to gather. Gather in the church building, yes, but also gather as the body of Christ in homes, schools, workplaces, and everywhere you can think of.

February 4

God, the blessed and only Ruler, the King of kings
and Lord of lords, who alone is immortal and who
lives in unapproachable light, whom no one has seen
or can see. To him be honor and might forever. Amen.

—1 Timothy 6:15b–16

Do you praise the King of kings and Lord of lords? Some will say they do. Some will say sometimes. Some will not know who that is. We all should praise the God of all.

How do we praise God? For many of us it is going to worship services on Sunday morning. The belief is that worshiping God once a week is enough. Perhaps. But do we really want to put our eternal life in jeopardy just because we want to do whatever we feel like? Do we really understand what hangs in the balance? It's a matter of living forever in perfection.

We all need to praise God each day. He is in control; we are not. That gives me great comfort. It also gives me confidence. If I'm praising Him and in step with Him, I know I will do the right thing and I have no reason to fear. Don't we all want to have that confidence and live without fear? If we do, we should pursue God with all our heart praising Him each day.

I pray we all praise the King of kings and Lord of lords each day. Give thanks to him for giving you another day to praise Him. Give thanks to Him for giving you another day to be the light He made you to be.

February 5

What good will it be for someone to gain the whole world, yet forfeit their soul? Or what can anyone give in exchange for their soul?

— Matthew 16:26

Are you a Jesus zealot? We might balk at that question at first. But what if we substituted fanatic for zealot? Are you a Jesus fanatic? The same basic question, is it not? What is your answer now?

Many of us want to avoid a negative stigma from our friends, family, co-workers, and so many others we are in contact with daily. We don't want them to think we are strange or weird. We want to fit in. We want to be accepted. Yet that is not who we are called to be.

Many of us are fanatics about many things. It could be our favorite sports team, our vehicle, our school, our kids, our parents, our spouse, or so many others. However, we are really called to be fanatics of Jesus. We are to be so in tune with Him that we can't imagine living without Him.

I pray we all become fanatics of Jesus, or put another way, fully dedicated to Jesus. Love Him with all your being rather than love this world.

February 6

If anyone speaks, they should do so as one who speaks the very words of God. If anyone serves, they should do so with the strength God provides, so that in all things God may be praised through Jesus Christ. To him be the glory and the power for ever and ever. Amen.

—1 Peter 4:11

What do you do when you don't have time for God? I'm sure each one of us has been so busy at work, at school, on travel, or any number of other tasks that we forget about God. Is this normal? Yes. Should it be normal? No.

Far too often we get busy and don't put God first. We continually rely on our own strength. We push through the task by our own will. Then we wonder why we're tired. If we would lean on God, we would find that we can do so much more without being so tired and fussy and complaining and generally in a bad mood.

How do we do this? We take God with us everywhere we go. We say short prayers at all times during the day. We make our task about God and not about us. No, this isn't easy when we first start doing it. It does get easier and becomes almost second nature as we continue to do so. As with any other road we travel we have to take the first step, then decide to take the next and the next and the next.

I pray we all decide to take God with us each and every day in everything we do. It really is for our benefit, not God's.

February 7

May the God of hope fill you with all joy and peace as
you trust in him, so that you may overflow with hope
by the power of the Holy Spirit.

— Romans 15:13

Do you trust God? That may sound like a straightforward question.
Do you trust God with everything in your life? That becomes a bit
tougher question, doesn't it? That question is challenging and perhaps
very daunting to answer in the affirmative.

Why is it we struggle with trusting God with everything? We
certainly have examples of people in the Bible who did. The answer is
likely a complicated one that includes us believing we are in control,
wanting what we can't have, and chasing after the things of this world.
Most importantly, we don't really believe God has our best interest
at heart.

I'm sure many will balk at the accusations above, but I challenge
us to stop and think long and hard on them. If we really believe God
has our best interest at heart, why don't we trust Him with everything?
We can't trust God with everything and continue to worry, continue
to chase after childish dreams, and be paralyzed by fear. We can't trust
God with everything and not be filled with hope.

I pray each one of us will decide to trust God with all our being
and everything we have. We all need the hope that comes from God
when we trust Him.

February 8

Praise be to the God and Father of our Lord Jesus
Christ, who has blessed us in the heavenly realms
with every spiritual blessing in Christ.

— Ephesians 1:3

How much do you praise God? Do you praise Him every day? Do you
have a full appreciation for what He did for you? Do you realize you
can never pay Him back for what He's done for each one of us? Do you
know that you owe everything you have and will ever achieve to Him?

This world seems to have two general types of people. Either
we are a person who wants to payback every person who ever does
something for us by doing something for them. Or, we are a person
who wants to take everything given to us and never pay anything
back. Which one are you?

We owe all we have and all we are to God. He created us, gave us
our talents, and continues to give us all we have. Most important of all,
He provided us with the hope of salvation and eternal life in heaven
with Him. Jesus stated He came to give us abundant life. (John 10:10)
If we are willing to believe this, why do we live our lives without His
continual guidance and without praising Him every day?

I pray we all decide to praise God today and every day. Let's all
contemplate all God has done for us. Praise the Father, the Son, and
the Holy Spirit, who are one God!

Marty Pressey

February 9

Do you not know? Have you not heard? The LORD
is the everlasting God, the Creator of the ends of
the earth. He will not grow tired or weary, and his
understanding no one can fathom. He gives strength
to the weary and increases the power of the weak.

— Isaiah 40:28–29

Do you live in step with God? I believe we all want to be at peace with
ourselves, family, friends, and co-workers. How do we find the peace
we are looking for? For many the answer is not what they want to hear,
but one we need to hear and seek.

The only way we acquire true peace is by walking in step with
God. We do that by participating in Christian gatherings, Bible
studies, small groups, Sunday worship services, and reading our Bibles
daily. This may seem a bit onerous, demanding, or overwhelming.

How much time do we spend watching TV or perusing social
media each day? How much time do we spend doing things that
neither bring us peace nor encourage us to do good? Many of those
things will only contribute to anxiety, hatefulness, judgmentalism,
grief, despondency, or depression. On the other hand, spending time
with God, growing closer to Him, will lift us up, give us strength, and
bring peace to us.

I pray each of us will set aside time to spend with God each day.
It is the only way we will ever feel at peace. I know this for a fact from
my own experience.

February 10

After his suffering, he presented himself to them and gave many convincing proofs that he was alive. He appeared to them over a period of forty days and spoke about the kingdom of God.

— Acts 1:3

Have you ever wondered why the apostles were so convinced that Jesus was who He said He was? Did you realize He walked the earth for 40 days after He was resurrected? No? He did and He continued to teach as He had done before.

Remember the discussion on the road to Emmaus in Luke 20? He talked with a couple men as they walked and yet He did not allow them to know who He was until He sat down to eat with them. When their eyes were opened to see Him for who He was, they were amazed and filled with joy.

Are we filled with joy when we think of Jesus? Do we rejoice because He is alive? Have we come to the realization that He is alive today and we are following a risen Savior? We all need to realize He is alive, He is our Savior. He is the living God that rules all the world, all of creation, for all of eternity.

The apostles who saw Him after His resurrection were filled with the Holy Spirit on Pentecost. He came upon them in the image of what appeared to be tongues of fire. They were filled with the Holy Spirit and emboldened to preach the Word of God to the ends of the earth. They baptized about 3,000 believers on the day of Pentecost! Amazing!

February 11

You make known to me the path of life; you will fill
me with joy in your presence, with eternal pleasures
at your right hand.

— Psalm 16:11

Are you living in the presence of God? I expect there will be different
answers depending on your background. I will tell you that you are
living in the presence of God. Now, what are you going to do about it?

I read a book titled A Table in the Presence several years ago
written by Navy Lieutenant Carey H. Cash. He was a chaplain for a
Marine battalion that went into Iraq in 2003 during the Gulf War.
The stories he recounts will send chills down your spine. He knew
they were living in the presence of God.

We all need to realize we are living in God's presence. He is in
everything we see, and He is in us. We may not believe it. We may
think we can hide from God. What will it take for us to realize we
are in His presence every minute of every day? For some, it takes a
catastrophe. For others, a near miss will wake them up. Don't wait
until you are up to your eyeballs in trouble. Believe in Him now.

I pray we all allow God to take control of our lives. Yes, you can
stop Him. All you have to do is be hard hearted and stubborn. He
allows you that choice. Stop thinking you are in control, instead live
in God's presence. He will show you great and wonderful things.

February 12

But in fact God has placed the parts in the body,
every one of them, just as he wanted them to be. If
they were all one part, where would the body be? As
it is, there are many parts, but one body.
—1 Corinthians 12:18–20

Are you zealous? Are you an extremist or fanatic for a cause? Some are, some are on occasion, and some are not. My guess is most of us fall in the middle. We are zealous about some things and not about others.

I am saddened when I hear Christians raging against other Christians because they attend a different church. I am also saddened when I hear a fellow Christian ask if he/she belongs to our denomination when they are told about a good book or speaker. Why are we unwilling to listen to or read what a Christian from another denomination speaks or writes about?

We are part of one body, and it is the body of Christ. We are told there are many parts in the body, and they are positioned exactly where God wants them. Therefore, we are part of Christ's body and right where God wants us. We need every part of the body of Christ to do His work here on earth.

I pray we all come to realize the body of Christ is a diverse body. It contains as many parts as our own physical bodies. Welcome the parts that don't look or act like you. We are all one in Christ Jesus. Be zealous for Christ and not your denomination.

February 13

Show me your ways, LORD, teach me your paths.
Guide me in your truth and teach me, for you are
God my Savior, and my hope is in you all day long.
— Psalm 25:4–5

Do you stand on your own two feet? Many of us will answer yes. If you are a parent, you probably want to teach your children to. Once we get into our late teens, we usually begin trying to do so, if for no other reason than we don't want to live with our parents anymore.

It is a tough world and it's difficult to make it on our own. We parents have made it tougher on our children. How so? We give them so many material things. We have set an example of spending lots of money on those material things and our children want them when they move out on their own. We failed to teach them those material things are not very important.

God should be who we seek. We should teach our children that He will provide for all their needs. We need to set the example of trusting God in all we do. By our example our children will also learn to trust God. When we fully trust God, we have no reason to fear. It does not mean we won't want nice things. It means we won't be driven by a desire for them. It means we will put God ahead of material belongings.

I pray each of us seeks out God and trusts Him above all else. We need to yearn after Him more than anything in this world. When we trust Him, we are at peace.

February 14

"Do not judge, or you too will be judged. For in the
same way you judge others, you will be judged, and
with the measure you use, it will be measured to you."
— Matthew 7:1–2

Do you judge others? Yes? No? Maybe? Sometimes? How well do
you like it when others judge you? Not so much? Hate it? Despise it?
Does it cause you to judge them even more? Maybe even harsher than
before?

Our communities have become so full of judgement. If we aren't
judging others, we stand out as being someone who thinks we are
better than others. If we don't judge others, we are an outcast or a
goody two shoes. Does that make it right to judge? No!

Many say we need to judge right from wrong. Don't mix up
judgement with discernment. Judging is exercising authority to
condemn others or set them free. Oh, now we say we don't judge? Do
we ever say "Really?!" when someone does something we don't like?
In most cases, we are consciously or subconsciously condemning the
other person. We are not to judge. We are to be a shining light to the
world. We are to show Christ to all those we encounter.

I pray we all stop judging others. Let's first get our own house in
order. Let's be the shining light to others. It's plain to see this world
needs to see Jesus in us. Show Him to them.

February 15

But the fruit of the Spirit is love, joy, peace, forbearance, kindness, goodness, faithfulness, gentleness and self-control. Against such things there is no law.

— Galatians 5:22–23

Do you demonstrate the fruits of the Spirit? Some of you may wonder what they are. There are nine of them. They can be found in today's Scripture reading. Some of you may be wondering how you can demonstrate these. You cannot demonstrate them on your own.

I know, some of us will say, "I can demonstrate love." Or, "I can demonstrate kindness." True. We may be able to demonstrate one or two of these for a short period of time on our own. We may even be able to for a few years. However, we cannot continually demonstrate several of these on our own.

You see, these are called fruits of the Spirit. That means these are the outgrowth from within when we are walking in step with God, allowing His Spirit to guide us in all that we do. When we are submissive to God's Spirit, we will demonstrate the fruits as a result. Do we want to be loving, kind, gentle, good, have joy and peace? We need to let go of our own will and submit to God's Spirit, His will.

I pray that each of us will allow God's Spirit to be our guide. I pray we all listen to Him, follow His lead, and become a fertile ground for His Spirit to work and grow and show His fruit.

February 16

"You have heard that it was said, 'Love your neighbor and hate your enemy.' But I tell you, love your enemies and pray for those who persecute you, that you may be children of your Father in heaven."

— Matthew 5:43–45a

Do you love? No, I mean really love. Do you love the way Jesus told us to love? Do you love unconditionally? Do you love your enemy? Or are you fooled by this world and lost to Satan?

Some will say it's pretty harsh to say someone is lost to Satan if they don't love like Jesus instructed us. It is uncomfortable, isn't it? However, if we hate people because they are different or have a different name or our friend told us to hate them or our country says to hate them, we have fallen into Satan's trap. He is laughing at us and has us snared in his claws.

You don't have to believe me, just do your own reading and studying of God's word. He doesn't spread hate. He tells us to love others. He shows us His diverse creation. He tells us to stand out as a person of love who others are attracted to.

I pray we all choose to love. Our world is so broken, and it needs so much love. Only we can make the choice to love. Only we can decide to make a difference.

February 17

"I have told you this so that my joy may be in you and that your joy may be complete. My command is this: Love each other as I have loved you."

—John 15:11–12

Do you have joy? We often equate joy to being happy. It can mean that. However, Jesus teaches us that joy is not just being happy, but it is completely fulfilled by His love for us and our love for each other. Do you have complete joy?

So many of us only find joy in worldly things. We become joyful or happy when we get shiny new things, whether it's a new house, new car, new clothes, new jewelry, etc. Some of us are joyful or happy when we eat certain foods or go out to eat at our favorite restaurant. Unfortunately, this joy is fleeting and only lasts for a short time.

It is really quite sad that we chase after joy in material things. We are trying to satisfy a need that can only be filled by God. His love for us will fill us with joy, if we will accept Him into our lives. Our joy is made complete by loving each other. Isn't that what we all seek? Perfect joyfulness? If that is what we seek, we need to accept God wholeheartedly into our life, accept His love for us, and love others in the same way.

I pray each of us will accept God's love and love others in the same way. We all seek joy. Let's seek God and allow Him into our lives. May each of us be filled with joy.

February 18

"Peace I leave with you; my peace I give you. I do not give to you as the world gives. Do not let your hearts be troubled and do not be afraid."

— John 14:27

Do you have peace? I mean real peace. The kind of inner peace that no matter what is happening around you, you know it will all turn out alright. Do you have that kind of peace? Do you want it? It is available to you.

So many in this world don't want peace. They thrive on drama. I've seen people complain about how much drama is going on or how much this person or that person seems to enjoy drama. Yet they jump right into the drama or overreact to someone making a simple statement. Do we like that person or their actions? Are we that person?

God will give us His peace, if we will only accept it. I've experienced it and continue to experience it. It doesn't mean we are indifferent or have no feelings. It does mean that we can remain calm and focused while not being caught up in the hysterics all those around us are caught up in. The peace Jesus Christ promises us is a quiet confidence in Him and His promises.

I pray each is us wants the peace of Christ in our lives. I pray each of us will seek a close, personal relationship with Jesus. By experiencing Him we obtain the peace He promises.

February 19

God presented Christ as a sacrifice of atonement,
through the shedding of his blood—to be received by
faith. He did this to demonstrate his righteousness,
because in his forbearance he had left the sins
committed beforehand unpunished—

— Romans 3:25

Do you exercise forbearance? Do you know what it means? It's not a word we often use in our daily language. Likely we don't exercise it because we don't know what it is. Perhaps if we were taught what it is, we would begin to exercise it.

Forbearance is patiently enduring something. For example, if our car payment is due the first of the month, but our creditor allows us to be up to 5 days late without penalty, that is forbearance, not grace. So do you exercise forbearance? As parents we often do with our kids. Sometimes we tell them to get something done by a certain time, they are late getting it done, but we overlook the tardiness and are thankful they did it at all.

How should we show forbearance to others? We might have planned an event, and someone assigned to help is running late. Being patient, not getting upset is exercising forbearance. Can we do it? Will we do it?

I pray we all show some forbearance. There are times when being on time is critical, but there are far more when it is not. Be willing to forbear others as God has us.

February 20

Once safely on shore, we found out that the island was called Malta. The islanders showed us unusual kindness. They built a fire and welcomed us all because it was raining and cold.

— Acts 28:1–2

Do you exhibit kindness? We are told that we should be welcoming to strangers and by doing so we might be entertaining angels. Even if we don't entertain angels, shouldn't we be kind to the children of God? And, isn't everyone a child if God?

Many in this world will justify retaliation, vengefulness, hatred, and downright evil because they feel they have been slighted in some way. The question is, are we a part of the world or living in God's kingdom? The world will lead us to destruction. Is that what we want?

We are to be kind to each other and to all we meet. We need kindness in this world. We need to be kind, be the ones leading the world in kindness. If we won't, who will? Those who are of this world will not.

I pray we all decide to be kind. Let the Spirit of God lead you and show through in you to others. Be kind.

Marty Pressey

February 21

Surely your goodness and love will follow me all the
days of my life, and I will dwell in the house of the
Lord forever.

— Psalm 23:6

Do you demonstrate goodness? I believe we often misinterpret this
fruit of the Spirit. I believe what is meant here is moral excellence or
virtue. This definition makes sense when you are talking about the
Spirit.

The world we live in likes to see goodness but doesn't want to
put forth the effort to live a virtuous life. They believe it is boring, no
fun, and drab. Well, it's not. A virtuous life will provide us an endless
adventure. Living a virtuous life is full of fun and joy. The question is,
are we willing to give up our sinful life for a virtuous life?

I see people who are young, old, middle age, women, men,
religious, and non-religious all rejecting God's goodness for temporary
fun. God's goodness will not just bring us temporary fun, but a joy that
lasts for eternity. If we surrender our sinful practices and submit to
God, the joy comes quickly. We are immediately in His spotlight.

I pray we all give up our own selfish desires and temporary fun for
eternal joy in God. From that we demonstrate the goodness of God as
His Spirit shines through us. Let's all show our moral excellence and
virtue for all to see.

February 22

Blessed are the meek, for they will inherit the earth.
— Matthew 5:5

Are you a meek person? Most of us will think that being meek means being weak. We often equate meek to the person who has shrunk into the back corner, hoping no one notices them. However, that is not the meek Jesus speaks about or exhibits Himself.

Meekness, as Jesus speaks of it, is being gentle and kind. Jesus Himself was gentle as demonstrated by how the children wanted to be around Him. He was kind to so many people. An example of His kindness is his treatment of the woman who was healed after 12 years of a bleeding disorder. Did He castigate her for touching His clothes? No, He was kind and stated her faith healed her (Matt. 9:20-22).

As we look at Jesus being meek, yet not allowing everyone to walk on Him, we learn meekness is not shrinking into the corner. Jesus clearly had righteous anger when he turned over the money changers' tables in the temple (John 2:13-17). He was upset because they were defiling the temple. It is a place to worship God.

We can also be meek and bold. Be gentle and kind to those in need and those you serve. But be bold in the defense of your faith and what is right in the sight of God. There is no discord in being both. Our example, Jesus Christ, showed us we can be both.

Marty Pressey

February 23

The apostles said to the Lord, "Increase our faith!"
He replied, "If you have faith as small as a
mustard seed, you can say to this mulberry tree, 'Be
uprooted and planted in the sea,' and it will obey you.

— Luke 17:5–6

Are you a faithful person? Some will say yes; some will say no. Why would someone say no? We all are faithful to something or someone. Many are faithful to their school, their favorite sports team, and their job.

Faith is a combination of believing in something and committing to it. If we didn't have faith the sun will rise, why would we plan on it? We all have this simple faith. What or who do we put our most important faith in?

Some will say they are Christians but have very little or no faith. Sure, they've been baptized, said the right words, but they don't really have faith. Perhaps they believe there is a God. But as we are told in James 2:19, even the demons believe and shudder. When we have a deep faith in God, we step out and do things He wants us to do, even when it doesn't make sense. Grow your faith by doing something small. Each time you do, your faith will grow.

I pray we each exercise our faith. That is how it grows. Sort of like exercising muscles. As our faith grows, we go further, and our faith gets deeper. God will provide. Don't forget that!

February 24

Be completely humble and gentle; be patient, bearing
with one another in love.

— Ephesians 4:2

Are you a gentle person? Some of us have heard of someone being
described as a gentle giant. But, what does it mean to be gentle? It
means to be kindly or amiable, not to be harsh toward others. Does
that describe you?

In today's world, we see far too much anger and hatred and harsh
treatment of others. The very same people who want people to calm
down are the ones who exhibit anger at the drop of a hat. Have we,
as a culture, become nothing but a seething bunch of human beings?
Waiting to explode on someone? Far too often it seems that way. The
least little thing that doesn't go our way, we become angry.

We are told that gentleness is a fruit of the Spirit (Gal. 5:22-23).
If we are not gentle, we are not in tune with the Spirit of God, and we
are not allowing the Spirit to guide us. We desperately need the Spirit
to be our guide. We desperately need to listen for the Spirit in our
lives. We desperately need to submit to God's holiness. Being gentle
to others will actually make us feel better, and we will gain more from
it than those we are being gentle to.

I pray we each listen for the Spirit, being gentle to each other and
those we meet. We all need gentleness in our lives. Why not be the
first to demonstrate gentleness to others?

February 25

So then, let us not be like others, who are asleep, but
let us be awake and sober.

—1 Thessalonians 5:6

Do you exhibit self-control? Self-control is largely lacking in today's
society. I remember my Grandma saying, "If you can't say something
nice about somebody, don't say anything at all." That was a form
of self-control. Today's society says whatever pops into their mind
whether it's true or not, whether it hurts someone or not, whether they
really mean it or not, and generally without self-control.

Why is it our society has lost all self-control? Some may say it's
because parents stopped spanking their children. Some will say
parents didn't teach their children right from wrong. Some will say
the schools have had discipline taken from them. Some will say ... you
can fill in the blank.

The real reason is people are not seeking to be in tune with God.
If you are truly in tune with God, you will have self-control. Not only
in what you say, but in what you do. The less we are in tune with God
the bigger the crack is to let Satan into our lives. Therefore, no self-
control results in an evil society.

I pray each of us seeks to be in tune with God and bear the fruits
of the Spirit. Without them we become another member of today's
society allowing evil to take control of us. Be a seeker of God. Bear
the fruits of the Spirit.

February 26

LORD, do not forsake me;
do not be far from me, my God.
Come quickly to help me,
my Lord and my Savior.

— Psalm 38:21-22

Who do you lean on? Many of us depend on family, friends, co-workers, or perhaps our church family to help when we need it. Often, that means physical help, but may also mean emotional help. Who do we ask for help when the odds are stacked against us?

I see a broken world. A world filled with struggling people. Some struggle for the basics of food, water, shelter, and clothing. These are obvious and outward struggles. Yet there are so many that struggle with inner fears, doubts, insecurities, and a host of other maladies.

Some will seek counseling from psychiatrists or professional counsellors. Some may seek counseling from their pastor. I would suggest these people read God's Word, search Him out in prayer, and ask others to pray on their behalf. Some of these ailments are chemical imbalances and can be treated medically. However, many of these are a result of Satan tormenting people. It takes faith and trusting the Lord to be there with us to remove Satan from our lives.

I pray each of us would lean on God throughout our lives. We all need Him. Lean on Him with your whole heart and He will answer. Never lose your trust and faith!

February 27

Remember the wonders he has done,
his miracles, and the judgments he pronounced,
you his servants, the descendants of Abraham,
his chosen ones, the children of Jacob.
He is the LORD our God;
his judgments are in all the earth.

— Psalm 105:5-7

Do you see the wonders of God all around you? Many of us don't. We see traffic, the hustle and bustle, chaos, deadlines, appointments, and so many other things. Why don't we take time to slow down and see what God has created?

The world we live in has become so demanding with all the technology or electronic leashes. We're always connected, and people are always asking something of us. And, we always think we have to answer immediately. Remember when an answer to a letter would come a week or two later? We are overwhelmed with demands and we don't even recognize it.

We all need to unplug. There is a reason God created the sabbath. We are to rest in order to be refreshed. We need to stop and see God's creation. We need to reflect on what God has done in our lives. We are created to be in communion with Him, to be loved by Him, and love Him back. When we rest, we are kind and loving toward others. When we don't, we are often overcome with anxiety and anger.

Take time to see the wonders God has created. Take time to rest and refresh. If not for those around you, do it for your own sanity.

February 28

but those who hope in the LORD
will renew their strength.
They will soar on wings like eagles;
they will run and not grow weary,
they will walk and not be faint.

— Isaiah 40:31

What do you do when you are worn out? Do you give up? Do you continue? Do you throw your hands up and ask, "why me?" Do you have a specific person you lean on? Do you try to hide? All of us get worn down, worn out, and come to a place in which we are ready to just give up. The key is how we react to that.

There are many people in this world who have no one to lean on. There are many who have no savings as a safety net. There are some who have had so many setbacks they have no will to continue. There are some who deal with ailments or pains for so long, they become depressed.

What can be done? The best we can do is lean on God. He has the power to provide us with the strength we need to continue. He will provide us with the desire to continue. God will sustain us in times of trouble, pain, anguish, and weariness. The question is, will we reach out to Him and lean on Him? Do we really trust Him for all that we need?

I pray we all trust God with our whole heart. That we give up our trust in material things and trust that God will provide. He has told us He will on many occasions. We need to trust Him and ask Him to increase our faith.

February 29

Praise be to the God and Father of our Lord Jesus Christ, who has blessed us in the heavenly realms with every spiritual blessing in Christ.

— Ephesians 1:3

How do you continue when it seems the whole world is against you? We all have times when it seems no matter what we do, it isn't right or it's not enough. We feel like the odds are stacked against us. When this happens, sometimes we just want to give up and move in a different direction. In some cases, that may be the best option. In other cases, it's not.

The people of first world countries have gotten so enamored with immediate satisfaction that we've lost the ability to endure hard times. Many people escape into the world of drugs and alcohol. Some just drop out of society. However, there are some hardy souls out there that keep going no matter what. What do they have that others don't?

I know some will argue with me, but a large portion of those that continue have a grounded faith in God. They realize that God is in control and they continue to follow Him. They pray. They trust. When we trust God and pray about our situations, He answers. Sometimes His answer is "no," sometimes it is "yes," and sometimes it is "not now." The bigger question is, will we trust Him and continue?

We all need God and we need to trust Him. Lean on Him in times of trouble, be joyous in Him in times of triumph, and praise Him always.

March

March 1

You, then, why do you judge your brother or sister? Or why do you treat them with contempt? For we will all stand before God's judgment seat. It is written: "'As surely as I live,' says the Lord, 'every knee will bow before me; every tongue will acknowledge God.'" So then, each of us will give an account of ourselves to God.

— Romans 14:10–12

How do you treat your family? This may seem an odd question, but we too often see squabbles, fights, and even disassociation. Why? It boils down to our failure to understand who we are, our position in life, and who God is. Bottom line, we don't have a proper relationship with God when we treat family members badly.

The world has become a "me" world. It's all about me. Am I happy? Am I being treated fairly? Am I getting what I want? Am I getting what I think I deserve? Am I, am I, am I?

God has called us to think as "we" or as "them." In other words, we are called to put others before ourselves in all things. That means putting others first when that person is being selfish, when others cut us off in traffic, and even when others hold us in contempt. It's not easy. It goes against our nature, our evil nature, that wants revenge. But God will reward us, if we put others first.

I pray we all come to understand the blessing of putting others first. It's only when we do that, that we come closer to God and can experience true joy.

March 2

Worship the Lord in the splendor of his holiness;
tremble before him, all the earth.

— Psalm 96:9

Do you worship God every day? Do you believe you should worship God every day? Does worship mean going to a building to you? Do you understand what worship is? All good questions and ones I believe we all need to wrestle with from time to time.

To really understand what worship means we don't need to nor should we go look it up in Webster's Dictionary. Sure, that would give us today's popular meaning of the English word. Unfortunately, it won't give us a comprehensive understanding of what it means to worship God. For that we need to study our Bible.

Worship should be done every day, all day long. How do we do this? We must allow God to fill us with His Spirit. We think of Him throughout the day. We pray throughout the day. We give thanks to Him all day for everything we have. We thank Him for the weather. We ask Him to guide us. We invite Him into our lives.

Worship is singing, praying, thanking, and praising God. It is to be done every day, all day, by living in Him.

March 3

Therefore, as God's chosen people, holy and dearly loved, clothe yourselves with compassion, kindness, humility, gentleness and patience. Bear with each other and forgive one another if any of you has a grievance against someone. Forgive as the Lord forgave you. And over all these virtues put on love, which binds them all together in perfect unity.

— Colossians 3:12–14

Are you willing to be a better you? Sound like an odd question? Who wouldn't want to be a better them? Truth be told, a large portion of our society doesn't really want to become a better them. Otherwise, they would pursue it.

Love is the one thing that overcomes all the imperfections, weaknesses, fears, hatred, and indifference. This is the true love of Christ. We can love others as Christ does. To do that we must pursue it. We must practice that love, even when we don't want to.

Most of us have either played a sport or a musical instrument or done something with a talent we have. In order to become very good at it, we had to practice, even when we didn't feel like it. We have to do the same to show the love of Christ. We may not want to, but we need to do it, just like we ran those laps when the coach told us to at the end of practice.

Today's Scripture lists some of the expressions of love we should demonstrate, even when we don't feel like it. I pray each of us determine to exercise these with everyone we meet.

March 4

Whoever brings ruin on their family will inherit only
wind, and the fool will be servant to the wise.

— Proverbs 11:29

How well do you take care of your family? Are you the protector? Are
you the instigator? Are you the victim? Are you the negotiator? Are
you the dictator? Are you the servant? We all probably fall in several
or all of these designations at some point or another.

The issue here is we are told not to be any of these types or
categories of people. We are told to be the one who mends, patches
up, takes care of, encourages, and protects our family. It's not just the
Dad or Mom who should be the protector, it's every member of the
family. As we might say today, we should have each other's back.

Does this mean we will seek revenge or pay back when something
bad happens to a family member? No! In fact, we are told specifically
that we are to allow God to be the one who pays back the evil person.
It's hard to do, but it is for our own good. What we are to do is be there
for our family. We are to be right there beside them, being a shield
rather than a sword, an encourager rather than a reviler, and a healer
rather than a destroyer.

I pray each of us will determine to protect, encourage, heal, and
uplift our families. Let's be people who love our parents, children,
siblings, grandparents, and grandchildren. Have the heart of God.

March 5

Love must be sincere. Hate what is evil; cling to what
is good. Be devoted to one another in love. Honor
one another above yourselves.

— Romans 12:9–10

How do you want to be remembered? Most of us want people to say
we were a nice, kind, compassionate, hardworking, solid citizen, or
something similar when we're gone. Okay, but what do you want them
to say right now? What do you want people to remember about you
when you've just walked away a few minutes prior?

We see so much strife, arguing, fighting, hate, anger, prejudice,
contempt, and general bad temperament in this world. Satan is truly
winning in far too many people's lives. How can we correct this? What
can we do? We can be the positive example others need to see and
follow. We can be more like Jesus.

Many will say Jesus lived in a simpler time. True, he didn't have
the internet, cars, electricity, and so much of what we have today.
However, you need to remember, Jesus lived amongst His enemies.
He was the positive example among the Pharisees, Roman soldiers,
and people overtaken by Satan. He expelled demons and forgave the
sinner. He is who we should strive to be like every day.

I don't believe many of us live in any more dangerous territory
than Jesus did. So, we too can be the positive example. We can
demonstrate forgiveness, compassion, and love toward those around
us every moment of every day.

March 6

So after they had fasted and prayed, they placed their
hands on them and sent them off.

— Acts 13:3

Do you lean on God for all your decisions? Do you ask Him to guide
you through each day? Have you ever fasted and prayed for God's
guidance in your life? Fasting and praying, earnestly seeking God's
wisdom and guidance, are powerful means to connect with God.

Some of us will say we can't go without a meal. Some of us will
get angry if we simply have to wait a few minutes extra for our meal.
We are foolish when we don't trust God to provide. God has promised
to provide for our needs. Food, water, and clothing are all needs.
However, we are so used to getting our wants that we forget eating 3
or 4 or 5 times a day is not needed.

If we really, really, earnestly desire to live better lives, lives without
hate and anger, we need to fast and pray and earnestly seek God's
guidance. There are no two ways around it. This broken world needs
it. I can tell you from personal experience that fasting is not easy. I can
tell you combining fasting and praying to seek God is a huge benefit
to us. God's people have fasted and prayed for thousands of years and
it has proven extremely beneficial.

I pray we all earnestly seek God's guidance, not as though He
were a genie in a bottle, but earnestly seek Him in prayer and fasting.
We need to do it for ourselves. We need to do it to make the world
around us better.

March 7

So I tell you this, and insist on it in the Lord, that you must no longer live as the Gentiles do, in the futility of their thinking. They are darkened in their understanding and separated from the life of God because of the ignorance that is in them due to the hardening of their hearts.

— Ephesians 4:17–18

How well do you know God's Word? Do you study it to have a better understanding? Do you know that by studying God's Word you will gain wisdom and insight into God's Will? Do you want to understand what God has planned for your life?

We need to read and understand God's Word by studying and discussing the Bible. We can read and study on our own, but we also need to discuss it with others. For God imparts wisdom to all who study His Word and we all can learn from one another. Theodore Roosevelt said, "A thorough understanding of the BIBLE is better than a college education."

There are many resources we can use. Obviously, the Bible itself. There are free web sites with many books from theologians and apps we can download onto our phones. We still have public libraries where we can check out books and people we can borrow books from.

We all need to study and understand God's Word, if we seek a truly successful life. It is only by leaning on God's Word, understanding how He will work in our lives, that we can confidently continue forward.

March 8

But seek first his kingdom and his righteousness, and
all these things will be given to you as well.

— Matthew 6:33

What is your morning routine? Pour a cup of coffee? Jump in the
shower and rush off to work? Get the kids up and off to school? Maybe
grab a bite of breakfast on your way out the door? Aren't our mornings
too busy and too rushed? Why?

We all push ourselves to do too much, and it all starts the moment
we wake up. We are tired from going too late into the night, so we sleep
until the last possible moment, which then causes us to start our day in
a rush and often stressed out before we even walk out the door. All of
this for what? To make an extra dollar? To buy one more thing? Most
of us have way more than we need already.

How do we eliminate our stress and anxiety? We first seek Jesus
our Lord. So, wake up just a few minutes earlier. Spend 5 or 10 or 30
minutes with Him each morning. Pray, study, meditate, and start your
day with the calming presence of God. You just might find out what it
means to have a really great day!

I pray we all take time each day to spend with God in prayer and
meditation, even if we don't have an opportunity to study that day.
Doing so will change our lives for the better.

March 9

Very early in the morning, while it was still dark,
Jesus got up, left the house and went off to a solitary
place, where he prayed.

— Mark 1:35

Do you start your day with God? Some of us might while others don't.
Some of us may simply wake up and say, "Thank you for another day
God." Some of us may wake up and say, "Where's my coffee?!" Some
of us may start our day by reading a devotional. Some of us may start
our day by reading from the Bible.

So much of this world starts the day with no thankfulness to
God, no desire to be with God, not even a thought of God. There is
no wonder this world has so much hurt and pain and hateful actions
toward one another. Only by seeking God can people truly change
for the better, experience the wonderful life of thankfulness and
blessings.

Each of us needs, whether we know it or not, to seek God first
thing each morning. We need to seek God each moment of each day.
Does that mean we don't work or any number of the other things we
do in our lives? No! It does mean that we do all of those things with
God in our minds; we are mindful of Him in all we say and do.

I pray each of us will seek God first and always. I pray that we
include Him in all we do. Trust God. Keep Him always in your mind.
He is always there with you.

March 10

Do not be deceived: God cannot be mocked. A man reaps what he sows. Whoever sows to please their flesh, from the flesh will reap destruction; whoever sows to please the Spirit, from the Spirit will reap eternal life.

— Galatians 6:7–8

Do you hold yourself accountable? So many in this world do not. We often don't like that word, accountable. It means we have to answer for what we do, good or bad. What we need to know and understand is God holds us accountable.

We often hear that God's grace covers all. That is true. His grace includes forgiveness and the strength to get through those tough times. What it does not include is the elimination of consequences for bad choices. God allows us the freedom of choice. He also holds us accountable for those choices.

I've given the advice that each choice we make opens some doors and closes others. I think nearly all of us would agree with that from a human perspective. But, do we see the same correlation in our spiritual walk? Do we fully understand that ignoring God or only cursorily following Him we don't live the abundant life He wants to give us?

I pray we all choose to live life abundantly, choosing to follow God with all our heart. I pray we come to a full understanding that grace does not eliminate the consequences of bad choices, but it does give us the strength to continue.

Marty Pressey

March 11

"Martha, Martha," the Lord answered, "you are worried and upset about many things, but few things are needed—or indeed only one. Mary has chosen what is better, and it will not be taken away from her."

— Luke 10:41–42

What are the consequences for your actions? Following up on yesterday's thought, we continue to look at the consequences of our choices. Each choice we make has an impact not only on us, but on others.

Who are the loneliest people and often completely overlooked? I would suggest the homeless who live under bridges or in alleys. If one of them makes a choice to drink themselves to death, doesn't someone need to recover their body? The city will not allow the body to lay where it is. Even the choice of someone we think is totally disconnected affects someone they don't know.

Now, think about how many people we are connected to or interact with on a daily basis. If we choose to do anything, even the smallest choice, we are affecting someone else. If we choose to be mean and ugly, we are negatively impacting someone else, perhaps someone we profess to love. If we truly love them, why would we choose to hurt them?

Every choice we make comes with consequences. When we make better choices, the consequences are better. I pray we all consciously choose to make better choices, for our sake and those around us. The world certainly needs it.

March 12

What shall we say, then? Shall we go on sinning so
that grace may increase? ... For sin shall no longer be
your master, because you are not under the law, but
under grace.

— Romans 6:1, 14

Do you accept God's grace? A fair question, but also a tricky question.
God's grace and mercy results in our forgiveness and blessings. Some
will accept it for what it is, meaning they realize they are a sinner and
honestly strive to change their ways.

God is a forgiving and loving God. He is also a just and jealous
God. We cannot continue to sin over and over and expect God to
continue to forgive us. Repentance is an honest sadness for our sin
and an honest commitment to change. It doesn't mean we will change
overnight. It does mean we make an attempt each day to become more
like Jesus.

Those who do make the commitment to try to be more like Jesus
each day will see their lives improve dramatically over time. I've
experienced it in my life and have seen it in others. Unfortunately, I
see it in far too few. We all need God, we all need His grace, we all need
His love, we all need to make a commitment to change.

I pray each of us will accept God's grace in our lives. I also pray we
honestly accept Him in our hearts and make every effort to become
more like Jesus. It is to our own benefit.

Marty Pressey

March 13

Very truly I tell you, whoever believes in me will do
the works I have been doing, and they will do even
greater things than these, because I am going to the
Father. And I will do whatever you ask in my name,
so that the Father may be glorified in the Son. You
may ask me for anything in my name, and I will do it.
— John 14:12–14

Do you pray? I'm sure most of us do. Maybe the better question is:
do you pray according to God's will? Many are confused and don't
know what God's will is. God's ultimate will is that all be saved and
live eternity with Him.

God ultimately cares about the condition of our hearts and wants
us to willingly submit to Him. In today's world, submission is a word
no one wants to hear. They believe submitting is a sign of weakness.
Honestly, we all submit to someone. None of us are all powerful.

Why don't we submit to the One who *is* all powerful? Have you
ever imagined what you could accomplish by having the God of gods,
King of kings on your side? Have you ever thought what great things
God will do in your life? He wants to do so many wonderful things in
our lives, if we will only submit to Him.

I pray we all choose to submit to His will. I pray we all come to
realize the wonderful blessings in store for us. Let's all submit and pray
in His will for ourselves, our family, our friends, our co-workers, our
leaders, and all the other Christians we don't even know.

March 14

"If you love those who love you, what reward will you
get? Are not even the tax collectors doing that? And if
you greet only your own people, what are you doing
more than others? Do not even pagans do that?"
— Matthew 5:46–47

Who do you love? Most of us will say our spouse, our children, our
family, our friends, and fellow church members. We will also likely
hear people say certain TV shows, movies, cars, pets, clothes, and
countries. Do we really love all those things and all those people? Or,
is it just a common saying or popular expression?

There are multiple forms of love. There is emotional love and
there is unconditional love. Some people say they love something or
someone when they really mean lust or desire. Words are important
and much of this world has forgotten how to choose words wisely.

Jesus tells us we are to love all people. The love he refers to is not
emotional or fleeting, but is unconditional and forever. We are to
remember that God created each person walking this earth. He put
each person here for a reason. We all should not only be searching for
our specific purpose, but helping others find theirs. Showing His love
to others is one piece to doing that.

I pray we all decide we will love everyone God created. I pray we
all show God's love to others and be a positive influence on their lives.
It's only by showing His love that we can become perfect like Him.

Marty Pressey

March 15

Then Jesus told his disciples a parable to show them
that they should always pray and not give up.

— Luke 18:1

What do you do when it seems God isn't answering your prayers?
So many will give up. Some will hold on to their faith. Others will
complain and seek as much attention as possible. What should we do
according to Scripture? What will we do next time?

In today's culture it's all about who can draw the biggest attention
to themselves. We see it in the TV shows, the news, and sports. "Hey!
Look at me. I'm in the spotlight. I'm great." Oh, I know, we will
say "I don't do that." But do we demand immediate answers to our
questions? Do we get upset when we feel ignored? Then we've acted
in the same manner as that childish person we complain about.

Jesus has taught us to be humble, be compassionate, love others,
serve others. He did not teach us to be the center of attention. He
taught us to be the mature person, the Christian who others want to
be around. He also taught us to pray and to continue to pray. Not as
though God were a genie in a bottle, but in accordance with His will
and don't give up, even if it seems God is not listening.

I pray we all mature in our Christian walk through a growing faith
and continually lean on God through prayer. It is through prayer that
God reveals Himself in a personal way. Keep at it.

March 16

Where there is strife, there is pride, but wisdom is
found in those who take advice.

— Proverbs 13:10

When do you turn to the Lord? Often, we don't turn to God until
we are in trouble. Perhaps it's financial, relationship, emotional,
or physical. Maybe we've reached the end of the line with drugs or
alcohol. Why don't we reach out sooner?

The simple answer to our question is pride. We think "we got
this." The real answer is "we ain't got nothin." We allow our pride to
fool us into believing we are in control. Or we act like we are in control
to be cool. We are such vain and foolish people. We know it, and yet
we don't change.

We need to seek God in all we do. His thoughts and His guidance
are far superior to ours. We can't just acknowledge that and not follow
it. That's like acknowledging the clouds and rain in the distance
moving toward us, but not putting on something to keep us from
getting soaked when we go out. The problem is, it's not as simple as
getting wet or not. It's a life and death issue.

I pray we all will spend more time in prayer and listening to God's
advice. We need Him and His guidance in our lives every day. Reach
out to Him before it's too late and listen to His still small voice.

March 17

You brood of vipers, how can you who are evil say
anything good? For the mouth speaks what the heart
is full of. A good man brings good things out of the
good stored up in him, and an evil man brings evil
things out of the evil stored up in him.

— Matthew 12:34–35

What comes out when you speak? In today's culture, we hear far too
much about people speaking their minds. It's really an excuse to be
obnoxious, hateful, selfish, rude, and just ugly toward each other. It's
an excuse to follow the evil Satan has put in this world.

You see, when we talk like that, it's not our mind that's speaking,
it's our heart. It is our inner most being that is coming out. It is
also what we've been taking in and committing to our heart. We've
heard the phrase "you are what you eat". That concept is even more
appropriate when it comes to how we speak and how we act.

If we want to speak nicely and act nicely toward others, we need
to take in and commit to our heart's nice actions and language. This
is a wakeup call to surround our self with good people, watch good
shows and movies, and listen to good music. If we're filling our head
and heart by taking in bad behavior, that's how we will speak and act.

I pray we all fill ourselves with good things in order to be good
people. After all, if you want people to like you, you kinda need to
be a good person. Seek the good things God has put before you and
bypass the bad things.

March 18

"Blessed are you when people insult you, persecute you and falsely say all kinds of evil against you because of me. Rejoice and be glad, because great is your reward in heaven, for in the same way they persecuted the prophets who were before you."

— Matthew 5:11–12

Do you love Jesus Christ? I don't mean do you say you do. I mean do you love Him deep in your soul. Is your heart filled with love for Him? If you still say you do, how is that demonstrated to others?

So many of us show our love for our favorite sports teams by wearing their shirts, hats, sweats, hoodies, and even sunglasses. We'll argue with a fan of another team about whose team is going to the playoffs and whose team is sitting them out. Those who are die-hard fans will support their team through those rough years.

Why is it we don't seem to support Jesus with the same enthusiasm? Why is it when asked if we are a Christian, we hesitate to answer, we answer with a meager "yes," or worse yet, "no." Why are we not thankful and joyous that we've been saved and want to let others know so they can be saved? We live in a broken and hurting world that needs Jesus now.

I pray we all decide to joyously proclaim we belong to Jesus Christ. In Him there is no fear, only love. Let's show our love for others by telling them about Jesus and how He will save them.

March 19

"What good is it for someone to gain the whole world,
yet forfeit their soul?"

— Mark 8:36

Who or what is your god? In today's culture there are so many gods
that compete for our worship. You may ask, "Really?!" Yes, it is true.
Very, very, true. Our god or gods are what take our focus, attention,
and energy.

For far too many people their god is success, popularity,
wealth, houses, cars, clothes, food, possessions, likability, gossiping,
celebrities, sports figures, and any number of other things or people.
Any and all of these take our attention away from who the real God
is. They take our focus, attention, and energy. We spend our time and
money on them. We focus on getting more of them. We make them
our god.

We are told not to worship idols, yet we watch TV shows that
purposely try to make various people our idols. We are told to put God
first in our lives, yet we often spend more time brushing our teeth than
we spend studying God's Word. We are told that God loves us, yet we
often deny Him and do things that violate His love for us.

We desperately need God in our lives. We also desperately need
to give our lives to God. We can be the richest, most popular, and
most possessive person in the world and completely lose out on the
abundant life in Jesus. I pray we all decide to make God our focus and
live the life of abundance Jesus came to provide for us.

March 20

Now he who supplies seed to the sower and bread for
food will also supply and increase your store of seed
and will enlarge the harvest of your righteousness.
—2 Corinthians 9:10

Are you taking care of what God has blessed you with? We often hear
that everything belongs to God. Usually, it's right before the offering
at church. Whether you agree to it or not, everything does belong
to God.

In this world, many pursue riches believing they will bring them
happiness. But how many of the rich and famous live sad lives and
come to a tragic end? How many of them suffer from drug, alcohol,
or some other abusive behavior? How many of them crumble under
depression, pressure, or failure? All this happening while they have
more possessions than anyone needs.

God provides what we need. We are also taught that we are to be
good stewards of what He gives us. That means we are to take care of
them. We are to make them last by performing normal maintenance.
It is our responsibility to take care of this earth, given to us by God,
and we do that by taking care of our possessions. We do that and God
provides more for us.

I pray we all understand that God gives us what we need. He also
entrusts more to those who take care of what they have been given.
Let's all decide to enjoy and care for all that we have been blessed with.

March 21

"Whoever belongs to God hears what God says.
The reason you do not hear is that you do not belong
to God."

— John 8:47

What organizations do you belong to? We all belong to various groups.
We are part of a family, a school, a class, a company, a team, and many
others. As we get older, we make decisions to join other organizations.
Have you decided to belong to God?

A very large portion of the people in this world do not belong
to God. Not in the way Jesus taught. Are they God's children? Yes,
in the sense that He created them, but not in the sense that they
have accepted Jesus as their Lord and Savior. Not in the sense that
they follow Him. It's obvious by their behavior. You see, our behavior
reflects who we belong to.

I know many of us have been told "Don't' do anything that will
reflect badly on our family name." Or we've been part of organizations
that have specific creeds or rules of behavior or expectations for
how we present ourselves. Do we not believe that God has similar
expectations? He has told us in His Word how to behave, how to treat
others, how to represent Him to the world. If we truly belong to Him,
we will follow His way.

I pray each of us determine to behave in a way that is pleasing to
God. Not just because He says so, but because we belong to Him and
we love Him.

March 22

Therefore confess your sins to each other and pray
for each other so that you may be healed. The prayer
of a righteous person is powerful and effective.

— James 5:16

How effective are your prayers? Some believe their prayers are
answered always. Some believe it does no good to pray and they are
never answered. Some believe some of their prayers are answered and
some are not. So, why are there so many different beliefs about prayer?

I'm sure we've all heard our prayers need to be in accordance with
God's Will at some point in our lives. We've probably also heard that
God doesn't answer prayers like a genie, and we shouldn't treat Him
as such. Yet, we've also heard that God provides for all our needs and
wants to bless us richly. So, how do we know if God will answer our
prayers?

I believe the answer lies in our own lives and experience. Think
about being a child. How do we know our parents will give us what
we ask for? First, we know they love us. Second, we know they care for
our safety. Third, we know they care for our needs. Finally, it depends
on how we are behaving. Do we think God is all that much different?

If we follow God's Word and Jesus' teachings, we are behaving the
way God wants us to behave. If our heart is fully dedicated to God, we
become the righteous person Jesus urges us to be. When we do these,
we can be confident in God answering our prayers.

March 23

"A new command I give you: Love one another. As I
have loved you, so you must love one another. By this
everyone will know that you are my disciples, if you
love one another."

— John 13:34–35

How do you express your love for someone? Many of us will say that
we tell the person we love them. There will also be many of us who
rarely tell people we love them, but we love them anyway. There will
be a few who don't really understand love nor how to express it.

Jesus used love as an action verb, not has an emotion descriptor.
So, when He talks about love, He is not talking about emotional,
often fleeting love. He is talking about a deep-down inside love that
takes on action to demonstrate the fullness of itself. Words can easily
be stated with little or no meaning. Actions are a result of a deeper
commitment.

What actions demonstrate our love for someone? Perhaps it's
doing the dishes, mowing the lawn, fixing a car, doing the laundry,
or holding their hand through a tough time. What it is not is buying
extravagant gifts. Those last a short time and fade away. Doing
something that requires our time and effort demonstrates our love
far more than gifts or words.

I pray each of us realize that love is expressed through actions.
Words are nice, but actions that require our time are much, much
more precious. Show someone you love them today.

March 24

To the Jews who had believed him, Jesus said, "If you hold to my teaching, you are really my disciples. Then you will know the truth, and the truth will set you free."

— John 8:31–32

Whose image are you made in? Many will answer in God's image. Some will say we are in human image and came about by evolution. Other's won't have any idea how to answer that question. What is your answer?

With all our science and technology today, there is an ever-increasing number of people questioning whether we are truly made in God's image. They have boiled us down to numerous biological equations. That is all fine and good when it comes to understanding the physical body. However, it does nothing for understanding our mental, emotional, and spiritual faculties.

When we hear we are made in God's image, it doesn't mean physical. It means we were given intellectual capabilities to reason, think, and understand what is happening around us, what is being taught, and interacting with others. It means we are to be in community with others. After all, God is one in three persons. God created us in His image to discern truth, not just be sheep led by the evils and falsities spread by so many today.

I pray we all realize we were made in God's image and we draw comfort from that. We were created to discern truth. Let's all seek truth and choose to follow God's truth.

March 25

It is for freedom that Christ has set us free. Stand firm, then, and do not let yourselves be burdened again by a yoke of slavery... You, my brothers and sisters, were called to be free. But do not use your freedom to indulge the flesh; rather, serve one another humbly in love.

— Galatians 5:1, 13

What does freedom mean to you? To many in this country, it means being free from oppression, free to do what you want. Other's may say it is being free to work where you want, buy what you want, and like whatever you want. But what does freedom mean to the Christian?

We've often heard freedom isn't free and that's true. However, that phrase is often used when talking about freedom as it relates to our country. It is also very true of our Christian freedom. Our freedom cost Jesus Christ His life. When was the last time we thanked Him for His willingness to die for us?

Our Christian freedom means we are free from sin. What does that mean? It means we are free to act out of righteousness rather than being a slave to sin. It means we are free to do the right thing. It means we are free to behave as Christ would behave. We are free to serve our Holy God in everything we do.

I pray we come to understand the freedom we have in Christ and we decide to use that freedom to follow Him. Let's be people who live out our freedom in all we do, being Jesus to others around us.

March 26

For the entire law is fulfilled in keeping this one command: "Love your neighbor as yourself." If you bite and devour each other, watch out or you will be destroyed by each other.

— Galatians 5:14–15

Who do you lean on in times of trouble? Who is there for you when you need them? Perhaps it is a spouse, a sibling, a parent, a close friend, a co-worker, or someone you go to church with. We all need that special someone we can count on.

Have we thought that having someone who will be there for us depends as much on us as it does the other person? For instance, if we are hateful toward other people, do we really think others will come to our aid? Or, if we are constantly crying wolf and being extremely needy, do we expect others not to grow weary of helping us?

We all need help at some point in our lives, but we need to do for ourselves when we can. We also need to be there for others. If we only take and never give, or don't give proportionately to what we receive, we become leeches in other people's eyes. We all need to participate and give of ourselves.

I pray we all give as much or more than we receive. In this way, we all get what we need without even asking. Be a giver, just as Christ gave for us.

Marty Pressey

March 27

"At that time many will turn away from the faith
and will betray and hate each other, and many false
prophets will appear and deceive many people."
— Matthew 24:10–14

Are you standing firm? So many people today believe they have to stand up to the tyranny they see, if only in their own mind. In fact, many see tyranny everywhere, from everyone who has any small amount of power, and especially when the others point of view doesn't coincide with their own. Should we stand firm?

We should absolutely stand firm; stand firm in our faith in Christ. Does that mean we should be offensive toward others? No! It means we stand in confidence that this life is temporary and so long as we stand firm in Christ, we have an eternal home in heaven; a home where there is no pain, no tears, no hate, no frustration, and no death! We have a perfect home with Him.

By standing firm in our faith, we may be persecuted, laughed at, cursed at, or even physically beaten. That is a small price to pay considering the price Jesus paid for each of us and the reward we will receive. It's not easy but striking out in anger at someone is not the right answer. In those situations we need to ask ourselves what Christ's example and teachings would tell us to do.

I pray we all will stand firm in our faith. Be the example for others. Be the person Christ has called you to be.

March 28

The law was brought in so that the trespass might increase. But where sin increased, grace increased all the more, so that, just as sin reigned in death, so also grace might reign through righteousness to bring eternal life through Jesus Christ our Lord.

— Romans 5:20–21

Do you live in grace? Do you accept grace? Do you know that God freely gives grace to you? Do you understand that God's grace sets you free? Do you realize you live a life of guilt, shame, frustration, and continual struggle, if you don't accept His grace?

This world will imprison us with all its judgmental attitudes. It will consume our minds with torment, fear, and anxiety. We will become overwhelmed with it. We will be jealous of those we think have it all together. How do we free ourselves of this?

Grace sets us free. Not free to do whatever we want, but free from the evil that wants to keep us imprisoned. The only way to feel that grace is to wholeheartedly accept it from God. Sometimes that isn't easy. Sometimes we need help doing that. God's people are there to help us. Go to church, go to Bible studies, ask questions, ask for help.

I pray each of us recognizes the devil would imprison us, if we will allow it. I pray each of us will commit to seeking the help we need from people we trust in our churches. We all need it and we all need God's grace.

March 29

Therefore God exalted him to the highest place and
gave him the name that is above every name, that at
the name of Jesus every knee should bow, in heaven
and on earth and under the earth, and every tongue
acknowledge that Jesus Christ is Lord, to the glory
of God the Father.

— Philippians 2:9–11

Do you bow down before God? Do you bow down to honor the Lord
Jesus Christ? Do you bow in honest worship? Or do you worship with
your lips, but not your heart? There is so much half-hearted worship
of God in this world today. One day that will no longer be the case.

We can only speak for ourselves. We cannot speak for others.
We know if we are honestly worshiping God. Oh, we may be a little
desperate at times and fool ourselves. In the end though, our heart will
tell us we are or are not worshiping Him honestly.

I can testify to you that honestly giving yourself to Him in all that
you say and do will set you free. I can also tell you, until you let go of
your own pride, self-centeredness, and truly humble yourself before
God, you cannot commit to Him fully. It's not easy to do.

I pray we all humble ourselves before God and ask Him to fill our
hearts with Jesus. I pray we all decide to bow to Him. In the end, all
will. The question is, will you be forced to do so as one who is judged
by Him or willingly do so and live eternity with Him?

March 30

Don't let anyone look down on you because you are
young, but set an example for the believers in speech,
in conduct, in love, in faith and in purity.
—1 Timothy 4:12

Do you want to change the world? Are you tired of all the arguing,
hate, anger, yelling, chaos, anxiety, prejudice, judgment, sniping,
gossiping, and so much more? How can you change the world? You
can make a change.

We've all heard somewhere, stated by someone, and perhaps many
someone's, that we can change the world. We've heard we must start
first with ourselves. We've heard we will need to work on one person
at a time. Many of us long to be able to tell everyone to stop being
so ugly to each other. Yet, we don't have that platform, the ability to
command the world. Or do we?

You know what? We do have the ability to begin the change. If
we first control ourselves, we can have a positive impact on others.
Why is it the person who wants others to stop judging them is often
the person judging others? Stop yourself. Look upon others with the
love of God. Show compassion, love, and grace. Be the person you
want others to be.

I pray each of us decides to show the love God has shown us to
every person we meet. Show it to your family, your friends, and the
grumpy person in the checkout line. Be who God has called you to be
and begin changing the world.

Marty Pressey

March 31

"My prayer is not for them alone. I pray also for those who will believe in me through their message, that all of them may be one, Father, just as you are in me and I am in you. May they also be in us so that the world may believe that you have sent me. I have given them the glory that you gave me, that they may be one as we are one—I in them and you in me—so that they may be brought to complete unity. Then the world will know that you sent me and have loved them even as you have loved me."

— John 17:20–23

Are you unified with your brothers and sisters? Are you unified in love? Do you accept that we are all different yet one in Christ? Are you willing to accept different opinions from those in the family?

We are a people that are called by Jesus Christ to be unified in love with our brothers and sisters in Christ. When we disagree, we are to disagree in love, allowing different opinions without being angry or judgmental.

Some of us may call this growing up and we would be correct. The true name is Christian Maturity. Christ has called us to be mature in His love. We are called to be mature, to eat spiritual meat rather than drink milk (Hebrews 5:12–14). If we are content to be babes in Christ, we are not fulfilling our calling.

I pray we all grow and mature in our walk with Christ. This is how we become one in love. We need to be one in love, because each of us will need the other at some point in our life.

April

April 1

For this son of mine was dead and is alive again; he
was lost and is found.' So they began to celebrate.
— Luke 15: 24

Are you alive? Or are you just living? So many in this world just live
and don't really come alive to live the abundant life Jesus has promised.
It is simple, yet very difficult to do. We all have a decision to make.

In this world there are many worries. We often let those worries
take over our lives. Not only that, but we worry about the smallest of
things. As we worry, the worries start compounding themselves until
we are one tangled mess of worry. We worry about our clothes, our
children, our work, our bills, and even something as small as how our
hair is combed.

This worry robs us of the abundant life. Cast off the worries;
throw them at the foot of the cross. Ask Jesus to remove them. Ask
over and over until they are gone. Does it take multiple times for Jesus
to remove them? No! It takes multiple times for us to release them.
We hold them tight like a safety blanket, wrapping ourselves in them.
Let them go!

I pray each of us will let go of our worldly worries and live the life
God intended for us. The only way to do that is to return to our one
true love. Let's all return to God and live the abundant life He has for
us in faith.

April 2

For by the grace given me I say to every one of you:
Do not think of yourself more highly than you ought,
but rather think of yourself with sober judgment, in
accordance with the faith God has distributed to
each of you.

— Romans 12:3

How do you see yourself? What is your view of yourself? Where do you see yourself fitting in? Do you look at yourself as being above others? Are you prideful? Are you haughty? Do you act as though you are better than others?

It seems everyone is posturing to get their piece of the pie. That may be to get their 10 minutes of fame or promotion or feel like they are better than the other person. We see it every day. We see it at work, school, on TV, in politics, in the news, and on and on and on.

God has called us to a higher standard. You see, the posturing to feel like we're better than someone else is really a low standard anyone can achieve. It's the higher standard of putting others ahead of ourselves and honestly looking in the mirror God has called us to. And here's the kicker, when we do, we are freed of the worldly view and culture of putting others down to make ourselves feel good.

I pray we all decide to stop the posturing, stop trying to make ourselves feel more important by putting others down. We all need to be set free from this prison. Determine to see people through Jesus' eyes. Determine to live in the freedom He provides.

April 3

Do you not know that your bodies are temples of the
Holy Spirit, who is in you, whom you have received
from God? You are not your own; you were bought
at a price. Therefore honor God with your bodies.

—1 Corinthians 6:19–20

Do you honor God? Better yet, do you honor God with your body?
How should we do that? Why should we do that? What does God have
to do with our bodies? Doesn't He just care about our hearts?

Our American culture is so duplicative. We look in wonder or
admiration at those who are in top physical shape, yet such a large
portion of our population is obese. We look at all the pretty faces in
the movies and on TV, then we try to make ourselves look like them,
while putting no effort into our physical health. Should we?

We are told in multiple places that we should take care of our
bodies. Does that mean we need to become fanatics? No. We should
do our best to eat right and exercise. Why? If we don't take care of
our bodies, how can we do the work God has put before us? We need
to be able to walk, lift, hug, hold, stand, assist, carry, run, sew, clean,
paint, and so much more. We need to take care of the place the Holy
Spirit lives.

I pray we all realize we must first take care of ourselves before we
can help others. That doesn't mean putting ourselves ahead of others,
it means preparing ourselves to help others. God has called us to be
His Holy Temple.

April 4

Endure hardship as discipline; God is treating you
as his children. For what children are not disciplined
by their father? If you are not disciplined—and
everyone undergoes discipline—then you are not
legitimate, not true sons and daughters at all.

— Hebrews 12:7–8

How are you holding up? Are you enduring your current trial? Are you
continuing in your belief? Do you continue to love God even when He
seems to be punishing you? Do you love Him when He appears to be
absent? We all need to hold onto our believe in Jesus Christ.

There are many in this world that will believe in something or
someone as long as they feel good about it. Many today leave the
person they are following the moment things get tough. People leave
their jobs as soon as their boss sternly reprimands them for not doing
something correctly. Perhaps there are circumstances in our world
where it's OK to walk out of a tough situation.

God is our father and He will discipline us sometimes. When we
go through difficult times, we need to turn to Him and ask what He
wants us to learn from it. He will show us and will bring us through
the tough time. We should then apply the lessons we learn to our
future steps.

I pray we all learn that discipline is good for us. I pray we all hold
on to God in our tough times and also in our good times. He does
discipline us; we need to recognize it as such and turn away from our
bad behavior.

April 5

"Whoever can be trusted with very little can also be trusted with much, and whoever is dishonest with very little will also be dishonest with much. So if you have not been trustworthy in handling worldly wealth, who will trust you with true riches?"

— Luke 16:10–11

Are you trustworthy? Can people count on you? Are you sure you know the answer to that question? Do you ever ask yourself, challenge yourself? We often fool ourselves into thinking we're trustworthy, but don't take a hard look in the mirror.

It is so common in today's culture to be untrustworthy, yet claim you are, that no one seems to bat an eye at it anymore. How many times have we heard someone say they will meet us at a certain place at a certain time and they show up 10 minutes late? Did it cause us to be at the wrong place at the wrong time, be in a hurry, and end up in a car accident?

Jesus tells us to be trustworthy in the smallest of things. Our word, our dedication, our commitment to follow through is worth more than gold. If we do not honor it, we have no ground to stand on. If we are not responsible with earthly things, how can we be trusted with the true riches of heaven?

I pray each of us take being trustworthy very seriously. We are human and will miss the mark at times, but we cannot make it a habit. Be trustworthy, be responsible, pursue God's riches.

April 6

Overhearing what they said, Jesus told him, "Don't be afraid; just believe."

— Mark 5:36

How is your faith? How do you know if your faith is good or not so good? We all have struggles and we all need to keep our faith in Jesus Christ, in God the Father, in the Holy Spirit. So, how do we know our faith is strong or if we are lacking in faith and really need to spend more time with God and His people?

We are told in 1 Peter 5:8 that the devil is prowling like a roaring lion looking to devour people. Who is he specifically looking for? He's looking for those who believe in Jesus. He's looking to weaken our faith. He'll use whatever means possible to make us question if God really cares. One of the most common means of achieving this is fear.

In Mark chapter 5 we see a few things happen. Jesus cleanses a demon-possessed man, rebuking the demons and leaving the man in a perfect state of mind. He also heals a woman who had a case of bleeding for 12 years. Finally, he raises the daughter of one of the synagogue leaders from the dead. It is all summed up in Jesus words in Mark 5:36. We must lose our fear by believing in Him.

I pray we all believe in and trust in Jesus. When we wholeheartedly do that, our fear goes away. It does not mean we can be reckless, but it does mean we can be confident that God is working in all situations according to His plan.

Marty Pressey

April 7

For this reason I kneel before the Father, from whom
every family in heaven and on earth derives its name.
— Ephesians 3:14–15

How is your family? Do you know which family you are part of? Are
you in a family? Do you want to be in a family? Are you contributing
to your family? We all need to be part of a family, specifically the
family of God.

A family is the basic model from which God works. We are told
that 2 people can stay warm when they huddle together in the cold
and can defend themselves. We are told a cord of 3 strands cannot be
easily broken (Eccles. 4:11–12). These examples indicate that God
made us to be together, to rely on one another, to work together. They
teach us that we are stronger when we collaborate, cooperate, and
work as a team.

We are part of a family in our local church, which is part of the
larger, global family. Our family must have a foundation of love to
fully serve the needs of each member. Our love should be based on
Christ's love for us. When we focus on our family in Christ and serve
in love, we reach our full potential and God works wonders in our
midst. This takes a commitment on our part to God and to each other.

I pray we all commit to each other in our family, serving one
another as Christ has served us. As we do so, we will see God blessing
us with the fullness of life. Live for each other.

April 8

When Jesus had finished saying all these things, he
said to his disciples, "As you know, the Passover is
two days away—and the Son of Man will be handed
over to be crucified."

— Matthew 26:1–2

Do you feel like the whole world is against you? Do you think other
people are plotting against you? Do you feel like you are not loved?
Do you feel like you are all alone? Imagine how Jesus felt on the day
He was betrayed.

As we live in this world, we can feel as though others are plotting
against us. Sometimes we may be right. All too often it's our mind
playing tricks on us. However, when we think about there being
roughly 7 billion people in this world and about 325 million people
in the U.S., we would be silly to think they are all plotting against us.
Sure, someone may plot against us, but we can overcome that.

We won't face the type of plotting against us that Jesus faced. He
was betrayed not only by someone who had been a close companion
for 3 years, but by a large crowd who wanted Him to face a gruesome
death. As we face challenges in our lives, let's remember that Jesus
faced a far bigger one and He gives us the strength to face ours.

Lean on Jesus and on the Spirit He gave us to face your challenges.
He will see you through whatever you are facing. He's overcome the
biggest challenge of all. Trust in Him.

Marty Pressey

April 9

He replied, "Go into the city to a certain man and tell
him, 'The Teacher says: My appointed time is near. I
am going to celebrate the Passover with my disciples
at your house.'"

— Matthew 26:18

How do you prepare for challenges? What do you do when you know
a difficult situation is on the horizon? Do you sit in dread? Or do you
celebrate with close friends? Do you trust God and know He is in
control?

We sometimes face some pretty daunting challenges. It could
be heading off to a combat zone. It could be taking a final in a very
difficult class. It could be a career change. It could be a major change
in a relationship. All of these can cause us to be stressed or experience
anxiety, worrying about what will happen.

God is always with us. He will be with us every step of the way
as we go through trials. Just as long-distance runners will carb up the
night before a big race, we need to fill our hearts and minds with God's
Word to prepare for our challenges. It is through His Word that we are
fed and strengthened. The more we fill ourselves with Him, the more
prepared we are for those tough times.

Let us all determine to feast on God's Word and come to trust
Him in all situations. As we learn to trust Him, our fears and worries
will disappear. Trust Him, prepare for the challenges ahead.

April 10

From noon until three in the afternoon darkness came over all the land. About three in the afternoon Jesus cried out in a loud voice, "Eli, Eli, lema sabachthani?" (which means "My God, my God, why have you forsaken me?").

— Matthew 27:45–46

Do you feel you've been forsaken? Perhaps you feel as though no one cares. Do you feel like you've been betrayed? Have you looked at your circumstances from a different point of view? Are you willing to sacrifice for others? Jesus took on the worst of humanity's sins or deeds in order to provide us with salvation.

Too often we are told to look out for ourselves. We are told, "if you don't look out for yourself, no one else will." It's a lie that Satan wants us to believe. It's one that, if we allow it to take root, will destroy us. Jesus is always looking out for us.

Jesus gave up His life to be the perfect sacrifice for us. His death darkened the world for a few hours. His death on that day caused many to lose hope. His mother and the apostles were distraught. So much so that the apostles could only huddle together in a room, trying to comfort one another and determine what to do next. All that changed three days later.

We all need to stop and really appreciate the pain and suffering Jesus went through for us. We need to recognize the love He has for us. When we do, we need to reciprocate that love with our love for Him.

Marty Pressey

April 11

The next day, the one after Preparation Day, the chief
priests and the Pharisees went to Pilate. "Sir," they
said, "we remember that while he was still alive that
deceiver said, 'After three days I will rise again.'"

— Matthew 27:62–63

How do you react when you have a really bad surprise? How would
you react if a mentor, teacher, close friend, a person you have lived
with and traveled with for 3 years suddenly died? Yes, I'm talking
about the apostles.

The apostles, much like the rest of the Jews, thought the Messiah
was going to be an earthly king. They expected him to sit on a throne,
throw the Romans out of Israel, and bring Israel back into prominence.
How could this type of king die and do what they expected?

You can imagine they were distraught, wondering what to do now,
the day after they had witnessed Jesus' excruciating death. We can
imagine them in a house together, hiding, hoping the Roman soldiers
didn't come around and take them to be crucified as well. There were
likely a lot of questions, gloom, shock, and mourning going on. What
is it like for you the day after someone close to you has died?

As we put ourselves in the apostle's shoes, we must remember they
were in fear for their lives as well. They were saddened by the loss of
someone they thought couldn't die. Yet, though they didn't know it,
they were feared by the religious elite.

April 12

So the women hurried away from the tomb, afraid yet
filled with joy, and ran to tell his disciples. Suddenly
Jesus met them. "Greetings," he said. They came
to him, clasped his feet and worshiped him. Then
Jesus said to them, "Do not be afraid. Go and tell
my brothers to go to Galilee; there they will see me."
— Matthew 28:8–10

How joyous would your celebration be? We throw lots of parties for
earthly events that have little consequence in the big scheme of things.
Why not celebrate with all our hearts on Easter? Why not be super
joyous and happy that we have been promised a life forever with God?

Can you imagine the joy the 2 Mary's would have had after they
saw the empty tomb, then see Jesus alive and talk to Him? They ran
as hard as they could with smiles as big as could be and hearts filled
with joy to tell the apostles He was alive! They were bursting with joy!

We probably don't fully appreciate the joy of seeing someone we
love resurrected. We can only imagine what it would be like. One day
we will see our loved ones resurrected. We will live forever with Him.
Our hearts should be filled with joy.

Let us all be filled with joy as we celebrate Jesus Christ rising
from the dead. Let us celebrate our redemption, our salvation, and
the promise of our resurrection! Be joyous and appreciative of the
greatest gift of all.

Marty Pressey

April 13

At that time Jesus, full of joy through the Holy Spirit,
said, "I praise you, Father, Lord of heaven and earth,
because you have hidden these things from the wise
and learned, and revealed them to little children. Yes,
Father, for this is what you were pleased to do."
— Luke 10:21

Are you joyous? Do you have true joy in your life? Do you know what true joy is? Do not mix up joy and happy, they are not the same. Did you know that true joy can be yours, even if you are not happy?

People are usually happy when they get what they want or something they've worked hard for. Some people are happy when they see others achieve a goal. There's nothing wrong with this, but it is fleeting. Our typical happiness only lasts a few moments or hours, then it is gone.

True joy comes from God, His gift of the Holy Spirit. Some will scoff at that, but they have not experienced it. Just like some do not understand the exhilaration of skydiving. When we submit and commit our lives to God, He blesses us with complete and endless joy. We just have to get out of the way.

I pray we all submit all our cares to God and ask Him for the true joy in our lives. He will give it to us. We can have joy even when going through trials and tough times. Step aside from your earthly desires and accept the joy of the Spirit.

April 14

He told the crowd to sit down on the ground. Then he took the seven loaves and the fish, and when he had given thanks, he broke them and gave them to the disciples, and they in turn to the people. They all ate and were satisfied. Afterward the disciples picked up seven basketfuls of broken pieces that were left over.

— Matthew 15:35–37

Give thanks for all that you have been blessed with. We often have big meals with our family. We are blessed with many people in our lives. But do we truly reflect on our blessing and give thanks to God for them?

If we were to go back just a few years and ask ourselves where we were, physically, emotionally, spiritually, what would we see? Would we see someone who was physically weak, emotionally distraught, and spiritually weak? Or would we see someone who has been physically healed, emotionally well, and faithful to God?

We all need to reflect on the path God has taken us and be thankful He is with us. He provides for us, even when we think it is not enough. He makes the smallest amount more than enough, if we are satisfied with what He gives.

I pray we all reflect on our blessings. I pray we all give thanks to God for His wondrous gifts. We have far more than we think. Let's truly appreciate what God has bless us with.

April 15

There was also a prophet, Anna, the daughter of
Penuel, of the tribe of Asher. She was very old; she
had lived with her husband seven years after her
marriage, and then was a widow until she was eighty-
four. She never left the temple but worshiped night
and day, fasting and praying.

— Luke 2:36–37

Are you dedicated to giving thanks? It's one thing to be taught to say
"Thank you" to someone who does something for you. It's something
different to be dedicated to giving God thanks with your entire being.

We teach our children to say thank you, because it's polite. But do
we teach them to truly be thankful from their heart? How does a child
begin to understand how to be thankful for what they have? There is a
simple, yet hard answer to that question. Make them endure hardship.

Who are the most thankful people in the world? The people who
have nearly nothing. Does seeing them or knowing them cause you
to be thankful? According to a study in 2016, if your net worth is
$3,210 you are in the top 50% richest people in the world and if your
net worth is $68,800 you are in the top 10% richest in the world. We
should all be very thankful.

I pray we all open our eyes and realize we have been richly blessed.
God knows our hearts and people usually do too. How? From our
heart come our words. Let's all have a change of heart and become
truly thankful.

April 16

One of them, when he saw he was healed, came
back, praising God in a loud voice. He threw himself
at Jesus' feet and thanked him—and he was a
Samaritan.

— Luke 17:15–16

How thankful are you? Do you fall at Jesus' feet with gratitude? Do
you submit your will to His? Have you realized He has your best
interest at heart? When will you let go? We all like to think we are in
control, yet we are not. We don't like to admit that God is in control,
not fully.

God can heal our hurts. He can eliminate our distress. He alone
can wipe out our anxiety and fear. All we have to do is fall at Jesus' feet,
praise Him, and let go of those things. He can free us from falling for
Satan's schemes. The world willingly follows Satan because they are
blinded by the shininess of Satan's lures. We are called to be different
from the world.

As we turn all our worries over to Jesus, let's also praise Him for
all He does. When we give thanks to Him and praise His wonderful
name, He is pleased. Not because of the words, but because our heart
has turned to Him. We become a new person—someone who shines
the light of Jesus on others.

Let's all turn our entire being, our whole hearts to Jesus, giving
Him our praise and thanks. He is our Savior yesterday, today, and
tomorrow. He was, is, and always will be right there with us.

Marty Pressey

April 17

When he had said this, Jesus called in a loud voice,
"Lazarus, come out!" The dead man came out, his
hands and feet wrapped with strips of linen, and a
cloth around his face. Jesus said to them, "Take off
the grave clothes and let him go."

— John 11:43–44

Are you thankful for the family you have? Are you thankful, even
when they irritate you? Do you let them know you are grateful for
them? We often hear people say, "No one is guaranteed another day."
But do we live that way?

Jesus has guaranteed us not just another day, but eternity.
However, that eternity will not be spent on this earth. We have a
limited time here and our decisions have an effect for eternity.
Specifically, we either accept Jesus as our Savior or we don't. There is
no gray area, we must make the decision for ourselves.

If we care about our family and understand the decision lasts
for eternity, we should strive for all our family members to decide to
follow Jesus. That doesn't include banging them over the head with a
Bible. It does include understanding each person so that we can teach
them in a manner they will understand. All will be raised from the
dead, but only those who choose Jesus will spend eternity with Him.

I pray we all choose Jesus. I pray we all choose to help our family
members to choose Him, too. Don't leave something undone in this
life.

April 18

For although they knew God, they neither glorified
him as God nor gave thanks to him, but their thinking
became futile and their foolish hearts were darkened.

— Romans 1:21

Who or what are you giving thanks for? Are you more thankful for the
things you have than the people in your life? Are you chasing more
things than relationships? This world is crazy for things. Have you
fallen into the same trap?

Our American culture is always chasing the next bright, shiny
thing. It might be a bigger house, a new car, new clothes, jewelry, or
any number of other things. We drive ourselves mad making another
dollar to buy something new. We, as Americans, have more things
than any other culture in the world, yet it's not enough. Why?

When we chase after things rather than a relationship with God,
we are left empty, yet never know how empty we are. If a bucket was
sitting in the yard and had never held water, would it know it was
supposed to hold water? No! But one day it rains, and the bucket gets
filled with water. Now it knows its purpose. The best way to build a
relationship with Him is to give thanks to Him.

I pray we all determine to seek a relationship with God and be
filled with His glory. When we seek to learn about Him, seek to
understand His will, seek to do what He would have us do, we will
be filled beyond measure. Give thanks to God for what He has done
for you.

April 19

I always thank my God for you because of his grace
given you in Christ Jesus. For in him you have been
enriched in every way—with all kinds of speech
and with all knowledge—God thus confirming our
testimony about Christ among you.

—1 Corinthians 1:4–6

Do you give thanks for those around you? Do you give thanks for their
spiritual gifts? Or are you jealous of them? Do you hold on to Christ
through all your joys and trials? We are to rejoice and be thankful
always.

This world tells us we are to be jealous, that we are to covet what
someone else has. It doesn't matter if it's their house or their car or
their boyfriend/girlfriend or spouse or any of the shiny things they
have. We are told by the world to continue to chase after those things
and to follow our eyes. We are fools when we fall victim to these false
teachings.

How do we combat the false teachings? We have to stand firm in
Jesus Christ. We have to learn His teaching and plant it firmly in our
hearts. When we do, our lives are enriched. We recognize the spiritual
gifts of others and the purpose for which they were put in our midst.
This leads to us having a deep joy that will see us through those trials
and will cause the mountain top experiences to be even higher.

I pray we all spend time learning about Jesus and plant His
teachings in our hearts. We all need that rock to keep us steady during
troubled times. Stand on the Rock.

April 20

The sting of death is sin, and the power of sin is the
law. But thanks be to God! He gives us the victory
through our Lord Jesus Christ.

—1 Corinthians 15:56–57

What are you thankful for? How do you show your thankfulness?
We can show thankfulness in so many ways. We can do so verbally or
physically. We have more options and chances to show thanks than
we often believe.

Thankfulness is often a foreign concept in today's world. So many
people believe they are owed everything. They believe that just their
mere presence dictates them being entitled to whatever they want. Of
course, this attitude is fed in today's world by commercials. We hear
"you deserve this" over and over.

Do any of us deserve anything? Yes! We deserve death because
of our sin. However, God has a very different plan. He provided
restitution for our sinfulness in the crucifixion of our Lord and Savior,
Jesus Christ, so we can fully enjoy the forgiveness and grace God
so freely gives. Shouldn't we, then, offer our thanks to Him for this
wonderful gift? If we were to put our thanks into action, couldn't we
begin changing the world into a better place?

I pray we all determine to give God thanks by both word and
deed. We need more deeds of thanks in this world today. As we do the
deeds of thanks, we will see a change in both the world around us and
ourselves. Give thanks to God.

April 21

Both the one who makes people holy and those who
are made holy are of the same family. So Jesus is not
ashamed to call them brothers and sisters.

— Hebrews 2:11

What is important to you? This is a good question for us. We should
ask this question of ourselves quite often. If it's important to you, you
will make it a priority. We hear that often, but often think it's a cliché.
The truth of the matter is, we have too many priorities, too much
chaos, and we are far too busy. We really do need to stop and assess
what's important to us. Most of us would say our family is important
and it should be. But do we act like it is? Do we put family first?
Sometimes we do. Sometimes we say no to the promotion or the
overtime or whatever is attempting to take our attention.

Do you know you are holy? Because you are in the family of God,
a brother or sister of Jesus, you are holy. Shouldn't that be important
to you? Shouldn't that be encouragement to you? Take comfort in
knowing you are holy. Be confident that nothing can change that.
Celebrate Jesus' wonderful life and remember He is our brother.

I pray we remember we are part of God's family. Let's be more like
our brother. Let's be holy.

April 22

"Who of you by worrying can add a single hour to your life? Since you cannot do this very little thing, why do you worry about the rest?"

— Luke 12:25–26

Are you anxious? Do you worry about loved ones, what gifts to buy, what food to serve, how you're going to fit it all in? These are common worries of lots of people. For some, you can include the worry of how will you pay for it all?

We are told that we are not to worry. So why do we do it? The very simple answer is, we think we should be in control. We somehow believe it all depends on us. We have been fooled into believing no one else can do what we do. We fall for the lie that Satan is telling us in our thoughts, in the commercials we see, in conversations with our friends, and the pressures from our boss.

We are not in control and we should not worry. It's easier said than done, but we can progress toward it. The more we rely on God, the more our confidence in Him will increase. We call that growing in our faith. We first have to trust Him in the small things. As our faith increases, we will trust Him in bigger things. As we trust Him more and more, our faith will increase, and our worries will decrease.

I pray we all learn to trust God more and reduce our worries. Let's not be anxious about anything, rather let's enjoy the wonderful love God has shown us and let Him be in control.

April 23

Be completely humble and gentle; be patient, bearing
with one another in love. Make every effort to keep
the unity of the Spirit through the bond of peace.
                                              — Ephesians 4:2–3

Are you patient? Or are you like the rest of our culture and want it all
right now? In our instant gratification culture, we think we need our
meal the moment we have the slightest inkling of hunger; we think
we need the new shiny object the moment we first see it; we think we
need the attention of someone the moment we ask for it. Is this how
we should be?

Do we realize impatience is a form of discourteousness? When
our impatience requires someone to answer us immediately, we are no
longer courteous to the other person, rather we are demanding they
stop whatever they are doing to attend to us.

We all need to realize we are not the center of the world nor are
we necessarily the center of any given group of people. There may
be times when all the attention is shown on us. There will be far
more times when we have to take the back seat and wait. Don't be the
grumpy, self-centered person who pouts or throws a fit because you
are not the center at the moment.

Let's all take on a little humility and not demand to have attention
at all times. When we are humble, we receive more recognition than
we can imagine. Wait patiently for your turn and be at peace.

April 24

"There was a rich man who was dressed in purple and fine linen and lived in luxury every day. At his gate was laid a beggar named Lazarus, covered with sores and longing to eat what fell from the rich man's table. Even the dogs came and licked his sores."

— Luke 16:19–21

Are you taking care of the needy? Do you see the needy around you? Do you recognize the truly needy? Do you see the person who sleeps in a cold alley not knowing where their next meal is coming from? The single mother who can barely pay for her tiny apartment and can't afford to buy clothes for her children?

We are told the poor in spirit are blessed. What does that mean? It means those who recognize all they have comes from God and they have been blessed so they can bless others. It means those who humble themselves before God and do His work.

Do we see the needy? They may have lots of money and lack spiritual humbleness. They may be the homeless person laying on the curb. They may be our co-worker who is going through a tough time and struggling to not have a nervous breakdown. They may be the person who meets us in Sunday morning worship with a smile, but deep down needs a hug and someone to tell them they are loved.

Let's all look for the needy and do something to provide for them. When we use God's blessings to bless others, we are blessed even more. Be a person who blesses.

April 25

"Rejoice in that day and leap for joy, because great is
your reward in heaven. For that is how their ancestors
treated the prophets."

— Luke 6:23

Are you joyous? Do you have the joy of Christ in your life? Or are you
only happy and only when things go your way? Joy is a deep-down
source of our well-being. Without it our lives are full of anxiety, hate,
anger, frustration, and self-pity.

Can we have those emotions, even with Christ in our life?
Absolutely. The difference is, we won't experience them every day
and probably not every week. Those emotions will come few and far
between. The more we have Christ in our life, the less often they will
come. The world will wonder what's wrong with us.

You see, the world is full of misery. That's why we see so much on
our TV's today of people putting other people down. It's the world's
way of trying to make us feel better. We don't need that to feel better.
We need Christ. Christ will fill us with His Spirit, the Holy Spirit, and
we will be filled with joy. We will no longer need to put others down
to feel better. Instead we will look for ways to lift others up.

I pray we all ask Christ to fill us with His Spirit. I pray we all seek
Him so we can be filled with joy. Let's all be the light to the world, the
joyful light the world needs, all day, every day.

April 26

We have different gifts, according to the grace given to each of us. If your gift is prophesying, then prophesy in accordance with your faith; if it is serving, then serve; if it is teaching, then teach; if it is to encourage, then give encouragement; if it is giving, then give generously; if it is to lead, do it diligently; if it is to show mercy, do it cheerfully.

— Romans 12:6–8

Do you give good gifts? I'm sure we all would like to think so. We may spend hours looking for the perfect gift. If we give the gift to someone and they don't like it, we feel bad, frustrated, and disappointed. Do we appreciate the gifts God gives us?

God graciously gives us wonderful gifts and we often don't appreciate them. How can I say that? Do we use our gifts? Do we bless others with our gifts as God has blessed us? Too often we don't. Too often our gifts from God are used for selfish purposes or not used at all.

God has blessed each of us in many different ways. As a parent, it is often disappointing when we give a gift and a child doesn't appreciate it. So how do we think God feels when He has said He will protect us and we choose to ignore it and live in fear instead?

I pray we all recognize the gifts God has given us and use them to further His kingdom. We should appreciate the gifts and show we appreciate them by blessing others. Let's all share our gifts and our blessings.

April 27

The man from whom the demons had gone out begged to go with him, but Jesus sent him away, saying, "Return home and tell how much God has done for you." So the man went away and told all over town how much Jesus had done for him.

— Luke 8:38–39

Are you home? This may sound like an odd question, but many are not at home. From a Christian point of view, we may say we won't be home until we are with God in heaven. But have you thought you can be home here and now? We can be—for a time.

We have been called by God for a purpose. He has work for us to do. We are to tell others what God has done in our lives. We are to lean on and learn from Him. We are to grow and become mature followers of Christ. As a child grows from an infant into adulthood, so we are to grow from being infants in Christ into mature Christians.

God's plan for us is not to live in fear, but to live with confidence in Him. Are we to be careless? No, we are to be judicious, yet confident. We can only grow and gain confidence in God when we trust Him a little more each day. As such, He has put us in our temporary home here on earth to complete the work He has put before us.

I pray we all learn and grow in Christ. I pray we all come to be at home in Him while we walk this earth. It will truly change the way we see things here and now.

April 28

Thanks be to God for his indescribable gift!
—2 Corinthians 9:15

Are you changed? Does a celebration bring out the best in you or are you still selfish? Do you appreciate your many blessings or are you still wanting more things? Are you appreciative of what it took to acquire the gifts given you or are you disappointed you didn't get just what you asked for? Those who live according to the world are disappointed.

We all have probably experienced disappointment on a Christmas morning or a birthday. The question is, how long did we allow that disappointment to control us? Was it a momentary flash and then gone? Or did it turn into a temper tantrum and turn the day into a dismal, black cloudy kind of day? So many in our country of wealth and plenty allow the day to become an ugly day because they didn't get the perfect gift.

Do we not know that we already have the perfect gift? There is no gift that can be given in this world that is more perfect than the gift God has given us. If all we got was a pair of socks, we should appreciate them as though it was a brand-new car or bicycle or purse or toolset or whatever we dreamt of as the perfect gift.

I pray we all realize the things we receive are gifts given with a loving heart. Be appreciative, for the perfect gift has already been given. Simply receive it and let it change you.

April 29

When they had gone, an angel of the Lord appeared
to Joseph in a dream. "Get up," he said, "take the
child and his mother and escape to Egypt. Stay there
until I tell you, for Herod is going to search for the
child to kill him."

— Matthew 2:13

Are you listening for God to speak? Do you hear the still, quiet voice?
Do you feel the Holy Spirit tugging at you on the inside? God still
speaks to us, just not from burning bushes like He did to Moses. He
still speaks to us, when we slow down and spend quiet time with Him.

You will notice it is far more common that God speaks to people
in the Bible through visions, dreams, or when they are in quiet places
seeking Him. Rare is the occasion that God speaks in a loud, booming
voice. So why do we think He will speak to us as if He is speaking
through a megaphone? Do we really think we are Moses? I'm not
convinced we want to be Moses.

Moses was out in the dessert, both figuratively and physically.
God had to speak loudly to get his attention. The only other time God
spoke loudly to Moses was when He was giving him the law. I doubt
we want to be Moses in either case. Wouldn't we rather be listening
for God to speak, spending some quiet time with Him? He will speak
to us, if we will only listen.

I pray we all slow down and spend some time with God. We need
it. Let's all listen to the guidance He is eager to provide to us. We'll be
far better off for it.

April 30

The true light that gives light to everyone was coming into the world. He was in the world, and though the world was made through him, the world did not recognize him.

— John 1:9–10

Are you following the light? Is it dim and in the distance? Or are you right there with it, close as close can be? Perhaps you see the bright light far off in front of you and you continue to seek after it, but you're still not completely out of the dark.

So many in this world live in the darkness, nearly all by their own choosing. They desire to live in the darkness to hide their selfish deeds. Or they have chosen to continue to live in their fears, afraid to step into the light and wash those fears away. It's a case of being comfortable in our situation, afraid of where we're at, but more afraid to take a chance on going into something different. There is no need for that fear. Christ is waiting to welcome us with open arms.

The true light is Christ. When we are close to Him, His light dispels the darkness that would so easily cause us to be lost. It's not that we can't see the darkness, but it no longer engulfs us. We stand in the light and are filled with the warmth and peace of being in the light.

I pray we all decide to step into the light. Let's all follow the true light and feel His loving warmth all around us. He knows our fears and is ready to take them away.

May

May 1

But you, man of God, flee from all this, and pursue
righteousness, godliness, faith, love, endurance and
gentleness. Fight the good fight of the faith. Take
hold of the eternal life to which you were called when
you made your good confession in the presence of
many witnesses.

—1 Timothy 6:11–12

What are the obstacles in your way today? What uphill battle are you
fighting? Do you feel as though you will never achieve it? Have you
asked if God wills it? Are you fighting the battle He wants you to fight?

We fight many battles in our lifetime. Sometimes they are tiny
battles and sometimes they are huge. We often fight battles because
there is something we want. Occasionally, we fight the battle God
wants us to fight.

When we are obeying God's will, we find the task may be tough,
but it is also very rewarding and achievable. We have a confidence we
will accomplish what He has set before us. We are to trust He is right
there beside us giving us what we need to do what He wants.

I pray we all discern the battles we should be fighting and fight
them according to God's will. I pray we all set about seeking His will
for our lives. Seek Him. Trust Him. Obey Him.

May 2

Last night an angel of the God to whom I belong and whom I serve stood beside me and said, 'Do not be afraid, Paul. You must stand trial before Caesar; and God has graciously given you the lives of all who sail with you.' So keep up your courage, men, for I have faith in God that it will happen just as he told me.

— Acts 27:23–25

Are you caught in a storm? Are you wondering what God has planned for you? Are you asking where He is and why He is allowing you to go through a tough time? Will you decide to trust in His plan?

We all go through tough times and they seem to never end. A day in a rough situation can seem like an eternity. We feel as though we have been abandoned or there is no way out. Yet, there is a new day dawning just ahead.

When we have those tough times, we need to rely on God to see us through. It's not always easy. We flounder and stumble and sometimes crawl. But God has a plan for us, and we are to trust in His plan.

I pray we all trust that God will see us through even the toughest of times. I pray each of us will build our trust in good times so we can hold onto it during the tough times. Trust in God. He will see you through.

Marty Pressey

May 3

And let us run with perseverance the race marked out for us, fixing our eyes on Jesus, the pioneer and perfecter of faith.

— Hebrews 12:1b–2a

Who do you look up to? Is there someone you view as a hero? Do you look at certain people as though they are superhuman? Do you look to Jesus as your Savior and Lord of your life?

We have more people in this world who are honored as heroes or looked to as being superhuman than we can count. It seems as though there is constantly someone being put on a pedestal. In many cases for not very good reasons.

There is One who should always be looked to and honored. He came to save us, a lowly people. When we honor Him with all we are and put our faith in Him, we find true life. When we put Him first in our lives, everything else falls into place.

I pray we all look to Jesus as our Hero, our Savior. I pray each of us will honor Him every day. I pray we will allow Him to guide us in everything we do. Jesus, Savior, God.

May 4

For we are God's handiwork, created in Christ Jesus
to do good works, which God prepared in advance
for us to do.

— Ephesians 2:10

We have work to do. We all have work to do, but often don't think about the work that God has called us to do. We too often think about the job, the house, the yard, the kids, the school, the you name it. Why is it we don't think about the work God has called us to do?

We claim our world is far too busy, and there is some truth to that. However, if we were to go back 2,000 years to Jesus' day, people still had jobs, kids, schools, meals to prepare, laundry to do, and so many other tasks that come with living. Perhaps the difference is, they didn't have the distractions of TV, internet, cell phones, nor even many books or scrolls.

We have the luxury of so many new gadgets that can be used to do the work God has called us to do. Yet we choose to use them to distract us. We have more resources, in the form of electronic availability, at our disposal to read, study, and expand our knowledge of God. We need to take advantage of the resources at our disposal rather than being so easily distracted. God has work for us to do. Will we work for Him?

I pray we all determine to do the work God has laid out for us. It's not that He needs us, we need Him, and we are invited to work alongside Him. Let's all work with God.

May 5

"A new command I give you: Love one another. As I have loved you, so you must love one another. By this everyone will know that you are my disciples, if you love one another."

— John 13:34–35

Are you following the new command? "What new command?" you may ask. The new command Jesus gave His disciples not long before His crucifixion. It was not that God had not expected the Jews to follow this command before, but Jesus made it explicit.

The world only looks to love those who love them back or who provides them something. Just look at who or what people say they love. The movie star on a pedestal. The new car for status. The boyfriend/girlfriend/spouse for comfort, security, appreciativeness. Friends for a sense of belonging. I'm sure we can all think of additional provisions.

Jesus commanded us, His followers, to love one another. Do we love the person across the aisle from us in church? Do we love the preacher when he says something hard to swallow? Do we love the person we don't agree with? How do we show that love? Do we give them a hug and a smile? Or do we talk badly about them when out of ear shot? Loving fellow Christians is a command.

I pray we love our fellow Christians. Yes, we should love each person, even if we don't love their actions. But we are commanded to love fellow followers of Christ. Let's commit to loving one another.

May 6

"Which of these three do you think was a neighbor to
the man who fell into the hands of robbers?"
The expert in the law replied, "The one who had
mercy on him."
Jesus told him, "Go and do likewise."
— Luke 10:36–37

Do you show mercy? Do you react negatively towards offenders,
perhaps even overreact? Or do you temper your reaction and attempt
to put yourself in the other person's shoes? Do you seek revenge or
show mercy to the other person?

In today's world it seems there is far too much vengefulness and
overreaction. If someone does something against us, we want to repay
them two-fold. If we are offended by someone, we want to offend
them back with double the effect. This is the world's mindset, not the
mindset we should have as followers of Jesus.

We are called to show mercy to others—the same mercy we've
been shown by Jesus. Mercy does not mean we approve of their
actions; it does mean we will not continue the circle of offenses. We
stop the escalation and bring about peace. We have the power to show
mercy and it does require power, self-control. Our power comes from
the Spirit that Jesus sent to us.

I pray we all show mercy toward each other. When we do, we find
inner peace within ourselves and we show the other person who Jesus
is. Let's all determine to show mercy rather than wrath.

Marty Pressey

May 7

"Ask and it will be given to you; seek and you will
find; knock and the door will be opened to you. For
everyone who asks receives; the one who seeks finds;
and to the one who knocks, the door will be opened."
— Matthew 7:7–8

Do you seek God? We all seek something. Perhaps it's wealth or
popularity or love or nice things or acceptance or you fill in the blank.
We seek after all these, yet don't seek the One who can provide what
we truly seek deep-down inside.

The world chases so many things to satisfy the desires we all have.
We want to climb the corporate ladder. We want to be in love with a
beautiful person and have them be in love with us. We work towards
having a big house and new cars. We are constantly seeking something
to fill a void that none of those things can fill.

We all need to seek God, who will fill our deepest desire and
need. Why don't we seek Him? Too often we think seeking God
means giving up all those other things. To some degree that is correct.
However, when we seek God, He fills our deepest desire and makes
those other things pale in comparison. We find our ultimate peace and
become satisfied with whatever God provides us. It is not becoming
complacent; it is becoming who we are meant to be.

I pray we all seek God, seek to know Him, seek to be who He
intended us to be. When we do, we find we are satisfied beyond what
we could ever dream. Let's all seek God.

May 8

"But seek his kingdom, and these things will be given to you as well."

— Luke 12:31

Do you seek the kingdom? Perhaps you don't know what the kingdom is. Perhaps you only seek your kingdom. Perhaps you only seek after your own selfish desires. Perhaps you only think you are seeking for your own desires and fail to realize you are seeking someone else's.

The world seeks after what it believes are its own desires. Unfortunately, the world does not realize it's not really their desires they seek. They seek the desires put before them by a fallen world, by Satan himself. It is true that seeking after worldly pleasures, worldly possessions, and worldly wealth is self-destruction.

We are to seek God's Kingdom. When we seek His Kingdom, His desires for us, we are given so much more than we can believe. Unfortunately, we don't really believe that, or we would seek His Kingdom constantly. I've personally experienced God blessing me beyond my expectations when I've sought Him and His desires for me. We all need to experience that but can only do so when we seek Him.

I pray we all decide to seek His Kingdom, His desires for us. I pray we all set aside seeking after worldly desires. I pray we all experience the rich blessings God will provide by seeking His Kingdom.

May 9

"Now this is eternal life: that they know you, the only true God, and Jesus Christ, whom you have sent."

— John 17:3

Are you hungry? That might seem like a silly question. We all get hungry, right? But are you hungry to know God, to know Jesus? Is it a desire of yours to know Him as much as you know your best friend, your spouse, your parents, your siblings? You can, you know.

Many people in this world are all wrapped up in relationships. That can be a very good thing. God made us relational. We need to interact with others to be made complete. God made Adam and Eve so that only when the two were together did they fully represent God. A person on their own can learn a lot by reading and studying, but they also need to interact with others.

We also need to interact with God, if we really want to know Him. How do we do that? One obvious way is to pray. When we pray, we should talk some and listen some. That's how conversations work. Another way to interact with God is to interact with His people. Yes, talking with fellow followers of Christ is interacting with God. His Spirit lives in each of us and prompts each of us to speak on His behalf, so long as we are also listening to Him.

I pray we are hungry to know God. I pray we spend time in prayer, both speaking and listening. I pray we continue to interact with the people of God. Let's get to know God really well.

May 10

"If you love me, keep my commands. And I will ask the Father, and he will give you another advocate to help you and be with you forever—the Spirit of truth. The world cannot accept him, because it neither sees him nor knows him. But you know him, for he lives with you and will be in you. I will not leave you as orphans; I will come to you."

—John 14:15–18

Do you feel all alone? In a world filled with billions of people, we can. Even when we see and interact with people every day, we can. Usually, it's more the feeling that people do not understand you than it is being alone.

We are not alone nor isolated. There is always someone with us and He knows exactly how we feel. The world will tell us it's not true and far too many of us don't really believe it. But that doesn't make it any less true. Jesus has sent the Holy Spirit to live in us, to be with us so that we are never alone.

Having been there done that, I feel for those who feel alone. I can say with full conviction that we are not alone. God is right there with us. He really wants us to lean on Him. We may have to do it several times before we really let go, but we need to lay our burdens at His feet. When we truly let them go, He takes them on, and we are free again. We are free to enjoy the abundant life He desires for us.

I pray we all realize in our hearts that God is always with us. I pray we lean on Him in times of loneliness and trial. Trust in God.

May 11

But may all who seek you
rejoice and be glad in you;
may those who long for your saving help always say,
"The LORD is great!"

— Psalm 40:16

Are you seeking God today? Do you seek Him every day? Or do you only seek Him when you are in trouble, in a bind, or in over your head? We should seek Him every day, to guide our thoughts, actions, words, and deeds. When we do, we find we are much better off.

The world will tell you to work harder, study harder, put more time into it, and there is a place for that. We get wrapped up in ourselves, our jobs, or whatever the hot topic of the moment is. Sometimes we are wrapped up in our sorrows, self-pity, dejectedness, or confusion. All these are fleeting and will not last.

What will last? God. If we put just a little time into getting to know God better, putting ourselves in His hands, committing to be His follower, seeking His guidance, our lives become so much better than the fleeting moments of this world. We can endure the hardships, we will see things more clearly, and we will be at peace with our lives. We will find the joy we seek.

God is eagerly waiting for us to come to Him. He wants to bless us. All we need to do is seek Him out. Let's all spend some time with Him each day, even if it's just a few moments.

May 12

"A new command I give you: Love one another. As I
have loved you, so you must love one another. By this
everyone will know that you are my disciples, if you
love one another."

— John 13:34–35

Do you believe in God? Do you believe in Jesus? How much do you
believe? Do you really believe He came to earth, died a horrible death
on a cross, was buried and rose on the third day? How do you speak
and act to show that is what you believe?

We are so often tricked into being like the world. We fight, argue,
bicker, point fingers, accuse, counter-accuse, and generally are ill
mannered toward our fellow Christians. Not exactly what Jesus called
us to do. In fact, far from it. What are we to do about it?

We are to follow one of only a couple commands Jesus issued when
He was walking on this earth. We are to love our fellow Christians.
Love does not mean we don't let someone know their wrong, if they
are wrong. It does mean we do it in a loving, compassionate way. It also
means we have to discern whether the other is really wrong or if their
approach or idea is just another way to do the same thing. We are to
show love to each other, even when we don't feel like it.

Let's decide to love each other and show that love to each other.
Let's stop acting like the world and be the light Jesus wants us to be.
Love our brothers and sisters.

May 13

Therefore, my dear brothers and sisters, stand firm.
Let nothing move you. Always give yourselves fully
to the work of the Lord, because you know that your
labor in the Lord is not in vain.

—1 Corinthians 15:58

How do you approach life? So many of us just kind of fumble our way through. Sure, we may set goals, but we don't really put forth the effort needed to accomplish them, then we wonder why we don't achieve the goal. Too often we don't live our lives with a purpose.

There are many different self-help books that will tell us how to set goals and achieve them. They will give us a 5-step process or some other set of steps that are "proven to work." Of course, all of this is dependent upon you being dedicated and having the discipline to follow those steps. Discipline is good, when it is applied to appropriate tasks and goals.

God also wants us to be dedicated to Him. We are instructed to give ourselves over to Him. That means to follow His Spirit and pursue what He has laid out for us. When we pursue His will for our lives, we are not disappointed. There may be struggles, but there will be much more joy. We simply need to trust Him and stay committed to the path He has for us.

God has a wonderful plan for us. I pray we all commit ourselves to Him and stay the course. It is not a vain pursuit.

May 14

You were taught, with regard to your former way of
life, to put off your old self, which is being corrupted
by its deceitful desires; to be made new in the attitude
of your minds; and to put on the new self, created to
be like God in true righteousness and holiness.

— Ephesians 4:22–24

What is your attitude? Do you get up in the morning with a negative
attitude? Do you wake up each morning thankful for another day? Do
you live like that? Does your attitude change drastically from moment
to moment? Do you allow external happenings, whether by people or
events, to change your attitude?

The world is a fickle place. So many are tricked into believing they
have to have a dramatic response to whatever happens around them,
what they see in the news, or something that happens in their favorite
TV show. The overreaction to these things is really a sad indicator of
the state of this world.

As followers of Christ, we are to know God intimately. When
we do, our attitudes don't necessarily reflect what's going on around
us. Instead, it reflects the attitude of God. That doesn't mean it's
impersonal. It simply means our attitudes represent a big picture view
of what's happening. It means we can be at peace when everyone else
is not.

I pray we all can be at peace and have a positive attitude all day
long, because we have the intimate relationship with God. Let's reflect
Jesus to all those around us.

Marty Pressey

May 15

Who shall separate us from the love of Christ? Shall trouble or hardship or persecution or famine or nakedness or danger or sword? ... For I am convinced that neither death nor life, neither angels nor demons, neither the present nor the future, nor any powers, neither height nor depth, nor anything else in all creation, will be able to separate us from the love of God that is in Christ Jesus our Lord.

— Romans 8:35, 37–39

How do you react during times of trial or hardship? Do you lash out at those around you? Do you curl up in a fetal position? Do you fight tooth and nail to maintain control? Or do you walk through it in peace?

The world will often tell us that we have to gut it out or fight back. Properly interpreted, that's good advice. Unfortunately, the world is saying it's all up to us! The world believes we make our own way. When we try to do it on our own, we're far more likely to fail.

When we trust God, we can persevere, we release control to Him, and we allow God to do the fighting for us. God will never leave us. He has promised to always be with us, and He does not break His promises. During those hard times, we are to trust Him even more and lean on Him to show us the pathway through them.

I pray we all trust and lean on God during both good and hard times. My personal experience has proven He doesn't disappoint. Trust that God is always with you.

May 16

"But seek first his kingdom and his righteousness, and all these things will be given to you as well."

— Matthew 6:33

Rejoice always, pray continually, give thanks in all circumstances; for this is God's will for you in Christ Jesus.

—1 Thessalonians 5:16–18

How much time do you spend with God? Tough question! It's tough for a few reasons. One, most of us don't like admitting our only time spent with God is Sunday morning. Two, even if we spend a little time reading our Bible, a devotional, or praying, we have a nagging feeling it's not enough. But what if you are one that absolutely thinks spending a little time on Sunday morning in church is enough?

In today's media dominated society, it's all about looking good. So, if we are at church on Sunday, we look good and we are good, according to the media mentality. But God isn't looking for media approval and neither should we. It's a false standard.

We are to seek God continuously. That means keeping Him at the forefront of our minds in every situation. It means we make decisions based on God's guidance. We need to seek to know Him as intimately as we know our spouse, parent, or sibling. In order to do that, we need to spend time with Him.

I pray we all seek God and spend time with Him. We need Him more than we know. Be in continuous prayer.

May 17

And pray in the Spirit on all occasions with all kinds
of prayers and requests. With this in mind, be alert
and always keep on praying for all the Lord's people.
— Ephesians 6:18

When do you reach out to God? Do you only reach out when things
are bad? Do you reach out when making big decisions? Do you reach
out when contemplating changing jobs? Do you reach out in all things
at all times? Do you keep that line of communication open to God?

Too often we just cruise along when things are going well, and we
forget about God. We think we have it all under control. Sure, we may
occasionally thank God for our blessings, but it often seems as though
it's an afterthought. Yet, when things go bad, we ask why and want to
blame God or question His love for us.

We need to be in constant communication with God. That
communication is commonly called prayer. We too often think of
prayer as those official sounding prayers we hear in church. But prayer
can be those short 5-word phrases we think of while sitting at the
stop light when we thank Him for our morning coffee. Prayer is also
listening, being open to hear God's Spirit talk to us while we are sitting
at our desk.

I pray we all keep the lines of communication open with God. We
need His guidance and He wants our thankfulness. Pray at all times
of the day and night.

May 18

The fear of the LORD is the beginning of knowledge,
but fools despise wisdom and instruction.
— Proverbs 1:7

Where do you start? We might say, "at the beginning." If we were going to gain wisdom and knowledge, where is that? Perhaps, we should start at the source of all wisdom and knowledge. Unfortunately, it seems the vast majority of people don't know where that is.

We study books throughout school as we grow up. We study books in our profession as we progress through our career. We read internet blogs, articles, magazines, and watch instructional videos. We do all of this to further our careers, to increase our knowledge of our professions, and to be promoted up the corporate ladder.

What are we doing to gain the wisdom and knowledge to truly enhance our lives? There is but one place we can go to get life instruction that will both enlighten and fulfill us, the Bible. God's Word instructs us how to live our lives in a successful manner. Does it tell us how to drive a car? No. It tells us how to live, how to behave, how to think, how to discern, how to worship, how to love, how to be in all we do. Start there.

I pray we all decide to start our pursuit of wisdom and knowledge by reading our Bible. Might I suggest you start with Proverbs and expand from there? Decide to become wise through God's Word.

May 19

She
I am a rose of Sharon, a lily of the valleys.
He
Like a lily among thorns is my darling among the
young women.

— Song of Solomon 2:1–2

How do you express your love? Do you say it with fancy words? Do you not say it much at all? Do you show it through actions? Do those you love know you love them? Good questions to think about.

Too often we get caught up in the rat race of life. We push ourselves to do "one more thing" before the end of the day. We have to get this task done before we can move on to the next. We hear the saying, "You need to stop and smell the roses" and immediately think, "The roses aren't blooming this time of year."

We should never be so busy that we can't say "I love you" to the ones we love. We should take time to do for those we love, expressing our love through action. Perhaps it's as simple as getting them a glass of water. We know what would make them happy. It's the small things done each day that makes love a wonderful thing, not the big, expensive, once a year gifts.

Spend time with your loved ones today. Do a little something for them, perhaps something unexpected. Love each other without question.

May 20

Sing joyfully to the LORD, you righteous;
it is fitting for the upright to praise him.
Praise the LORD with the harp;
make music to him on the ten-stringed lyre.

— Psalm 33:1-2

Are you joyful? Are you in high spirits? Did you wake up this morning looking forward to another day in God's presence? If not, did you make the decision to consciously be joyful and praise God today? It is true, we do get to make that choice every morning.

There are lots of self-help books out there on the bookshelves. Many of them will tell us nearly the same thing the Bible does, they just won't mention it came from the Bible. The basic principle is that we can choose to be joyful. The one thing missing in most of those books is God.

The Bible tells us we can have joy every day of our lives, when we lean on God. When we wake up in a bad mood, we simply need to stop, pray, and ask God to bring His joy into our lives that day. At first, that may be a bit difficult. But once we begin to experience it, just a little, we find it becomes easier and we experience the truth of it.

I pray we all raise our hands, hearts, and minds to God in praise each day. Seek the joy that only He can give. Praise Him and experience His joy for yourself.

May 21

May his name endure forever;
may it continue as long as the sun.
Then all nations will be blessed through him,
and they will call him blessed.

— Psalm 72:17

Do you know how long forever is? Do you understand the concept of eternity? Is forever a word you use to mean a long time, as we count time, but doesn't really mean it goes on for infinity? Ponder forever, eternity, infinity for just a moment.

In today's use of language many words take on different meanings. In order to understand some conversations, we need to understand the context. We hear people say, "I haven't seen you in forever." What they really mean is, "I haven't seen you in days (or weeks or months)."

When we read about forever in the Bible, it means exactly what the word was intended to mean. It means time without end. We don't often think in these terms; we're usually too tied up thinking about today and maybe tomorrow. Sure, we'll plan vacations months in advance, but we don't typically think about time without end. Or more appropriately, time has ceased to exist. Forever does exist.

I pray we all take time on occasion to think about forever. It will give us a little perspective on the short time we have in this life. Pause, think, and appreciate it today.

May 22

My son, if you accept my words
and store up my commands within you,
turning your ear to wisdom
and applying your heart to understanding—
indeed, if you call out for insight
and cry aloud for understanding,
and if you look for it as for silver
and search for it as for hidden treasure,
then you will understand the fear of the LORD
and find the knowledge of God.

— Proverbs 2:1–5

Are you looking for wisdom? Are you looking for knowledge? Why are you looking? What do you expect to find? What are your motives for searching for it? Is it to be rich and famous?

Many in this world are looking for a way to "get ahead." Get ahead of what? Usually, to get ahead of everyone else. That may mean to get a promotion, a raise, be popular, be a person others look up to, or any number of reasons to feel important. Is this what we really want?

We should seek wisdom and knowledge. We should seek these to become a better person, to show God to others, to be an example of what a godly person looks like. When we seek wisdom to glorify God, we get so much more. Sure, we may get the promotion or pay raise, but that should not be the reason for seeking wisdom.

I pray we all seek wisdom to be better followers of Jesus Christ. When we do that, we receive the abundant life He promised us. Seek God's wisdom.

Marty Pressey

May 23

It is for freedom that Christ has set us free. Stand
firm, then, and do not let yourselves be burdened
again by a yoke of slavery.

— Galatians 5:1

How do you remember Memorial Day? I'm sure each of us will answer
that question in different ways. For some, it's a day off work and an
outing with the family. For others, it's a day to catch up doing things
around the house. Still others are working on this day.

By and large, we Americans pause and remember the veterans who
laid down their lives in defense of freedom. It is good we remember.
However, there is a much larger sacrifice that should be remembered
every moment of every day that set us free for eternity.

Jesus Christ left heaven, came to our broken world, lived, taught,
and was an example for us. He sacrificed himself as the perfect lamb of
God, was buried, and rose again on the third day. He did all this to set
us free from sin and destruction. He is the reason we can be confident
in our eternal freedom and salvation. We should remember Him every
day and be thankful for His sacrifice every day.

I pray each of us would wake each morning being thankful for
Christ's sacrifice. Let each of us commit to live in the freedom Christ
has provided; freedom to live without hate, vengefulness, chaos,
judgment, bad attitudes; freedom to live in joy, peace, and love.

May 24

"Come to me, all you who are weary and burdened, and I will give you rest. Take my yoke upon you and learn from me, for I am gentle and humble in heart, and you will find rest for your souls. For my yoke is easy and my burden is light."

— Matthew 11:28–30

Are you humble? Do you seek to follow Jesus as a humble servant? Do you understand that being humble is not the same as being weak? A Clydesdale is one of the most powerful horses in the world but submits to its master and follows his lead.

The world will tell us that we have to be strong, stand up for what's ours or we will be pushed around and trampled. So, people are in constant opposition, fighting for what they believe they deserve. Of course, all this fighting causes a lot of stress, heartache, let downs, and occasionally joys and success.

Jesus tells us to follow Him, to take on His yoke. When we do, our burdens are lifted, and we acquire peace and joy that we never knew before. Taking on His yoke is fully trusting that He is in control. When we come to the realization that we don't really need all the stuff we pursue and we allow Him to provide as He sees fit, we live with virtually no anxiety, worry, stress, anger, hatred, and jealousy.

I pray we all decide to humble ourselves and submit to Jesus, taking on His persona. Allow Him to lead the way. Humble yourselves in the sight of the Lord.

Marty Pressey

May 25

Blessed is the one
who does not walk in step with the wicked
or stand in the way that sinners take
or sit in the company of mockers,
but whose delight is in the law of the LORD,
and who meditates on his law day and night.
That person is like a tree planted by streams of water,
which yields its fruit in season
and whose leaf does not wither—
whatever they do prospers.

— Psalm 1:1–3

Are you planted by streams of water? That may sound like a silly question. But water is life sustaining. How long can you go without water? According to modern science, our bodies can only go about 3 days without water.

We need water to sustain our physical body. Many of us drink several glasses a day. It may be coffee, tea, lemonade, soda, or any number of other drinks. We drink multiple glasses a day to sustain our physical bodies.

Why don't we drink spiritual water several times a day to sustain our spiritual life? Jesus said those who come to him and drink of Him would have a well spring up within them. We need to drink of His Word several times a day.

I pray we all realize we need God's Word each day as much as we need water. It is only in taking in His life sustaining Word that we will grow and mature spiritually. Drink in God's Word each day.

May 26

Be very careful, then, how you live—not as unwise
but as wise, making the most of every opportunity,
because the days are evil. Therefore do not be foolish,
but understand what the Lord's will is.

— Ephesians 5:15–17

Are you wise? Do you use wisdom in your decision? Or do you admit
being unwise and laugh it off? Do you think it's cool to act unwise?
How can you become wise? All good questions and ones we should
wrestle with.

Wisdom does not come easy in this world. It seems each generation
has to learn the hard way, making bad decisions, and suffering the
consequences. When we are young, we think we know it all. I'm not
sure if it's the hormones blocking proper functioning of our brain or
the desire to feel like we fit in as an adult.

In Proverbs it states a wise man listens far more than he talks. We
also see in James we are to ask for wisdom and God will give it to us.
His Holy Spirit provides wisdom. Wisdom is not just knowledge, it is
gathering the facts, reviewing them, and making a sound decision. It
is also making the best decision with limited information by thinking
through the situation, looking at possible outcomes, and choosing the
best option for us.

I pray we all decide to do more listening, particularly listening to
those with experience, and ask God for wisdom. Use the wisdom God
gives us in all decisions. Seek wisdom, it won't disappoint.

Marty Pressey

May 27

A voice came from the cloud, saying, "This is my Son,
whom I have chosen; listen to him."

— Luke 9:35

How do you make decisions? Do you have a set of close friends
that advise you? Do you listen to your parent's advice? Do you seek
counselors that you trust based on their position? Or do you lay out
all the pros and cons to help you make your decision on your own?
Perhaps you use some combination of all of those options.

We normally use some combination of these, even if we don't
think we do. As we grow up, the influence of our parents stays with us.
If we received bad advice from them, it takes commitment to reverse
that when we are adults. We usually also seek out someone we trust
to help us with our decisions by providing a different perspective and
perhaps advice.

We should seek God in our decisions. That is not just in prayer,
but also by reading His Word. No, there is nothing in the Bible about
making a decision to buy a new car. However, there is guidance in
the Bible about how to handle the money God has blessed us with.
We should especially look at how He provided insights to living an
abundant life. Finally, we have the Holy Spirit living in us. Learn to
listen to Him and trust Him.

I pray we all spend more time getting to know God: the Father,
the Son, and the Holy Spirit. Learn to reach out to Him for advice and
listen to Him. Pray, read, and listen.

May 28

And you also were included in Christ when you heard
the message of truth, the gospel of your salvation.
When you believed, you were marked in him with
a seal, the promised Holy Spirit, who is a deposit
guaranteeing our inheritance until the redemption
of those who are God's possession—to the praise of
his glory.

— Ephesians 1:13–14

Do you feel left out? Do you feel like you are on the outside looking in?
Do you want to be on the team, in a relationship, part of the group? I
invite you to be in a relationship with Jesus Christ, in the group who
follows Him, and you will be part of the best group for eternity.

We don't think of being a Christian as being part of a team. Jesus
did not come to institute Christianity. He came to speak truth and
invite us to be a disciple. We are invited to follow Him more closely
than we follow our favorite celebrities, mentors, and teachers.

It is when we decide to be a true follower of Jesus and throw off
the false facade that we truly experience His love. It is then that we feel
like we are part of the team and understand that He put His stamp of
approval on us. When we commit ourselves fully to Him, we finally
understand the meaning of the guarantee He gave us of spending
eternity with Him.

I pray we all choose to be on Jesus' team. Accept and understand
the inheritance provided by Him. Give the glory to God for your
salvation.

Marty Pressey

May 29

"I know your deeds, that you are neither cold nor hot.
I wish you were either one or the other!"
— Revelation 3:15

Are you fully committed to God? Or are you only partially committed?
Perhaps you are only committed when you participate in church
activities. Perhaps you act like a follower of Christ only when you are
around others who are. God wants all of who we are.

Many will go to church, sing the songs, bow their heads for
prayers, and listen to the sermon, yet not really be committed to God.
Many will walk out those church doors on Sunday and be just like the
rest of the world for 6 1/2 days a week. Are we one of them? Do we
realize we are breaking our Heavenly Father's heart?

Jesus called us to follow Him. He wants us to be a cold, refreshing
glass of water to others. He wants our hearts to be on fire for Him. He
wants us to follow Him with all our being. He wants us to dedicate
our lives to Him. It doesn't mean we don't live in this world and don't
have needs. It does mean we see this world through His eyes and treat
others as He would.

I pray we all be the cold water that refreshes and the heart of fire
that burns for Him. Let's be Jesus to *everyone* we encounter. Commit
yourself to Jesus today.

May 30

Then we will no longer be infants, tossed back
and forth by the waves, and blown here and there
by every wind of teaching and by the cunning and
craftiness of people in their deceitful scheming.
Instead, speaking the truth in love, we will grow to
become in every respect the mature body of him who
is the head, that is, Christ.

— Ephesians 4:14–15

Who or what do you serve? You may say proudly, "I serve no one!" Or
you may say, "I'm a slave to money." Or perhaps you will say, "I serve
my boss." Whether we realize it or not, we all serve something or
someone and ultimately it is someone who is behind the something.

The someone we serve is totally dependent on our hearts. It
ultimately comes down to who is most important in our life. True,
we all have people who are important in our lives: our spouses, our
parents, our kids, our friends, and many others. Those are not who
I'm referring to.

We will ultimately serve Satan or God. There is no gray area. It
is very black and white. It is good vs evil. We can try to rationalize
it away, but it doesn't work in the end and we know it. We are either
moving toward God or toward Satan. Just as a boat is moving toward
land or away from it, so it is with us.

I pray we all choose to serve God. We can do so as part of our
everyday lives. Serve and move toward God.

May 31

Thanks be to God for his indescribable gift!
> —2 Corinthians 9:15

Do you thank God for what He has blessed you with? Not just a passing "thank you," but a heartfelt thanks. Do you really understand what He has done for you? Perhaps you've not thought much about it but have taken it for granted.

So many of us are so busy, not always because we need to be, but because we have put so much on our plates. We have to paint that room, go buy a new shirt, mow the yard, decorate for the next holiday, watch that TV show, clean out that shed, or any number of other things. Do we really *need* to do those things?

We really do need to thank God for what he's done for us. We need to spend a little time and appreciate His blessings. We take them for granted so much of the time. The very clothes on our back are a blessing from Him. The fact we have a job is a blessing from Him. He deserves our thanks all day, every day. When we take time to thank Him, we receive the blessing of peace. He continues to give to us His immeasurable grace.

Stop, take just a few minutes and give thanks to God today. We owe all we have to Him. Give Him the thanks He deserves for just a few minutes.

June

June 1

"I tell you that in the same way there will be more rejoicing in heaven over one sinner who repents than over ninety-nine righteous persons who do not need to repent."

— Luke 15:7

What do you do when you fail God? Do you just slough it off and say, "none of us are perfect" or do you pray for God's forgiveness? Do you continue down the path you are on or do you honestly ask God to make a change in your life? There *is* a right and wrong answer.

We are human and we do make mistakes. We do sin. We do fall short of God's glory. But it doesn't have to be the end. Because of the pathway Jesus made for us, we can go straight to the Father, repenting of our sin and asking for forgiveness. We have the promise that He will forgive us.

When we repent, honestly looking for change, and we ask God to make that change in us, He will do so. We don't have the power to overcome ourselves, but He does. He will bring about the change we need. But we have to let go. We have to release ourselves into His hands to make the change. When we do, all of Heaven rejoices.

We need to let go of ourselves—putting ourselves in God's hands to mold and change us as He sees fit. Until we do, not only are we living a fleshly life, but we are fighting God. Release yourself into His hands.

June 2

Surely he will save you
from the fowler's snare
and from the deadly pestilence.
He will cover you with his feathers,
and under his wings you will find refuge;
his faithfulness will be your shield and rampart.

— Psalm 91:3–4

Who do you run to? We might run to our parents in joy or sorrow. We might run to greet our friend, spouse, children, or parents after being gone for an extended period of time. We might run to a close friend for advice. There is One whom we should always run to.

We often find ourselves in a tough spot. It could be a decision looming ahead of us. It could be bills are due. It could be a relationship in trouble. It could be persecution for our faith. God is always there.

When we are feeling distraught, afraid, persecuted, or depressed, we should always seek God in prayer. Spend time with Him—read His Word. He is always there and will always get us through. Sure, we can seek our family and friends. In fact, God often uses our family and friends to be His hands or His voice. We must remember that God works through people around us.

Seek God to be your shelter, your protector during times of trouble. He will never leave you. Spend time with Him. He will grant you the protection, strength, courage, and peace you need.

June 3

Again Jesus called the crowd to him and said, "Listen to me, everyone, and understand this. Nothing outside a person can defile them by going into them. Rather, it is what comes out of a person that defiles them."

— Mark 7:14–15

Are you clean? Or are you defiled? Are you misled? Do you misunderstand? How can you be sure if you are clean? There is quite a misunderstanding of what or who is clean in this world today.

We see people spending lots of time and money to be clean. Millions of dollars are being spent on hand sanitizer. Some people take multiple showers a day. Some will ask for a new fork if there is a water spot on it. Yet none of this has anything to do with being clean and presents a false sense of cleanliness.

Jesus chastised the Pharisees because they questioned His disciples eating without washing their hands. We have forgotten or failed to listen to Jesus when it comes to being clean. Our world is filthy, and we are failing to make it better. We need to stop teaching little kids it's okay to be sassy and teach them to be nice. We need to stop being ugly toward others and be kind to them instead. We need to stop talking like sailors and speak as Jesus would.

Let's dedicate ourselves to cleaning up the world, not by using some chemical, but by cleaning up our actions and words. Jesus has given us guidance regarding being clean. Be clean as Jesus was clean.

June 4

Since, then, you have been raised with Christ, set
your hearts on things above, where Christ is, seated
at the right hand of God. Set your minds on things
above, not on earthly things. For you died, and your
life is now hidden with Christ in God. When Christ,
who is your life, appears, then you also will appear
with him in glory.

— Colossians 3:1–4

Have you missed God? There's more than one question in that
question. Have you missed being with God? Have you missed God
when He's been all around you? Have you missed being close with
God? Have you missed the opportunities He's putting before you?

We can easily miss God. When we are blinded by anger. When we
are selfish—looking out for only ourselves. When we are focused on
an object of our possession. When our minds are focused on someone
who wronged us, we miss God's beauty all around us.

We have become so busy, focusing on jobs, on selfish pursuits, on
possessing things, rather than spending our time focusing on God. We
don't have to read the Bible every moment of every day to spend time
with God. But perhaps we could stop and "smell the roses." Maybe we
can appreciate the meal God provided for us. We could see the love
God blessed us with.

God is all around us. Let's take time to slow down a bit and see
Him. Let's take time to focus on Him and give thanks to Him for all
His blessings. Set your mind on God.

June 5

Jesus answered, "Very truly I tell you, no one can enter the kingdom of God unless they are born of water and the Spirit. Flesh gives birth to flesh, but the Spirit gives birth to spirit. You should not be surprised at my saying, 'You must be born again.'"

— John 3:5–7

Have you been born anew? Have you been born of water and spirit? Have you been born into the family of God? Have you become a brother or sister of Jesus Christ? Jesus tells us we must do this to enter into God's kingdom.

We all love newborn babies. They are cute and cuddly, and coo and cry and we love to take care of them. It's amazing to see them grow those first few months and years. There are so many firsts and so many new things they do.

When we are born again, we face many of those same firsts again, but in a different context. We grow in our walk with Jesus, in our faith in Him, in our understanding of His teachings. We are newborn babes and we depend on others to help us grow and understand. If we don't, we are defying the normal course of growth. We wouldn't expect a newborn baby to reject its parents, would we? We must also accept the help of others as we grow.

Newborns are fun to be around, 2-year old's not always. As we grow in our walk of faith, we mustn't become 2-year old's. We need to listen, grasp understanding, and continue to grow in our faith. I pray we all grow into mature faith in God.

June 6

But Jesus called the children to him and said, "Let the little children come to me, and do not hinder them, for the kingdom of God belongs to such as these. Truly I tell you, anyone who will not receive the kingdom of God like a little child will never enter it."

— Luke 18:16–17

Where are you headed? Seems like a simple question. I'm headed to the store. I'm headed to work. I'm headed home. We go to so many different places during our day. Have you ever stopped to count how many places you go in a week?

Where are we headed can be the most important question we answer. Are we headed for heaven or not? How do we know? Are we sure of our answer? We can be sure.

We can know without a doubt. Perhaps we're not sure. Perhaps we have doubts. Perhaps we think that God could not possibly love someone like us. There is a simple, yet sometimes hard to do, answer to our doubts.

I pray we all have the faith of a child. Let's all trust God in everything we do, with all our heart. He does and will provide. Have a child's faith.

June 7

With this in mind, we constantly pray for you, that
our God may make you worthy of his calling, and
that by his power he may bring to fruition your every
desire for goodness and your every deed prompted
by faith.

—2 Thessalonians 1:11

What do you want? Okay, what do you really want, deep-down in your
heart? Are you sure that's what you want? Are your wants aligned with
God's? Do you need to reevaluate your wants? What are you doing to
achieve your wants?

We hear a lot of wants, don't we? We probably have a lot of wants,
if we're honest with ourselves. But are they superficial wants or deep
desires? We hear people say, "I want to get in shape," but lay around on
the couch and watch TV. We hear people say, "I want to be a scientist,"
but they don't go on to school to get the education needed to be one.

We also hear all kinds of excuses. Ultimately, it comes down to
how bad we want it. That's where the deep desire comes in. We hear
stories of people who were raised poor—in inner cities with a mother
working 2 or 3 jobs just to put food on the table, yet these children
grow up and become PhD's. How? They have a deep, driving desire.
You see, we do what we want and often take the easy path, what some
may call being lazy.

We all need to desire God. We all need to desire to follow His
Son Jesus Christ. We all need to desire to do His work here on earth.
Desire His Will and pursue it with all your being.

June 8

"Ask and it will be given to you; seek and you will find; knock and the door will be opened to you. For everyone who asks receives; the one who seeks finds; and to the one who knocks, the door will be opened."

— Matthew 7:7-8

What are you doing to better yourself? We can find all kinds of self-help books. We also hear plenty of advice from others. Often we don't want to hear it, because we don't want to face our faults. Yet, we are called to be better than we are and to pursue righteousness with the help of the Holy Spirit.

We will quickly acknowledge that none of us are perfect, yet we often act as though we are. We quickly get defensive when others point out something we did was wrong or incorrect. Why? Our pride is often the culprit. Sometimes we will think about it later and realize the person was right. Sometimes not. Sometimes we keep our head in the sand.

Jesus told us to ask and we would receive. Why not ask for an open mind and open heart to hear the Holy Spirit speaking to us? He speaks to us through other people. Too often we don't want to hear it. We don't want to ask, and we don't want to change. Most assuredly, we don't want to humble ourselves before Him and recognize He is speaking to us through others.

Ask God to change your heart and mind. Ask Him to remove the pride that keeps you from becoming who He desires you to be. Ask Him and He will give it to you.

Marty Pressey

June 9

"You are witnesses of these things. I am going to send you what my Father has promised; but stay in the city until you have been clothed with power from on high."

— Luke 24:48–49

Do you believe you are gifted? No? Maybe? Yes? You are gifted, whether you believe it or not. When you accept Jesus Christ as your Savior and are baptized, you receive the gift of the Holy Spirit. He then gives you one or more gifts to do the work God has set before you.

We see a lot of prejudice in the world today. Not just racial or gender, but prejudice based on the talents or gifts of others. The evil in this world wants to divide us. If we allow that to happen by continuing our prejudices based on whether someone is good at a particular thing or not, we have allowed evil to win.

Rather than put someone down because they can't do something we can do, let's celebrate the things they can do. In doing so, we are celebrating the diverse gifts we have as a community of Christ followers or disciples. Our combined gifts were given to us to proclaim the saving power of Jesus through the many works God assigned to the body of Christ, the Church.

Each one of us has a gift or gifts. Jesus conquered death, not only to save us, but also to gift us. Celebrate each other and celebrate God. Let's do the work God assigned to the Church.

June 10

The Spirit you received does not make you slaves,
so that you live in fear again; rather, the Spirit you
received brought about your adoption to sonship.
And by him we cry, "Abba, Father."

— Romans 8:15

Do you like being told lies? I'm venturing to guess the vast majority of
us do not. Yet we listen to them and go along with them far too often
each day. The lies we hear and listen to are lies telling us to be afraid,
to live in fear.

Lies come to us from a variety of places. Sometimes it's friends
or co-workers or family. Sometimes it's from the TV shows or news
we watch. But more often than not, it comes from Satan. We will say,
"Oh, it's only in your head." And we would be correct, because it's
Satan who has gotten in our heads. You see, Satan is the father of lies,
as Jesus tells us in John 8:44.

There is a way to remove the lies and the fear from inside us. It
requires us to surrender to God and welcome His Spirit to take over
our inner beings. He will not only remove the fear from us, but also
create in us a far better person. He is a guide we can depend on to
always lead us down the right path.

I pray we all allow the Holy Spirit to be our guide, to lead us, to
teach us, to change us. Be strong in the Spirit and leave fear behind.

Marty Pressey

June 11

"Do not let your hearts be troubled. You believe in God; believe also in me."

— John 14:1

Are you troubled about something today? Don't be. Turn it all over to God, to Jesus. He is our Savior who conquered death and is living today. He sent His Helper to be with us always.

We don't often have the peace we should because we don't trust in God. It may sound simple, but it's not. We all are made up of so many different genes and experiences. We have been conditioned by life, what we've seen, and what we've heard. We have to be retrained.

Our ultimate trainer is the Holy Spirit. Will we listen to Him? We need to. Only when we listen and follow His leading will we be able to let go of who we are and become who He desires us to be. Jesus sent us His Spirit to be that leader—that trainer to teach us so we would have peace rather than troubled spirits.

I pray we all learn to trust God and believe what Jesus has told us. Allow His Spirit to fill you and give you peace, to calm your spirit. Trust in Him.

June 12

"Simon, Simon, Satan has asked to sift all of you as wheat. But I have prayed for you, Simon, that your faith may not fail. And when you have turned back, strengthen your brothers."

— Luke 22:31–32

What do you do when you falter? Do you give up? Do you continue down a bad path? Or do you recognize it and make a course correction? Are you willing to turn back to the right path? How much do you desire that wonderful destination?

So many people in this world are lost and don't know it. When one is awakened to their lostness and turns to Christ, it's a wonderful thing. Angels rejoice! Unfortunately, too many don't wake up or they won't commit to the narrow path.

It takes a commitment to make the change. It's especially hard in the beginning, which can last for several months or even a few years. As we continue down that path, it does get easier to stay on the path, but it still takes commitment. It still requires us to have the desire to be with Jesus. Much like Peter, we can lose heart for a while, but we can turn back to Him and be strengthened in our faith.

I pray we all pursue being with Jesus. I pray we all wake up and stay awake, looking around us and thinking deeply about where we are at. Let's all commit to follow Jesus and keep that commitment.

Marty Pressey

June 13

Then Jesus came to them and said, "All authority in
heaven and on earth has been given to me. Therefore
go and make disciples of all nations, baptizing them
in the name of the Father and of the Son and of the
Holy Spirit, and teaching them to obey everything I
have commanded you."

— Matthew 28:18–20

Are you fishing? Do you know you should be fishing? We have all
been commissioned to be fishers of men. We are all to be trying to
bring others into the body of Christ. If we are fishing, we are doing
God's will.

How do we fish? We fish with lures and all kinds of bait, much
like we fish for anything. We are kind to others. We smile and open
doors. We show them the love of God. We tell them of the wonderful
life in Jesus Christ. We become "all things to all people" as Paul states
in 1 Corinthians 9:22.

Are we all to fish? Yes! It doesn't get much clearer than Jesus
telling us to. Does it mean we all have to be preacher's? No! In fact,
preachers bring fewer people into the church than members do. It's
by demonstrating the love of God and talking about Jesus that new
people are brought into the church. So go fishing and bring in new
disciples.

I pray we all recognize we are representing God with every word
and action during every moment of every day. Through our words
and actions we will be fishers of men. Be good fishers. Be a good
representative of God.

June 14

And whatever you do, whether in word or deed, do
it all in the name of the Lord Jesus, giving thanks to
God the Father through him.

— Colossians 3:17

What are your struggles? What challenges will you face today? What
joys will you experience today? What mundane tasks will you do
today? Will you do all of these as though you were doing them for God?

We all get frustrated, angry, upset, or bored with our jobs, our
homes, our lives. We look for new and exciting things to do. We look
for entertainment, excitement, or simply a change. If we think we are
to be constantly excited or entertained, we are sadly mistaken.

We all have tasks to do. We should do them as though we were
doing them for God. He sees us at all times, day or night, every
moment. He knows if we are not putting forth 100%. He knows if we
are slacking. For our own sake we need to do the best we can at all
times. It is how we grow. If you are an athlete, you don't train to be
better by doing the minimum, you push yourself. The same holds true
in every other aspect of our lives.

I pray we all dedicate ourselves to do everything for God, doing
the best we can and praying that He will help us grow and mature our
entire lives. Do it all for God and be blessed.

Marty Pressey

June 15

Submit yourselves, then, to God. Resist the devil,
and he will flee from you. Come near to God and he
will come near to you. Wash your hands, you sinners,
and purify your hearts, you double-minded.

—James 4:7–8

What are your priorities? Who are your priorities? Do you say one
thing and do another? Many will say family is a priority, but not show
it with their actions. Many will say they want to pursue a specific
profession, but not pursue the education to achieve it.

We are often bombarded with many people, tasks, and thoughts
that are vying for our attention. We need a filter, a set of priorities
that guide our decisions and actions in order to do what's best. If we
don't have the priorities firmly set, we will be tossed about like a ship
on the ocean.

Our best option is to have God be our filter. He can only be our
filter, our guide, if we spend time with Him. We spend time with
Him by reading His Word and in prayer. When we make Him our
guide and allow His Spirit to fill our hearts, souls, and minds, our
priorities will be made much clearer. We will better determine the
best profession for us. We will increase in self-discipline and self-
motivation to pursue what's best.

I pray that we all spend time with God today and every day. We
need so spend time with Him as much as we need to eat. Make God
your priority.

June 16

May the God of hope fill you with all joy and peace as
you trust in him, so that you may overflow with hope
by the power of the Holy Spirit.

— Romans 15:13

Do you feel all alone? Do you feel as though you are fighting an uphill
battle? You feel like your friends have abandoned you? Have you lost
hope? There is One in which our hope is not lost and in Whom we can
trust every minute of every day.

This world can be tough. After all, it's broken. Sometimes we feel
as though we are abandoned, over tasked, buried in work, nowhere
to turn for help, or just down in the dumps. There are many who will
kick us when we are down. Or we are told to pick our own selves up
by the boot straps, yet we just don't know how.

The good news is there One who never leaves us. We are never
alone nor abandoned. Our hope is in Him—the One who continues
to bless us through many different avenues. Our hope is in Him and
we can talk to Him at any time in any place through prayer. When we
do that, He is there with us.

Remember Jesus is with You at all times through the Holy Spirit.
Don't let it be just a mental acknowledgment but know it in your heart.
Hope and trust in Him.

Marty Pressey

June 17

"Come to me, all you who are weary and burdened, and I will give you rest. Take my yoke upon you and learn from me, for I am gentle and humble in heart, and you will find rest for your souls. For my yoke is easy and my burden is light."

— Matthew 11:28–30

What do you do when you feel overwhelmed? Where do you run to get away from it all? How do you cope with the flood of information in today's world? How do you deal with the pressures of life?

The world is full of pressures today. Pressure to perform, to be accepted, to be pretty, to be happy, to put on a smiling face, to show we have it all together. Pressure from more angles than ever before: from social media, from news sources, from bosses, from friends. Sometimes we need to escape it all.

There is One who will always be there to listen to us—One who will take the pressure off of us. He can carry the burdens and allow us to walk tall again. Far too often we don't go to Him like we should. We need to say short prayers all day long, asking for His help in every situation. It is by reaching out, asking for His help, that we release ourselves from carrying the burdens we often carry on our own.

Reach out to Jesus today. Ask Him to relieve you of your burdens, to give you strength to carry on. Realize that your burdens of today will be gone tomorrow. Trust in Jesus. Pray often throughout the day.

June 18

In the same way, the Spirit helps us in our weakness. We do not know what we ought to pray for, but the Spirit himself intercedes for us through wordless groans.

— Romans 8:26

How often do you pray? Do you pray continuously as Jesus told us to? Do you pray multiple times per day? Do you pray at meals? What do you pray about? Do you pray for others or only yourself? Do you pray only when in need?

A recent survey by the Pew Research Center shows that only 55% of adults pray at least daily and that percentage has dropped over the years. Is it any wonder we have so many troubles? Is it any wonder we see so much crime? Is it any wonder our society, schools, workplaces, and families experience so much disfunction?

We need prayer in our lives. We need it multiple times per day. We need to pray for others, for ourselves, for our country, for our co-workers, for those we love, for those we prefer not to be around, for everyone we meet. We need to be a praying people, seeing others as God sees them. Most of all, we need to thank God for all He has blessed us with.

Pray about each decision you make. Pray that God guides you in your work and studies. Yes, pray when you are in need, but also pray in thanksgiving for your many blessings. Pray when you don't know what to pray for or how to pray. Pray without ceasing.

June 19

For this reason I kneel before the Father, from whom every family in heaven and on earth derives its name. I pray that out of his glorious riches he may strengthen you with power through his Spirit in your inner being, so that Christ may dwell in your hearts through faith.

— Ephesians 3:14–17a

Are you searching? Are you confused? Do you feel lost sometimes? Do you feel like you are floundering about, trying to find your way in a big world? If you are, you are not alone. In fact, you are one of many in the same spot.

There are many people who are searching for their place in this world. In fact, all of us go through that at some point in our lives and often multiple times throughout our lives. We try to figure what our profession will be. Sometimes we change professions. We look for a lifelong mate. Sometimes we join clubs in our efforts to fit in. We search and search.

There is one place we all belong, the family of God. When we are an active participant in God's family, His Church, we find a place where we are loved and fit in. We find our faith increases, we find peace, we become filled with God's wonderful Spirit. We are empowered and free to do the work He puts before us.

Find your place in God's family. Go to Him, fall on your knees, and ask Him to show you where you belong, how you can contribute. He will not disappoint. Be part of God's family.

June 20

"This, then, is how you should pray:
'Our Father in heaven, hallowed be your name, your
kingdom come, your will be done, on earth as it is in
heaven.'"

— Matthew 6:9–10

Are you doing God's Will? Do you want to do God's Will? Do you
pray to do God's Will? Are you committed to that or just saying the
words? Do you understand what you are saying when you pray The
Lord's Prayer? Have you really thought through the words?

Jesus taught His disciples a pattern in which to pray. We often
state it word for word, but it really is a pattern for prayer in general.
Even so, the words Jesus taught His disciples are powerful. One of
the specifics He calls out is God's Will being done on earth just like
it is in Heaven. Since God works through us, we are the ones to carry
out His Will.

We may ask what His Will is. Jesus made it pretty clear. We are
to love God and love our neighbor. Who is our neighbor? It is every
person we come across. If we love God and love our neighbor, do
we show that in our actions? This does not mean giving money to
charities. It means smiling, saying kind words, being kind, being
honorable, regardless of how we feel and who they are.

We pray the words far too often without thinking about them.
Do yourself a favor and ponder on them. Allow the words and Jesus
to make a change in your life. Do God's Will.

June 21

I know what it is to be in need, and I know what it
is to have plenty. I have learned the secret of being
content in any and every situation, whether well fed
or hungry, whether living in plenty or in want. I can
do all this through him who gives me strength.

— Philippians 4:12–13

How do you react when in need? Do you ask for help? Do you reach
out to family, friends, or co-workers? Do you just work harder to make
it all work out? Do you eventually come to a breaking point? Do you
reach out to God?

We all have struggles, frustrations, and setbacks. It doesn't matter
who we are, we will face them. It doesn't matter if we are rich or
poor, married or single, male or female, in school or in the workforce,
Christian or non-Christian. We will all face bumps in the road.

The issue at hand is how we react to them. Do we see the help
available and do we reach out for it? God does provide us strength
and help all the days of our lives. Do we see it around us? We need
to recognize it in the people God puts in our lives. He provides
abundantly the help we need.

When going through struggles, reach out to those people God has
put in your life. Each of us is put in situations for a reason. Sometimes
we are the helper and sometimes we are the helped. We need God and
the people He put in our lives. Reach out.

June 22

Now about your love for one another we do not need to write to you, for you yourselves have been taught by God to love each other. And in fact, you do love all of God's family throughout Macedonia. Yet we urge you, brothers and sisters, to do so more and more, and to make it your ambition to lead a quiet life: You should mind your own business and work with your hands, just as we told you, so that your daily life may win the respect of outsiders and so that you will not be dependent on anybody.

—1 Thessalonians 4:9–12

How do you express your love? Do you express it at all? Do you tell those you love that you love them? Do you show your love through actions? Do others recognize love in you? Love is far more than words.

Love as demonstrated and demanded by God is an active verb. It requires action on our part. It includes our actions toward those we encounter on a daily basis.

What does that love look like? It might include serving others during a church or family activity. It may be coordinating events. It may be teaching classes. We could show our love by volunteering to clean the church building. We could go visit those who are sick. We may show it through many, many actions.

Remember that love as demonstrated and expected by God is action. Don't say empty words, rather put your words in action. Demonstrate your love for God and others by doing.

June 23

"If you love me, keep my commands. And I will ask
the Father, and he will give you another advocate to
help you and be with you forever—the Spirit of truth.
The world cannot accept him, because it neither sees
him nor knows him. But you know him, for he lives
with you and will be in you. I will not leave you as
orphans; I will come to you."

— John 14:15–18

Do you sometimes feel as though you have strayed off the right path?
Do you feel like you are being pulled into a dark and dangerous
situation? Do you wish there was a way to get back to the narrow way?
Are you willing to follow the One who can get you there?

There are more distractions in this world than we can count. We
see people falling for drugs, alcohol, materialism, bad relationships,
and attempting to belong. It all boils down to our desire to worship
something bigger than ourselves. So, we create idols of many kinds.

We can erase our desire to worship all those things by worshiping
the Creator of all things, the God of the universe, the Savior of the
world. But the first thing we need to do is love Him. If we love Him,
we will do as He has instructed us to do. He has sent His Spirit to be
our guide in following Him.

I pray we all decide to love God and follow His instructions. By
doing this, we are given peace, joy, and love. Choose to love God and
His Son and accept His Holy Spirit into your life.

June 24

Then the LORD God formed a man from the dust of
the ground and breathed into his nostrils the breath
of life, and the man became a living being.

— Genesis 2:7

Do you believe in miracles? Have you ever really contemplated the concept? Do you know what a miracle is? Can you accept that God can and will do things that man cannot explain? Are you willing to put your faith in Him—the One who is all powerful?

We see things that are unexplained all the time. Yet we often don't attribute them to God. We explain them away by saying we don't understand them, but there is someone smart enough who can. Or we think we can explain them even if we can't. We just don't want to give God the credit.

If we really dig deep and try to understand life on this planet, we will find that even the brightest minds and most studied scientists cannot explain everything about life. There are so many different enzymes, molecules, and sub-components of them in our very own bodies that science has yet to identify them all. Who, but God, could have created something as complex as our very own selves?

Open your eyes and see the miracles around you. See others as God sees them. See them as miracles and determine to love them as a creation of God.

Marty Pressey

June 25

The thief comes only to steal and kill and destroy;
I have come that they may have life, and have it to
the full.

— John 10:10

Are you struggling to find your place in this world? Are your looking for a career, a club, a school, a partner, or something else? Do you think you'll never find it? Have you thought that you are really looking for peace, joy, and love?

When we listen to this world, we go chasing after so many attractions and distractions. We chase after the limelight, the promotion, the elaborate, the glitzy, the spotlight. We believe the ludicrousness of Hollywood. We seek to look like the movie stars. We try to be the tough guy on the silver screen.

What we are really looking for is the peace, joy, and love of acceptance. Our true acceptance comes for God. We can't believe it is free for the taking, because everything in this world has a cost. Well, it's not exactly free. You have to give up the lies of this world to experience the freedom offered by Jesus Christ.

I pray we all decide to trust and follow Jesus, to accept His gift of freedom and experience the peace, joy, and love He provides. Trust Him. He won't disappoint.

June 26

Rejoice always, pray continually, give thanks in all
circumstances; for this is God's will for you in Christ
Jesus.

—1 Thessalonians 5:16–18

Does your faith waiver? Do you sometimes wonder how many times
you can fall and still get back up? Do you sometimes feel like it's just
too hard to keep going? Does your strength run low? Lean on the One
who has an endless strength.

We all fall. We all feel down and out at times. We all feel like we
are at the end of our rope. The world presses in with a heavy load and
we're ready to give up. We struggle to keep going. We lose sleep. We
don't want to get up. We feel like we're trudging through the day as
though wading through knee deep mud.

We all have the option to reach out to God and trust Him.
When we do, He blesses us with the strength we need to keep going.
Sometimes it is nothing more than a nudging to take one more step,
then one more step. It can be hard, because we may not really want
to do that. But if we keep going and leaning on God, He brings us
through it and we are much better on the other side.

Don't stop moving forward. Keep leaning on God. He will give
you the strength you need. Pray to Him at all times, continuously, in
short prayers all day long. He is there and your faith in Him will grow
stronger and you will too.

Marty Pressey

June 27

"My sheep listen to my voice; I know them, and they follow me. I give them eternal life, and they shall never perish; no one will snatch them out of my hand. My Father, who has given them to me, is greater than all; no one can snatch them out of my Father's hand. I and the Father are one."

— John 10:27–30

Do others know you are a Christian? Do they see the Holy Spirit working through you? Do you exhibit the fruits of the spirit? Is it obvious by your actions and words that you are a follower of Jesus Christ? Or do you look more like everyone else in the world?

We can have a big influence on those around us by simply allowing the Holy Spirit to lead us in all situations. Jesus will change us, if we are willing to follow. He will fill us with His Spirit. If we choose to follow Him, we cannot help but change. Unfortunately, some only choose to follow when it's convenient.

Being a follower of Jesus is not always easy and sometimes flat out hard. But we need to keep our hearts and our heads focused on Jesus, on listening for the Holy Spirit. He will lead us in a positive direction, toward the place He wants us to be, a life far better than any we can imagine.

I pray we all determine to follow Jesus, to listen for His Spirit to speak to us. Follow Him into a life you cannot imagine and won't be able to put into words. Continue to follow Him.

June 28

"I have told you these things, so that in me you may
have peace. In this world you will have trouble. But
take heart! I have overcome the world."

—John 16:33

Do you sometimes wonder if God really cares? Do you ask, "Where
are you God?" Do you wonder if He really loves you? Do you think
that God could not possibly love you? Have you experienced His love?
Have you trusted Him?

We have many different situations thrown at us as we go
through this life. Sometimes we have several thrown at us all at once.
Sometimes we think God obviously isn't taking care of us because we
are overwhelmed. This world is broken and comes at us at breakneck
speed.

We need to hold onto our faith in God. He will always be there
for us. It seems trite or simple to say that, but He really is there for us.
We are a pretty spoiled society and most of us don't know what it is to
depend on God to provide each meal we have or the water we drink.
This hinders us sometimes from trusting Him.

I pray we all decide to trust God. He loves us and will always be
with us. He has conquered this world and promises us a much better
place. Hold on to your faith in God.

June 29

"So do not worry, saying, 'What shall we eat?' or 'What shall we drink?' or 'What shall we wear?' For the pagans run after all these things, and your heavenly Father knows that you need them. But seek first his kingdom and his righteousness, and all these things will be given to you as well. Therefore do not worry about tomorrow, for tomorrow will worry about itself. Each day has enough trouble of its own."
— Matthew 6:31–34

Who is your anchor in the storm? Do you have someone you can depend on? Are you an anchor for others? Perhaps you are the rope that connects the true anchor to others. Perhaps you are the one that needs the anchor.

We all have stormy times in our lives. There are times when it's all we can do to get up in the morning. There are times when we are the one encouraging others. The world throws many difficulties our way. It could be losing a job, relationships, health issues, financial struggles, or destruction of our belongings.

God is always there for us. When we go through struggles, we need to turn to Him and hold on to Him. We are also told to prepare for these tough times ahead of time by studying His Word, building a relationship with Him, and learning to trust Him.

Turn to God to be prepared for those tough times when they come. They will come and you will need Him. Don't wait, turn to God today. Begin or restart your walk with Him today.

June 30

"As the Father has loved me, so have I loved you.
Now remain in my love. If you keep my commands,
you will remain in my love, just as I have kept my
Father's commands and remain in his love. I have
told you this so that my joy may be in you and that
your joy may be complete. My command is this: Love
each other as I have loved you. Greater love has no
one than this: to lay down one's life for one's friends."

— John 15:9–13

Do you know how much you are loved? Are you sure? Do you know
that God loves you more than ice cream? More than chocolate? More
than a brand-new car? More than an expensive dress? More than
anything you can imagine?

If we don't know this, we should read His Book and see just how
much He loves us. It is a love we don't want to miss out on. It is a
love that we desperately desire, even if we don't know we do. We are
looking for this love for our entire lives until we find it in Him.

We need search no more but read His Word and find it. We are
loved beyond our imagination and we are to share it with others. We
are to show Jesus through the sharing of His love for each person we
meet. We are to share this love with family and friends. When we find
it, we will be so filled that we can't contain it.

Wake up! Recognize the love God has for you. Share that love
with others. Show Jesus in all you do, especially through your actions
toward those you meet. Be loved and show love.

Marty Pressey

July

July 1

May the God of hope fill you with all joy and peace as
you trust in him, so that you may overflow with hope
by the power of the Holy Spirit.

— Romans 15:13

How much do you trust God? Do you trust Him when things are
going badly? Is your trust in Him deep, taking root in your heart?
Does your trust in Him fill your whole being? When it does, you can
be calm and confident in the toughest of trials.

Trust seems to be losing in today's world. We are suspicious of
nearly everyone. We look at people we don't know as though we think
they are going to wrong us, steal from us, cheat us, or harm us. We are
leery when a stranger approaches us to ask a question and perhaps
think they are odd or weird.

We can trust God in all things. We can trust Him to always be
with us. Our trust in Him in strengthened by learning more about
Him and by experiencing Him being there for us. We often don't
realize He is there or that He got us through something until we look
back and reflect on our experiences. We all need to reflect back on our
lives and identify when God took care of us.

I pray each of us will learn to trust God more each day. Let Him
take root deep in your heart. Come to know He is in control no matter
the situation. Trust God.

July 2

Love is patient, love is kind. It does not envy, it does
not boast, it is not proud. It does not dishonor others,
it is not self-seeking, it is not easily angered, it keeps
no record of wrongs. Love does not delight in evil
but rejoices with the truth. It always protects, always
trusts, always hopes, always perseveres.

—1 Corinthians 13:4–7

When you tell someone you love them, do you mean it? Do you
know what love really is? Do you reflect love in all you do? Or do you
selectively show love? Will you show the world and everyone you meet
the love of Christ? If we did, this world would be a better place.

The love of this world is often mere words and often fleeting. Let
someone do something we don't like, and we hate them. We don't
treat others we meet with love most of the time, but maybe with a
little kindness or fake smile. We may attempt to be courteous, but it's
not really genuine.

We are commanded by Jesus to love one another, to love our
enemies, to show the world the love He showed. We are to be the
light of the world, yet we cannot be the light without love. We are to
be self-sacrificing in order to show Christ's love. Love is much more
than a word.

I pray we all decide to not just say the word but be the word. Be the
love that Jesus was. Love others as Jesus does. Show love to the world.

Marty Pressey

July 3

Jesus said, "My kingdom is not of this world. If it were, my servants would fight to prevent my arrest by the Jewish leaders. But now my kingdom is from another place."

— John 18:36

Are you part of God's kingdom? Do you know where His kingdom is? Do you know that Jesus is the king in that kingdom? Are you following Jesus and bringing others into His kingdom? After all, the best recruiters are the ones who are already part of the company, team, or organization.

We see the corruption in the world we live in on a daily basis. It seems there is so much destruction in people's lives. Of course, part of that is the news never ends and it covers the entire world. So, we're seeing the news of a small-town school shooting in the headlines today, when we wouldn't have 30 years ago.

The thing is, we don't need to focus on the negatives of this world. Yes, they will happen, and we are told that by Jesus Himself. However, He also told us He was the king of a different kingdom. His kingdom is coming. Are we ready to be in His kingdom? Or do we cling to the drudgery of this one?

I pray we all look forward to the kingdom where Jesus is king. I pray we all understand that He defeated the ruler of this world, Satan. Live in the freedom that Jesus provided you and look forward to being in His kingdom forever.

July 4

But you, man of God, flee from all this, and pursue
righteousness, godliness, faith, love, endurance and
gentleness. Fight the good fight of the faith. Take
hold of the eternal life to which you were called when
you made your good confession in the presence of
many witnesses.

—1 Timothy 6:11–12

Are you fighting the good fight? Or do you succumb to the ways of
the world—the ways of Satan? Do you use the weapons God has
given you? Or do you flail about on your own, not having learned to
use your gifts?

Despite popular belief, there is a battle going on every day. We
have become so blind to it that we don't even notice. We don't discuss
it nor discuss how to fight it so we can be victorious. We have become
complacent and lazy when it comes to fighting the good fight.

God has given each of us the freedom of choice. If we choose
to follow Him, He gives us everything we need to fight the good
fight. He blesses us with spiritual gifts, with knowledge, with energy,
and with courage to be a warrior. Our part is to be willing and to be
obedient. If we will do our part, God more than does His.

I pray we all decide to be willing and obedient to God. I pray we
take up the good fight and follow Him in all we do. I pray we all work
at learning to handle the weapons God has blessed us with.

July 5

But thanks be to God! He gives us the victory
through our Lord Jesus Christ.

—1 Corinthians 15:57

Are you celebrating the victory? Are you asking yourself, "What
victory?" Do you realize you are victorious in Jesus Christ? Do you
know that He provided a victory for us over sin and death? So, let's
celebrate that victory.

This world wants to bring us down. Satan wants to bring us down.
We have too much to do. We have too many bills. We worry about
everything under the sun. We hold on to those worries. We allow them
to eat us up. We allow them to bring us down to the pit.

We have a great and wonderful victory because of what Jesus did
for us. We don't have to worry anymore. That's not to say we should
do nothing. It is to say that we are to do what God has called us to do
and leave the rest to Him. We are to trust in the victory He provided.

I pray each of us will let go of our worries, do what we know God
has called us to do, and celebrate the victory. We are victorious! Let's
be the victors!

July 6

In fact, this is love for God: to keep his commands.
And his commands are not burdensome, for everyone
born of God overcomes the world. This is the victory
that has overcome the world, even our faith. Who is it
that overcomes the world? Only the one who believes
that Jesus is the Son of God.

—1 John 5:3–5

Have you overcome the world in your faith? Do you realize you have
the power to overcome the world? Are you victorious through your
love for God? Do you truly believe in Jesus? When we do, we are
victorious.

This world will put us down nearly every day if we let it. The
world is full of people who want to keep climbing an invisible ladder
and they think the way to do that is by putting others down. This is a
lie that Satan tells us.

It is through our love for God, obeying Him, and loving others
that we are victorious. It is by taking one step forward in our faith,
then another step that we grow and realize the victory that God has
set before us. As we experience His love and share it with others, we
continue to grow and experience the victory that results in freedom.

I pray we all experience the love of God. I pray we all share that
love. I pray we all grow in our faith by taking one step at a time and
continue taking those steps. Love God, share His love, and step out
in faith.

July 7

On a Sabbath Jesus was teaching in one of the
synagogues, and a woman was there who had been
crippled by a spirit for eighteen years. She was
bent over and could not straighten up at all. When
Jesus saw her, he called her forward and said to her,
"Woman, you are set free from your infirmity."
Then he put his hands on her, and immediately she
straightened up and praised God.

— Luke 13:10–13

Are you living free? Do you know you are set free? Truly free? Do you
understand what being free means? Have you accepted your freedom
in Jesus Christ? He is willing and capable of setting you completely
free.

We are often bound by so many chains from so many different
people or things in this world. We are bound by our love for money.
We are bound by our desire to be accepted. We are tied up and twisted
with seeking out popularity. We are crippled by our lust for new things
or experiences.

What we really need is to accept our freedom that is offered by
Jesus. He will break those chains that bind us. He will set us free from
our worldly desires. Does it mean we won't need to work or buy things
or mingle with other people? No. It does mean that we won't be held
hostage by them.

I pray we all experience the freedom Jesus offers and we learn to
live free. It is through this freedom that we learn to truly live. Live
free. Live an abundant life.

July 8

My goal is that they may be encouraged in heart
and united in love, so that they may have the full
riches of complete understanding, in order that they
may know the mystery of God, namely, Christ, in
whom are hidden all the treasures of wisdom and
knowledge.

— Colossians 2:2–3

Who do you lean on? Do you have someone in your life that helps get
you through those tough times? Do you have someone who will be
honest with you, even if they know you won't like it? Will you allow
someone to be close to you?

This world is full of people who would take advantage of our
vulnerability, which makes most of us hesitant to be open with others.
We won't be open and transparent with others due to fear of being
taken advantage of or made fun of. We don't let others know when we
are struggling.

Have we thought that God put someone in our life that will be
there for us? That person will be honest, yet not judgmental. It may
be our spouse, our boyfriend or girlfriend, a best friend, a sibling, a
parent, or someone we go to church with. That person will not leave
us when we are going through tough times, through trials, through
struggles.

I pray we all recognize the person God has put in our lives to be
there for us no matter what. I pray we recognize that person as a gift
from God. I pray we recognize that person as God's hands holding us.
Accept God's servants.

July 9

Live in harmony with one another. Do not be
proud but be willing to associate with people of low
position. Do not be conceited. Do not repay anyone
evil for evil. Be careful to do what is right in the eyes
of everyone. If it is possible, as far as it depends on
you, live at peace with everyone.

— Romans 12:16–18

How do you want to be remembered? How do you want people to look
at you today? What do you want people to say about you today and
tomorrow? Do you think a reputation is built on a single day?

We often hear so and so is this or that type of person. We may
wonder sometimes what people say about us. We will hear some say
they don't care what others think. That is usually said in a selfish
and negative manner, because those folks only care about their own
desires.

We have to face the fact that people will say things about us when
we are not around. The question we should wrestle with is, "What do
we want them to say?" If we want them to say good things, we need
to do good things and behave in a good manner. If we want a good
legacy, we need to start building it as soon as possible and stick with it.

God wants us to do His will. If we want people to respect us and
say good things about us, we need to do God's will. Think about what
you want people to say about you and begin fulfilling that legacy. Do
the right thing. Do God's will.

July 10

Suddenly a furious storm came up on the lake, so that the waves swept over the boat. But Jesus was sleeping. The disciples went and woke him, saying, "Lord, save us! We're going to drown!"

He replied, "You of little faith, why are you so afraid?" Then he got up and rebuked the winds and the waves, and it was completely calm.

— Matthew 8:24–26

How do you handle the storms of life? What is your reaction when things go haywire? Do you overreact? Or do you remain calm? You can remain calm, if you rely on God.

I'm sure someone will say, "God isn't going to hand me the money I need for rent from heaven." True, but I've seen Him provide rent money to people in a variety of ways, including getting an unexpected refund check in the mail. Perhaps we don't believe that is God. Perhaps we should read how He has worked throughout history.

When we trust God to handle our troubles, He will. He may not handle it the way we want. Instead, He will handle it in a way that will fulfill His will and His purpose for us. We are to trust Him to calm the storms in our lives, to bring us through to the other side, and to show us the rainbow.

I pray we all decide to trust God at all times, but especially as we go through the storms of life. He will lead us through them, sometimes carrying us when we can't carry ourselves. Trust God always.

July 11

He gives strength to the weary
and increases the power of the weak.
Even youths grow tired and weary,
and young men stumble and fall;
but those who hope in the LORD
will renew their strength.
They will soar on wings like eagles;
they will run and not grow weary,
they will walk and not be faint.

— Isaiah 40:29–32

How do you keep going when you grow weary? Do you give up? Do you get depressed? Do you decide to be lazy and sleep all day? Or do you have a source of strength that you can tap into?

It seems we are always on the go and always busy in today's world. It seems our jobs have gotten more demanding. Computers were supposed to save time, but they've really increased the amount of work we have on our plates. We are also more aware of news and can get infinite details in an instant. All this causes us to grow weary.

We can rely on God to lift us up. He will not only give us the strength we need to keep going but will bring us to new heights. We are to trust Him, turn our problems, issues, doubts, worries, and weakness over to Him. It is only then that He will lift us up.

Trust all things to God. Allow Him to show you the way, to lift you above the scruff. Soar above the fray with God.

July 12

Then I heard every creature in heaven and on earth
and under the earth and on the sea, and all that is in
them, saying:
"To him who sits on the throne and to the Lamb
be praise and honor and glory and power, for ever
and ever!"

— Revelation 5:13

Are you worshiping God every moment of every day? Do you fully
understand His mighty power? Do you trust in Him? Do you know
that He has already conquered this world and all the evil in it?

We often get lost in our daily lives, our daily struggles, our daily
chaos, our daily needs and wants. We lose focus on God. We forget to
praise God for being the Almighty. We forget to thank Him for our
many blessings. We become lost along our way because we take our
eyes off Jesus.

We need to remember that the things of this world will pass away.
We need to understand that this world is a temporary place for us. Our
permanent home is with God, with Jesus in the new heaven and new
earth. That is where eternity will be spent—in the presence of God.

Keep God in the forefront of your mind. Focus on Him being in
control. Know that He is God. Know that Jesus sacrificed for you.
Know that you will be with God forever.

July 13

Those who live according to the flesh have their
minds set on what the flesh desires; but those who
live in accordance with the Spirit have their minds
set on what the Spirit desires. The mind governed
by the flesh is death, but the mind governed by the
Spirit is life and peace.

— Romans 8:5–6

Who do you want? Do you want a wish granter, a genie? Are you
looking for someone who will give you all you could ever want? Are
you hoping for your every wish to come true in the snap of your
fingers?

The world is full of dream chasers. Chasing dreams can be
good and it can be destructive. Many will chase dreams of success,
promotion, and notoriety at any cost. Their view of success is
distorted by idol worship. Their idols are fame, money, and elaborate
possessions.

True success is love, peace, and joy. Those can only be achieved by
focusing on God, doing His will. When we focus on God, understand
what He has gifted us to do, and pursue His will, we will find true
success. Rather than chasing fleeting dreams, we should be chasing
God's will for us.

Seek God first and find success. Trust in His guiding Spirit and
find peace beyond description. Trust in the revolution started by
Jesus. Follow in His footsteps.

July 14

We know that anyone born of God does not continue
to sin; the One who was born of God keeps them
safe, and the evil one cannot harm them. We know
that we are children of God, and that the whole world
is under the control of the evil one.

—1 John 18–19

Do you have a safe place? Do you feel safe in this world? Do you trust
that everything will be alright? Do you seek the assurance and safety
of God? He provides us the assurance of being in His presence for
eternity.

There are certainly times when we feel unsafe or insecure in
our surroundings. The world can be a tough and tumble world that
threatens our physical, mental, and emotional safety. People can be
destructive toward others and even themselves.

However, we have the assurance in God that we rest in His arms
always. It doesn't mean we won't have hard times. It does mean He will
provide what's needed for us to get through those hard times. We need
to cling to God and His assurance that He is in control.

Pray at all times that God gives you strength. Hold on to His
promise that He will not leave you alone. Be confident in God. Trust
Him always.

July 15

Jesus answered, "I am the way and the truth and the life. No one comes to the Father except through me. If you really know me, you will know my Father as well. From now on, you do know him and have seen him."

— John 14:6–7

Are you crazy about following Jesus? Do you understand the radicalness of what He did? Will you commit to the revolution He started? Are you willing to turn your world upside down for Him?

Jesus turned the Jewish and Roman world's upside down when he walked this earth. He told the Jews the real meaning of the laws God had given them. He showed the Romans they could not stop the King of the World. He eliminated boundaries.

Jesus did not care if we were an outcast, diseased, what our race was, or if we were man or woman. He loved and cared for all. He lived righteously according to God's laws. He was the perfect example for us to emulate. If we are to be His followers, we should imitate Him.

Be part of the revolution Jesus started and still leads. Be crazy for Christ. Be a person who stands out. Be humble, generous, forgiving, caring, and loving. Follow Jesus with all your heart.

July 16

"If you love those who love you, what reward will you get? Are not even the tax collectors doing that? And if you greet only your own people, what are you doing more than others? Do not even pagans do that? Be perfect, therefore, as your heavenly Father is perfect."
— Matthew 5:46–48

What does your love look like? What actions of yours demonstrate love? Do you only love those who love you? Are you vengeful toward those who don't love you? When will you decide to follow Jesus and love your enemies?

There is already too much hate and indifference in this world. We see it in the personal attacks, battles, wars, street violence, and the ignoring of others. We are often part of the problem. We don't really go out of our way to help others, to show the love of Christ.

We are called to love everyone. That is hard. How do we love the one who offended a family member? The only way to do that is to allow Jesus to fill us with His Spirit. We must submit to His will, follow His commands. We are called to be better than the rest of the world. We are to see everyone as Jesus sees them.

I pray we all commit to continue to improve ourselves. I pray we commit to love everyone. I pray we see the broken, the violent, the tormented as Jesus does. Make every effort to see others as Jesus does and love them as He does.

Marty Pressey

July 17

"But if serving the LORD seems undesirable to
you, then choose for yourselves this day whom you
will serve, whether the gods your ancestors served
beyond the Euphrates, or the gods of the Amorites,
in whose land you are living. But as for me and my
household, we will serve the LORD."

— Joshua 24:15

Who or what do you serve? Do you know who or what you are serving?
Are you aware of who you serve? Are you aware you serve material
things? Do you consciously think about who or what you are serving?
The vast majority of people in this world do not.

We often are serving material objects without even realizing it.
For instance, how much time and effort do we put into what we wear?
How much time do we spend waxing that car? How much time do we
spend making our home beautiful by decorating or planting flowers?
How much time do we spend watching TV?

None of these things are bad in and of themselves. However, when
we spend an inordinate amount of time worrying about them, we are
worshiping them and not God. We are to serve God and He demands
our time. That means spending time with Him and spending time
doing for Him.

I pray we all decide to spend more time with God and more time
serving Him. We serve Him when we serve others. Serve God. Serve
others.

July 18

"To whom will you compare me?
Or who is my equal?" says the Holy One.
Lift up your eyes and look to the heavens:
Who created all these?
He who brings out the starry host one by one
and calls forth each of them by name.
Because of his great power and mighty strength,
not one of them is missing.

— Isaiah 40:25–26

Where is your strength? How do you keep going? Are you weak or strong? Do you boldly take on challenges or shrink away and hope someone else does? Are you willing to step into the unknown or stay in your cocoon? There is strength at your disposal.

The world we live in can be a scary place, but only if we let it. That's not to say we should be careless, but to say we don't need to be afraid of doing new things with people we haven't met in places we haven't been. We often shy away from those things.

Most of us have been and will be put in situations where we don't know the people in a group setting in which we find ourselves. Some of us are shy and will stand in the corner. Others are more outgoing and will mingle. For those who are shy, we can mingle with the confidence that God is with us.

Be confident God is with you always. Lean on His strength to overcome challenges you face. He won't let you down. Trust God to work through you and in you.

July 19

For the message of the cross is foolishness to those
who are perishing, but to us who are being saved it is
the power of God.

—1 Corinthians 1:18

Are you perishing or saved? Are you confident in your answer? Do you
live out the salvation provided by Jesus? Or do you depend on yourself
rather than Him? Are you willing to give up your desires to fulfill His?
Tough questions for each one of us.

We are inundated with the selfishness of the world and our
own. We watch far too many TV shows that promote taking care of
ourselves and forget others. We see others around us doing this, too,
and begin believing we should do that same. When we do that, we
become like the world.

We are called to be different than the world. If we are going to do
that, we must fill our sight, our hearing, our entire hearts and minds
with God. We have heard the saying, "You are what you eat." The
same is true of our hearts and minds. They will be filled with what
we focus on.

I pray we all make a conscious decision to fill ourselves with
God and not the world. I pray we commit to that decision and follow
through. We all need God. We all need to be filled by Him. Choose
to be filled with His Word.

July 20

I know what it is to be in need, and I know what it
is to have plenty. I have learned the secret of being
content in any and every situation, whether well fed
or hungry, whether living in plenty or in want. I can
do all this through him who gives me strength.

—1 Corinthians 4:12–13

What are you up to? Are you doing things you never dreamed? Are
you surprised how far you've come? Have you given credit for that
progress to God? Or do you really think it's all you? Where did you
get your talent, your abilities?

We progress naturally in life to some degree through your
experiences and by learning from them. We progress through study,
education, new ideas, new theories. We can also train ourselves to
perform certain tasks. All of these are abilities.

Where did we get the ability to learn, to train? Sure, people can
point to genetics. But who created the genes, the very first genes?
God is the creator of all things, including the genes that make up our
physical bodies. He is the one that provided the ability to think. He
provided the ability to do.

I pray we all recognize and give credit to God for our many
accomplishments, for our progression. He has gifted us with many
abilities. When we lean on Him, He blesses us with additional insights
into how to use those abilities and progress further than we can
imagine.

July 21

And let us consider how we may spur one another on
toward love and good deeds, not giving up meeting
together, as some are in the habit of doing, but
encouraging one another—and all the more as you
see the Day approaching.

— Hebrews 10:24–25

Do you realize there are people you can lean on? Do you reach out
to them? Do you depend on them? Do you know you cannot follow
God all on your own? Do you understand you need others in the
church? We all need others in our lives. We will either depend on those
following God or those following the world.

We see people fall into the wrong crowd all the time. Why? Because
we all need community. We all need to feel as though someone cares
for us, someone has our best interest at heart. This is why gangs are
so successful. They draw kids in by giving them a place where they
feel they belong.

As a church body, we must make others feel as though they belong.
We need to welcome everyone in with open arms. As individual
Christians, we need to continue to meet with the church, with other
Christians. If not, we will drift away and end up with the wrong crowd.

I pray we all commit to both continue meeting with other
Christians and welcoming newcomers into our group. This will not
only grow God's Kingdom but will save the person from a doomed
end. Greet each other with open arms. Care for each other. Love one
another.

July 22

"You have heard that it was said, 'Love you neighbor and hate your enemy.' But I tell you, love your enemies and pray for those who persecute you, that you may be children of you Father in heaven."
— Matthew 5:43–45a

Who do you love? Do you love everyone you see, meet, know, or don't know? Do you pray for people you don't know, even if it's just a brief prayer for someone you see while out on errands? Are you willing to see others as God sees them?

Jesus taught that we are to love, not only our neighbor, but our enemies as well. We are to see the lost, those who don't know Jesus intimately, just as we see a brother or sister. We are to love all people, maybe not their actions. There is quite a difference in how we look at people when we do this.

When we love people as Jesus did, we will pray for them, we will reach out to them, we will provide loving correction rather than hatefulness and being judgmental of them. When we love our neighbor and our enemy, we will serve them like Jesus. We are to become more like Him, following in His footsteps.

I pray we all decide to love each person we meet. I pray we all decide to love our family members. I pray we all decide to treat others as Jesus did. Let's all become more like Him.

Marty Pressey

July 23

God is our refuge and strength, an ever-present help
in trouble. Therefore we will not fear, though the
earth give way and the mountains fall into the heart
of the sea, though its waters roar and foam and the
mountains quake with their surging.

— Psalm 46:1–2

Do you take refuge in God, fully knowing He is in charge, trusting He
will protect you? Do you trust Him with everything in your life? Do
you run to Him when you are feeling depressed, oppressed, or fearful?

Sometimes it's hard for us to go to God. Sometimes we don't want
to trust in someone we don't see. But do we trust our spouses when
we're not near them? I dare say the vast majority of us do. So why don't
we trust God, even if we can't see Him?

We all need to have faith in someone or something. God is the
One we should put our faith in. It may be difficult at first. But as we
continue to do so and experience His protection and His guidance, it
will get easier. It will get to the point that it becomes second nature.

I pray we all decide to put our faith in God. I pray we take the first
step and the next step and keep taking those steps to trust God. He is
faithful and will always be there for us.

July 24

Shout for joy to the LORD, all the earth.
Worship the LORD with gladness;
come before him with joyful songs.
Know that the LORD is God.

— Psalm 100:1–3a

Do you worship the Lord? Do you really worship Him with all your heart? Do you bless His Name? Do praise Him for all you have, for all your experiences (good or bad), for the people He has put in your life, for the job you have? Do you realize you live, breath, and have material possessions because of His blessings?

We may occasionally thank God for the good things in our lives. We may occasionally thank Him for our families. We may even remember to thank Him for our jobs, but usually only when we get a job we like or think we will like. But do we thank Him for the trials we face?

God allows us to face trials. Yet he never leaves us alone. He is always right there with us. Do we listen for Him or look for Him in those situations? Do we thank Him for being with us? We should not only ask God for help in tough situations but thank Him for being there with us and helping us get through them.

I pray we all decide to praise God in all situations. Praise Him for His wonderful blessings, including carrying us through the tough times. Praise God and sing wonderful songs to Him.

Marty Pressey

July 25

When Jesus heard this, he said to him, "You still lack
one thing. Sell everything you have and give to the
poor, and you will have treasure in heaven. Then
come, follow me."

— Luke 18:22

Are you willing to follow? Are you willing to follow Jesus? Are you
willing to follow His commands? Will you follow His teaching? Will
you follow in His footsteps so that others see you are a disciple of His?
Will you give up yourself to be His?

So many times, we say we will follow Jesus. Perhaps we tell others
we are followers of Jesus. Or we simply state we are Christians. We
may think of ourselves as followers or, in another word, disciples. But
do we exhibit that on a daily basis?

Jesus demands we give up ourselves to follow Him. He demands
we give up chasing others or other things. He is not asking us to
stop living and pursuing a good life, but He is demanding us to stop
making those other things our idols.

I pray we all decide to follow Him and His teaching with all our
heart. Let's stop putting other things higher in priority above Jesus.
Show His true light to others.

July 26

And the disciples were filled with joy and with the
Holy Spirit.

— Acts 13:52

Do you have joy in your life? Do you seek joy? Do you really and
honestly desire to have joy in your life? Are you seeking joy from the
correct source? There is only one way to acquire true joy.

So many in this world think they seek joy. Really, they are seeking
happiness and exhilarating experiences. They want to be excited,
happy, laughing, enjoying things or people. Unfortunately, it's a false
pursuit. No one will have a life with every moment filled with those
experiences.

We can experience joy in our lives. Joy is akin to peace. It is an
inner contentment. It does include happiness but is not limited to just
that. It is much more than momentary happiness. A joyful life can
only be achieved by living in the Holy Spirit. He is the only One that
can fill us with joy.

I pray we all decide to invite the Holy Spirit into our lives. Ask
Him to fill you up and move your old self out. Ask Him to take control
of your life. Only when He does will you be able to experience the true
joy that is available to all of us.

Marty Pressey

July 27

For the grace of God has appeared that offers salvation
to all people. It teaches us to say "No" to ungodliness
and worldly passions, and to live self-controlled,
upright and godly lives in this present age, while we
wait for the blessed hope—the appearing of the glory
of our great God and Savior, Jesus Christ, who gave
himself for us to redeem us from all wickedness and
to purify for himself a people that are his very own,
eager to do what is good.

— Titus 2:11–14

Are you living the new you? Do you believe you have been made new?
Or are you still trying to make the new you? Do you understand that
you cannot make a new you? Are you willing to submit to the One
who can remake you?

There are tons of self-help books out there. They provide all types
of advice. They talk about self-discipline, setting priorities, setting
goals, make a plan to achieve our goals. Many will also discuss self-
reflection, looking in the mirror.

The best self-help book in the world is the Bible. We will find all
the ideas put forth in other self-help books and one more that is key.
The key is to submit to God and allow Him to make the change in us.
Our faith and trust in Him are the key to be who we were meant to be.

I pray we all decide to read God's Word and trust in Him. Ask
Him to make the change in you. Then be patient and follow where
He leads. God will make the change in you.

July 28

Rejoice always, pray continually, give thanks in all circumstances; for this is God's will for you in Christ Jesus.

—1 Thessalonians 5:16–18

How often do you pray? Do you pray at all? Do you pray at least once a day? Do you pray 3, 6, 8, 10 times a day? How often do you think you should pray? Only at mealtime? Only when you go to bed? Perhaps when you wake up?

I often wonder about praying and what our different thoughts are on the subject. Do we really believe prayer works? If we do, why don't we pray more often? I believe we need prayer in our lives, and we should be constantly praying.

We often pray only when we are in deep trouble or when we want God to do something for us. We should be thanking God in prayer for all He does for us. If we truly want to change our lives for the better, we will pray, continually. We will have a continual conversation with God.

I pray that we all decide to pray every day and multiple times during the day, to the point that we are praying continually. Let's all give God the thanks He deserves every day and be less demanding that He do something for us. After all, He is not a genie in a bottle, He is God.

July 29

May the God of hope fill you with all joy and peace as
you trust in him, so that you may overflow with hope
by the power of the Holy Spirit.

— Romans 15:13

Do you trust in God? Do you trust that He will lead you through any
situation? Do you trust Him with all of your decisions? Do you trust
Him when things don't go the way you want? Are you willing to let
go of your anger, hatred, frustration, and judgmental attitude and
trust Him?

We see quite a lot of anger in this world today. We see a lot of
judgmentalism. We see hateful barbs being spewed back and forth.
We often shake our heads and ask, "What are these people thinking?"
Then we do the same thing, even if it's on a smaller scale.

When we trust God with everything, we can let go of that behavior
and those attitudes. You see, our lashing out is almost always selfish or
out of fear. When we trust in God, we lose both of those. We realize
there is nothing to fear, because God is in control. We realize, if we
want to be more like Jesus, we are to be unselfish and look out for
others.

I pray we all decide to trust God with everything. I pray we all lose
our fear and our selfish attitude. When we do, our world becomes a
better place. Put your trust in God.

July 30

Who is wise and understanding among you? Let
them show it by their good life, by deeds done in the
humility that comes from wisdom. But if you harbor
bitter envy and selfish ambition in your hearts, do
not boast about it or deny the truth. Such "wisdom"
does not come down from heaven but is earthly,
unspiritual, demonic.

— James 3:13–15

Are you selfish? That's a hard question, isn't it? If you are selfish, you
probably don't even realize it, but those around you do. How can you
come to the realization that you are selfish? It's not easy.

The people of the world will tell us to take care of ourselves first.
They will tell us to go take what is rightfully ours. They will say to
step on others to get to the top. They will tell us that we deserve it.
But the world is wrong.

When we step on others or take care of ourselves first, we become
a very unlikeable person. We become the person no one wants to be
around. We are told in the Bible to be unselfish, to do things for others,
to put others ahead of ourselves. Jesus lived this as an example for us.

I pray we all take a long, hard look at our actions and attitudes.
I pray we all ask God to remove our selfish nature from us. I pray we
make the hard choice of breaking the chains of selfishness.

July 31

Do not repay anyone evil for evil. Be careful to do
what is right in the eyes of everyone. If it is possible, as
far as it depends on you, live at peace with everyone.
Do not take revenge, my dear friends, but leave room
for God's wrath, for it is written: "It is mine to avenge;
I will repay," says the Lord.

— Romans 12:17–21

Are you a vengeful person? No?! Do you not want to pay back someone
who does you wrong? Don't you give the cold shoulder to a person who
did something bad to you or someone close to you? Don't we all want
revenge at some point in our lives?

Perhaps someone "took my parking spot" and we become furious,
spewing obscenities. Maybe someone "stole" a boyfriend or girlfriend
and we decide we can no longer talk to that person. Or a co-worker
tells our boss that we have been cheating on the time clock and we
refuse to speak to them and maybe even start looking for dirt on them
to tell the boss.

This is not what we should be doing. We are to bless our enemies
and even serve them. Is it easy? No! But we are called to be above the
world in our actions and attitudes. We are to be the shining light of
Jesus. How can we be His light if we act just like the world?

I pray we all decide to be above the world and show Jesus' light.
Let's bless our enemies. Let's change our attitudes to be like Jesus.
Let's change our actions to reflect Him.

August

August 1

Finally, brothers and sisters, rejoice! Strive for full restoration, encourage one another, be of one mind, live in peace. And the God of love and peace will be with you.

—2 Corinthians 13:11

How much credit have you built up? What are your expectations of others? How does your personal credit compare to your expectations of others? What do these two have to do with each other? If you expect others to be kind to you, how kind are you to others?

Far too often, we don't realize how unkind we are to others. Yet we expect others to treat us kindly. If we want others to treat us kindly, we need to be kind first. We need to build credit. If our credit is not good, how can we expect others to treat us any better?

We are told we are to love each other, to encourage each other, to take care of each other. All of those require a positive attitude, a kind heart, putting others in front of ourselves. When we are selfishly putting our own desires first, we lose credit. When we put others first, we build credit. When our credit is high, we receive unexpected blessings in great multitudes.

I pray we all decide to be kind and encourage each other. Let's build our credit so as to be treated according to our expectations. Encourage one another. Love one another.

August 2

Dear children, do not let anyone lead you astray. The
one who does what is right is righteous, just as he is
righteous.

—1 John 3:7

How are you today? Are you following God's commands? Are you
following Jesus' example? Do you know for sure you are? Have you
slowly slipped away? It is an easy thing to slowly slip into bad attitudes
and bad actions.

We are inundated with all kinds of negative pressures every day.
Whether it's TV shows, commercials, billboards, friends, co-workers,
or some random person we meet. We often think, "Well, it's just this
one little thing." That is the beginning of slipping down the slippery
slope.

We are to be vigilant in doing right. We are commended for doing
right by God. We are rewarded for following Jesus' example and doing
the will of God. Rewards may or may not come in this lifetime, but we
have assurance our reward will come following this life.

I pray we all decide to do what is right. I pray we don't let the little
things trip us up. I pray we hold to our faith and follow our Savior. Stay
strong, do what is right.

August 3

But now that you know God—or rather are known
by God—how is it that you are turning back to
those weak and miserable forces? Do you wish to be
enslaved by them all over again?

— Galatians 4:9

Do you know the real you? Or are you wrapped in who you project you
are? Are you trying to make everyone believe you are someone you're
not? Are you allowing external forces to cause you to be someone
you're not? Won't you decide to be who you really are?

The world pressures us to be someone we're not. We try to be
glamorous like the movie stars. We try to be the walk-off home run
hero. We try to be the fictional hero who rescues the maiden. We try
to be the heroin who stands up for the less fortunate.

Underneath all this, we are who God created us to be. When we
decide to follow Jesus, we often have an incredible energy to do so. But
somewhere along the way, we lose it. Why? We start letting the world
dictate our lives for us again.

I pray we all decide to regain the energy we once had to follow
Jesus. We need Him to be first in our lives to be who God created us
to be. Follow Jesus, not the world.

August 4

"Come to me, all you who are weary and burdened, and I will give you rest. Take my yoke upon you and learn from me, for I am gentle and humble in heart, and you will find rest for your souls. For my yoke is easy and my burden is light."

— Matthew 11:28–30

Do you feel like you are being overwhelmed at times? Do you feel like there is too much to do? Do you feel inadequate for the task? Do you feel like you are left on an island by yourself? There is hope.

The world we live in demands a lot of us. We also demand a lot of ourselves. Often, we put undue pressure on ourselves. We try to fit in too many tasks, too many TV shows, too many visits, too many of whatever it is we're trying to fit in. Part of that is our own desires and part of it is the world we live in expecting it of us.

Jesus told us to lay our burdens at His feet. He will carry them for us. That doesn't mean we won't ever feel pressure or need to meet deadlines, but it does mean He will take away our anxiety and worry. He will provide us the strength, patience, and peace going forward.

I pray we all learn to turn our burdens over to Jesus. Allow Him to carry the heavy load, just as He has promised. Let go and let Him.

August 5

He replied, "Because you have so little faith. Truly I tell you, if you have faith as small as a mustard seed, you can say to this mountain, 'Move from here to there,' and it will move. Nothing will be impossible for you."

— Matthew 17:20

What are you facing today? Are you struggling with something? Do you need someone to lean on? Will you accept the help if it's available to you? Are you willing to make the change needed to walk the right path?

We all make mistakes. We all fail to be perfect. We all need improvement. We all know our own failures. We often feel ashamed of those failures. Many of us get trapped in the past, failing to let go of it and move forward. What can we do about moving that mountain?

We can take a step in the right direction by putting our faith in Jesus Christ. We can continue moving in a positive direction by better understanding the promises He made. We can exercise our faith, whether little or great, and see our faith grow.

I pray we all exercise our faith and move forward one step at a time. I pray we all see the wonders of God. I pray we all accept His promises and apply them in our lives. When we do, we can move mountains.

August 6

"All this I have spoken while still with you. But the
Advocate, the Holy Spirit, whom the Father will send
in my name, will teach you all things and will remind
you of everything I have said to you. Peace I leave
with you; my peace I give you. I do not give to you as
the world gives. Do not let your hearts be troubled
and do not be afraid."

— John 14:25–27

What are you afraid of today? Are you afraid of commitment? Are
you afraid of admitting you don't know? Are you afraid of taking the
step toward learning new things, of gaining a better understanding?

There are many people in this world who don't want to commit
to God. They are afraid they will give up having fun. They are afraid
they will have to give up their friends. They are afraid they will look
foolish when they attend church or a class, because they don't know
a lot about God.

The best thing any of us can do is take the step toward learning
more about God, His plan for us, and knowing His Son Jesus Christ.
None of us know everything there is to know about God. We all need
each other to share what we know and learn from one another.

I pray we all commit to learning more about Jesus. I pray we all
overcome our fears of foolishness and commit ourselves to Him. Seek
knowledge, understanding, and wisdom.

Marty Pressey

August 7

For what I received I passed on to you as of first importance: that Christ died for our sins according to the Scriptures, that he was buried, that he was raised on the third day according to the Scriptures, and that he appeared to Cephas, and then to the Twelve.

—1 Corinthians 15:3–5

Do you know the gospel? Do you know the good news? Do you think it's complicated or confusing? What if I told you it is simple? Would you believe me?

Many people in this world think being a follower of Jesus Christ is confusing, complicated, too many rules, or hypocritical. Some think it is too simple to be true. Many will reject Him because they just don't want to believe.

The gospel is simple. Jesus, the Son of God, came to this earth, lived, died, was buried, and rose again. He did this to save the world from its sin. He came to save each one of us. It's a shame if we try to complicate it and don't share it.

I pray we all decide to accept the gospel and share it with others. Let's not complicate it. Let's convince others to believe and be saved. Be a disciple, a follower of Jesus.

August 8

Rejoice always, pray continually, give thanks in all circumstances; for this is God's will for you in Christ Jesus.

—1 Thessalonians 5:16–18

What are you doing today? Are you making a positive change? Are you striving to be a better you? Are you looking to help someone else? Are you asking God to lead you? Are you continually praying?

Many of us start out our young professional lives looking to make changes. Many of us continue to try to make changes throughout our careers as we see things not being done right. Many of us try to do this through our own power and according to our desires.

God calls us to make positive changes according to His plan. The only way we know that plan and can make those positive changes is through prayer. We are to pray continually, asking for His guidance, listening for His voice, and applying that in our lives.

I pray we all decide to pray continually. May we all listen for God's small, sweet voice like the gentle breeze and decide to apply His guidance in our lives.

August 9

But now that you know God—or rather are known
by God—how is it that you are turning back to
those weak and miserable forces? Do you wish to be
enslaved by them all over again?

— Galatians 4:9

Do you know you are known by God? Do you understand that He
knows you better than you know yourself? Do you realize that He
knows every thought, every action? Will you perform every action,
think every thought, and speak every word knowing God is watching?

So many in this world will "speak their mind" as if they have
no one to answer to. They fail to realize that God is always there,
always watching, always listening. We might compare their actions
and words to 2-year old's who are completely ignorant of what is right
and wrong.

As Christians, we are called to be the light of the world. We know
better than to think God is not watching. We are to be the example
for others. We are to live our lives as representatives of God. That
is a powerful responsibility. If we do everything, think everything,
and say everything as though we are doing it for God, we will be the
example the world needs.

I pray we all realize God is always there, not just to help, but
also to observe us. We are never alone, which is both comforting and
challenging. Let's all decide to be a good representative of God.

August 10

If anyone, then, knows the good they ought to do and
doesn't do it, it is sin for them.

— James 4:17

What is sin? We often think of the "big" sins: murder, adultery, theft, ...
We don't think of our everyday sin. We don't want to think about it.
We like thinking to ourselves, "I'm not nearly as bad as so-and-so."
Really?! That is not what we are taught in the Bible.

Do you realize that sin is when you should do the right thing, but
don't? That could be something as simple as opening the door for an
elderly person. We, too often, don't act as though God is watching our
every move. We are under constant scrutiny by God.

Sure, God is a loving God. But He is also a just God. That means
he sees us when we don't do what's right and we know it. He does keep
track of it. We will answer for it one day. Yes, thankfully, Jesus will
be right there and cover that sin for us. But do we really want to be
standing in front of God answering the "why's" for not doing what's
right? That will be far more embarrassing and worse than answering
to Mom why we got in the cookie jar.

I pray we all really think through our actions and inactions. I pray
we all stop to think about doing what's right rather than just skipping
past it because we don't feel like it. I pray we all decide to serve others
and God in even the smallest of ways. God expects it.

Marty Pressey

August 11

For my eyes have seen your salvation,
which you have prepared in the sight of all nations:
a light for revelation to the Gentiles,
and the glory of your people Israel.

— Luke 2:30–32

Have you seen the light? Have you seen the salvation provided by Jesus Christ? Have you decided to follow the light? Are you sharing His light with others? His light removes the darkness forever.

Many in this world live in darkness. Unfortunately, some call themselves Christians. There are many who willingly choose to live in the darkness and there are others who have been overcome by it. In either case, there is a way to the light that will disperse the darkness forever.

Jesus said He was the light of the world. That He is. We are to accept Him as the light and walk in darkness no more. We can do so by releasing our inner selves to Him. When we empty ourselves of our own preferences and desires, allowing Him to take over, we will walk in His light.

I pray we all turn ourselves over to Jesus and His light. Why continue to suffer or wander in the darkness? Give up your self-centered ways and allow Jesus to be your Guide. Live in His light.

August 12

Now that you have purified yourselves by obeying the truth so that you have sincere love for each other, love one another deeply, from the heart. For you have been born again, not of perishable seed, but of imperishable, through the living and enduring word of God.

—1 Peter 1:22–23

Are you who you want to be? Are you searching for something more? Do you feel as though you're stuck in a rut? Do you want to live life to the full? God has provided a way for us to live an abundant life.

So many in this world are searching. They're searching for their place in the world. They're searching for the perfect job. They're searching for a lifetime mate. They're searching for the meaning of life. Unfortunately, they're looking for those things in the wrong places.

Fulfillment comes from doing for others. Experiencing the joy of helping someone else is a wonderful feeling. It doesn't have to be grand; it can be the smallest thing. We simply need to realize that God has blessed us, and we are to bless others, sharing His love with them.

I pray we all take on the mindset of helping others through the love of Christ. Let's share our blessings, which may simply be that we are capable of opening a door for the lady with her hands full of kids and groceries. Let's show who Christ is.

August 13

The LORD lives! Praise be to my Rock!
Exalted be God my Savior!

— Psalm 18:46

Who do you praise? Do you praise your children? Do you praise your parents? Do you praise your co-worker? Do you praise the athletes? Do you praise the movie stars? We all praise someone. Who should we praise?

We see many people all wrapped up in praising people on this earth, though it's often reflected in different ways. It may be that we are clapping or cheering during a sports event. It may be saying, "I just love so-so in such-such show." It may be telling our children they did a great job in the school play.

Too often we neglect to praise God and give Him thanks for all we have, who we are, and our many blessings. We too easily forget that everything belongs to Him. He does want our praise and our thanks. In fact, He expects it and He expects it to be genuine.

I pray we all realize that everything on this earth belongs to God and we praise Him for it. Give thanks to God for providing for you and praise Him for His wonderful blessings. Our God is an awesome God.

August 14

"Be dressed ready for service and keep your lamps burning, like servants waiting for their master to return from a wedding banquet, so that when he comes and knocks they can immediately open the door for him. It will be good for those servants whose master finds them watching when he comes."

— Luke 12:35–37a

Are you ready? Ready to serve? Ready for Jesus to come again? When will He come? No one knows. What if He comes in the middle of the night? Are you ready? What if He comes while you are at your job? Are you ready?

We often live our lives like we've got a hundred years left to do whatever it is we want to do or what we think we should do. We run a rat race trying to get the next big thing or next cool gadget, but don't seem to have a sense of urgency when it comes to following Jesus. Are we ready?

We are told to be ready at any given time for Jesus to arrive. We are to serve others, bring them to Christ, provide for them when needed, and love all people just as Jesus did. We are to show others Jesus through our own lives, our actions and our words. Are we ready?

I pray we all decide to be more urgent about doing and speaking what Jesus taught us. I pray we all decide to show Jesus every moment of every day. Let's all be ready, just in case He shows up today.

August 15

Submit yourselves, then, to God. Resist the devil,
and he will flee from you. Come near to God and he
will come near to you. Wash your hands, you sinners,
and purify your hearts, you double-minded. Grieve,
mourn and wail. Change your laughter to mourning
and your joy to gloom. Humble yourselves before the
Lord, and he will lift you up.

— James 4:7–10

Who is first in your life? Is it your spouse, your siblings, your parents?
Perhaps you have a very close friend that means the world to you.
Catch that phrase? "Means the world." Are you willing to trade heaven
for this world?

So many put success in this world above all else. They may define
success as wealth, fame, or relationship. It doesn't matter how it's
defined, they put it above all else. In fact, that is why they become the
best at what they do. They sacrifice everything to be the best.

God wants us to put Him first. He wants us to be disciples of His
Son, Jesus Christ. If we are willing to put God first, He blesses us
beyond our wildest dreams. No, that doesn't necessarily mean wealth
and fame. It does mean our needs are provided for, including love,
peace, and joy. Those are riches money can't buy.

I pray we all put God first in our lives. We need to do so for our
own sake. Only He can provide for us what this world cannot and what
we desperately need. Put Him first in your life.

August 16

We do not want you to be uninformed, brothers and sisters, about the troubles we experienced in the province of Asia. We were under great pressure, far beyond our ability to endure, so that we despaired of life itself. Indeed, we felt we had received the sentence of death. But this happened that we might not rely on ourselves but on God, who raises the dead.

—2 Corinthians 1:8–9

Are you struggling today? Do you have some heavy thoughts on your mind? Are you facing a difficult situation? Perhaps it's to do with a job, a medical issue, pursuit of a dream, or just everyday life. Are you willing to give up those struggles for something better?

Our God is able to protect us, save us, and provide for us in any situation. He often does so, even though we fail to recognize it or give Him credit for it. Our God can quiet the wind and waves. He can raise the dead. He can stop the arrows of Satan from hurting us.

We are to put our hope and trust in Jesus Christ, the Savior of the World. His healing power, protecting arms, and life changing Spirit are there for us every day. All we need to do is submit ourselves to Him, fully, wholeheartedly, and with all our being. Sounds easy. It's not. We want to rely on ourselves.

I pray we all submit ourselves to God, putting our faith, hope, and trust in Jesus Christ, His Son. Be comforted by the thought that He will protect you. Trust in Him.

Marty Pressey

August 17

A fool finds pleasure in wicked schemes,
but a person of understanding delights in wisdom.
What the wicked dread will overtake them;
what the righteous desire will be granted.
When the storm has swept by, the wicked are gone,
but the righteous stand firm forever.

— Proverbs 10:23–25

Are you cool? Are you one of the few who hang out with all the cool people? What is it costing you to be one of the super-cool? Do you know the price of admission?

We are inundated with commercials on TV, signs in the stores, and our friends telling us all about the newest thing. We are urged to go get it; we must have it. Or it is impressed on us that all the "in crowd" go to certain restaurants and we must go, if we want to be part of them. Or worst case, we are compelled to mistreat others to be part of the group.

All of this boils down to wickedness and evil. Anytime we look down on another person, a creation of God's, we are doing evil. We are foolish to think that God doesn't see us. The very words from our mouths betray our thoughts and our hearts.

I pray we don't pursue being cool in this world but be the wise who demonstrate Jesus to others. Fools always fall. The wise will always stand firm, even in the fiercest storm. Be wise, know God, follow Jesus.

August 18

And we know that in all things God works for the
good of those who love him, who have been called
according to his purpose.

— Romans 8:28

Do you wish you could go back to a happy time in your life? Is it
because you are in a dark time? Is it because a loved one is no longer
with you? Is it because your health is not what it once was, and you
can't do what you used to do? Or is it because your spiritual life has
taken a downturn?

As we go through our lives, things change. Some for the better and
some for the worse. At least, it seems that way in our minds. Yes, we
go through sufferings and we go through exuberant highs. Sometimes
we are flying high and sometimes we are in the dumps.

Our lives sometimes seem to be rollercoaster rides. It is only when
we lean on God, fully trusting Him, that the ups and downs become
less extreme. It is only in our faith that we can rejoice in our sadness.
God is always there. We must recognize that and trust Him.

I pray we all come to realize that God will work good out of every
circumstance and situation we go through. Let's all trust Him. Know
that you are loved, and God is at work.

Marty Pressey

August 19

Praise be to the God and Father of our Lord Jesus
Christ, who has blessed us in the heavenly realms
with every spiritual blessing in Christ.

— Ephesians 1:3

Do you praise God in all situations? Do you praise Him at all? Do
you realize that praising Him is not really the same as thanking Him?
Could it be that we often call giving thanks to God, praising God?

In our lives we may hear or say thanks for many things to many
people. If we were told "thank you" by someone, would we consider
that praise? I don't believe we would. So, what is praise? It is admiration,
stating wonderful things about someone, or worshiping someone.

God wants us to praise Him in all situations. Why? Regardless
of the situation, we belong to Him and have a place reserved in His
presence for eternity. We may go through trials on this earth, but they
will pass, and we have an eternity with God to look forward to. So, sing
praises to God for such a wonderful promise.

I pray we all tell God how wonderful and awesome we think He
is. I pray we all praise God every day. Lift your eyes to the heavens
and praise God.

August 20

"Peace I leave with you; my peace I give you. I do not give to you as the world gives. Do not let your hearts be troubled and do not be afraid."

— John 14:27

What is weighing on your mind today? What are your struggles? Are you depressed? Are you seeking a new job? Are you concerned about a loved one? Are you looking to change who you are deep inside?

This world will cause us to think about so many different things. We have thousands of thoughts per day. Too often those thoughts are worries or fears or concerns. We will often allow them to consume us—take over our lives, which leaves us immobile.

When we turn those thoughts over to Jesus, He gives us peace. We may need to do so multiple times. Why? Because we don't really want to let them go. It takes us trying to let them go over and over before we finally let go of all those worries and allow Jesus to take them.

I pray we all learn to let go and let Jesus grant us peace. We need to feel that peace in our lives, which means we need to let go. Give it all to Jesus.

August 21

As the body without the spirit is dead, so faith without deeds is dead.

— James 2:26

How do you show your faith? What are you doing that others see your faith? How do you treat others that demonstrates your faith in Jesus? How do you look at or speak about those who are different from you?

We read where Jesus told us to take care of the poor, the widows, the orphans, and to feed the hungry, give a drink to the thirsty, visit those in prison, attend to the sick. Are we doing well at those things? Or are we just taking care of ourselves?

Our faith can only be demonstrated to others by doing. Our faith is a gift from God. Our actions are a result of our faith. If our actions are minimal or nonexistent, our faith cannot be very strong. We are called, not only to faith but to action.

I pray we all realize our shortcomings in deeds and look to build our faith through actions. As we step out to take action, our faith will grow. Trust God, step out in faith.

August 22

LORD, our Lord, how majestic is your name in all
the earth!
You have set your glory in the heavens.
Through the praise of children and infants you
have established a stronghold against your enemies,
to silence the foe and the avenger.
When I consider your heavens, the work of your
fingers, the moon and the stars, which you have set in
place, what is mankind that you are mindful of them,
human beings that you care for them?
— Psalm 8:1–4

Are you amazed? I am! As I went out this morning to turn on the
sprinkler to water the newly seeded grass in our yard, I looked up and
was amazed. The sky was so absolutely clear, with the light of the sun
just beginning to peek up over the eastern horizon. I could make out
the entire moon, but just a sliver of it was shining brightly. The stars
were all visible, even seeing some in the far distance.

Isn't it amazing what God has created?! Yes, we have our worries
here on earth. Yet many of those worries are self-induced. Our fears
are often self-made fears. Too often we forget God is in charge and has
already won the battle.

We need to remember His amazing creation, not just this earth,
but far beyond, and we need to live our lives in amazement. If our
focus is on God, our worries will fade away. Focus on God. See His
wonderful works.

August 23

"'These people honor me with their lips,
but their hearts are far from me.
They worship me in vain;
their teachings are merely human rules.'"

— Matthew 15:8–9

What is your heart full of? We've heard of hearts full of love, hearts being broken, hearts full of hope, hearts that are seeking. But seeking for what? There's a big difference between a heart seeking true love versus a heart seeking worldly love.

We see people every day who are depressed, broken, downtrodden, or putting on a facade. In most cases, it's because they don't know the true love. It's because their heart is full of worldly desires rather than full of hope in Jesus Christ. It's only when we accept the truth and determine to make a change, that we begin to fill our hearts with God.

Why are we so afraid to seek Jesus? Is it because we want our co-worker, our fellow student, or our family to accept us? I rarely see schoolmates anymore. I've had more co-worker's than I can count. What have I gotten from any of them? A few lessons. A few ideas. My family and church family have given me more than all of them combined.

I pray we all seek God, allow Him to fill our hearts, and empty our hearts of worldly desires. When we do, we become free. Free of worry, anxiety, and fear. We become filled with faith, hope, and love.

August 24

Paul replied, "Short time or long—I pray to God that
not only you but all who are listening to me today
may become what I am, except for these chains."
— Acts 26:29

Is today the day for you? Will you turn yourself over to God? Will
you decide to be the person God intended you to be? Will you make
the commitment to follow Jesus? Are you ready for a life of peace and
contentment regardless of the situation?

This world is filled with all types of disorders. Many of those
disorders are fed by our very own minds. They are also fed by the
things we listen to, whether a friend, family member, or someone
else. If we are told we are worthless long enough and often enough,
we will believe it.

God has a different plan for us. He intends to give us an abundant
life. It is our decision to take it up or disregard it. We must believe
He has the power to give it to us. It can't be just a passing fancy, but a
wholehearted belief. We call that faith.

I pray we all commit, today, to believe that God will provide the
abundant life He promised. We can make the commitment, if we
decide not to continue to believe the lies of this world. Commit to
Jesus and His teachings.

August 25

I will extol You, my God, O King,
And I will bless Your name forever and ever.
                                              — Psalm 145:1

Do you bless God? Do you bless His name? Do you bless God in all situations? Do you bless Him forever? Do you understand what it is to bless? God deserves our praise, thankfulness, and our blessing.

We are to bless God's name. We are told that in various places in Scripture. But what does that mean? It means to sanctify His name. It means to hold His name in reverence. Now, does the 3rd of the Ten Commandments, "You shall not take the name of the LORD your God in vain," (Exodus 20:7) make sense?

We are to praise God and lift His name on high, above all others. The Israelites held His name is such high regard that they would not even say it. We, too often, disregard His name without even thinking. How do you feel when people disregard your name?

I pray we will decide to bless God's name, hold it in the highest of regard and respect. Do not misuse His name. Let's all show respect, honor, and awe for God's name.

August 26

The LORD had said to Abram, "Go from your country, your people and your father's household to the land I will show you. ... So Abram went, as the LORD had told him; and Lot went with him. Abram was seventy-five years old when he set out from Harran.

— Genesis 12:1, 4

Are you willing to go where God has called you? Do you listen for His guidance? Will you trust Him when He does call you? He promises to be with you always, wherever you are, wherever you go. Especially, if He calls you there.

We don't often talk about God calling us to go somewhere. In fact, we don't often talk about God calling us, speaking to us, or nudging us in a particular direction. Sure, the vast majority of us will never here the booming voice of God like Moses did. Instead, we will feel our conscience tugging at us or our gut telling us to go do this.

Of course, those feelings could be selfishness. However, when we are truly following Jesus and listening for His voice, those nudging's will be from His Spirit. We will know it is coming from Him. When we are confident it is His voice calling us, will we trust Him enough to go?

I pray we all trust in Jesus and follow His lead. I pray we listen for His voice and go where He is calling us. Trust Him. He will not lead you astray.

August 27

He traveled through that area, speaking many words
of encouragement to the people, and finally arrived
in Greece.

— Acts 20:2

Do you speak words of encouragement, words of life? Or do you speak
words of discontent, words of death? There is no gray. Your words are
either encouraging or discouraging, life or death. What words will
you speak?

We are often bombarded with words of hate, discontent,
argumentative, or prejudice. The question is, will we do the same?
When we do the same, we are no better than anyone else. When we
do the same, we are worse than others, because we know better.

Jesus has called us to speak words of life, uplifting, encouragement,
benefit, or comfort. When we do this, we are doing the work Jesus
called us to do. When we do this, we become a blessing to others. We
should be especially cognizant of this with family.

I pray we all decide to speak words of life to all people we come
in contact with. Be the one who encourages. Speak the words Jesus
would have you speak.

August 28

We have much to say about this, but it is hard to make it clear to you because you no longer try to understand. In fact, though by this time you ought to be teachers, you need someone to teach you the elementary truths of God's word all over again. You need milk, not solid food! Anyone who lives on milk, being still an infant, is not acquainted with the teaching about righteousness. But solid food is for the mature, who by constant use have trained themselves to distinguish good from evil.

— Hebrews 5:11–14

Are you trying to understand? Are you putting forth an honest effort? Are you proceeding toward maturity? Are you really studying, learning, evaluating, and applying the lessons to your life?

How many times do we hear someone say, "They just need to grow up."? Usually, it is said by someone who also needs to grow up. Usually, it is said because one person did something the other person thinks is childish, yet the second person reacts just like the first.

We are to grow up in Christ. We are to become mature in our thinking. We are to become more like Jesus. It is only when we do, that we find true contentment and are able to recognize others for who they really are, a child of God.

I pray we all mature in Christ. I pray we all seek the knowledge of Him, seek His understanding and become more like Him. Seek maturity, don't stay as a child.

August 29

He replied, "Because you have so little faith. Truly I tell you, if you have faith as small as a mustard seed, you can say to this mountain, 'Move from here to there,' and it will move. Nothing will be impossible for you."

— Matthew 17:20

How are you doing today? Are you facing obstacles in your life? Do you sometimes feel like they are so big you can't overcome them? Are you facing those bigger obstacles with the same faith you face the smaller ones?

There is no doubt we all face obstacles in our lives. Some of them are small and some are rather large. Some are job related and some are family related. Some are physical health issues, and some are spiritual health issues. What can we do about any and all of them?

We are to keep our faith in God. We are to turn *all* our troubles over to Him. He has promised to take our burdens and shoulder them. He has promised to give us His yoke and it is light (Matthew 11:29). As we turn our concerns over to Him and truly release them, we will see that He is faithful, and our faith will increase.

I pray each of us decides to turn *all* our troubles and obstacles over to God. Trust Him and trust His Word. He will not fail you.

August 30

But when the kindness and love of God our Savior
appeared, he saved us, not because of righteous things
we had done, but because of his mercy. He saved us
through the washing of rebirth and renewal by the
Holy Spirit, whom he poured out on us generously
through Jesus Christ our Savior, so that, having been
justified by his grace, we might become heirs having
the hope of eternal life.

— Titus 3:4–7

Do you know you are loved? Do you comprehend the love God has for
you? In all likelihood, no. God has a love for you that goes far beyond
any love a person here on this earth can show you.

Most of us have parents who provide for us, teach us, and generally
care for us. Our parents do this out of love. There will be some who
are not so fortunate. It is even more important for them to understand
God's love.

If we have parents who love and care for us, we have a glimpse of
God's love. We trust our parents because we've experienced this love.
If we trust our parents and they can only show us a glimpse of God's
love, shouldn't we trust God all the more?

I pray we all come to have a better understanding of God's love
and increase our trust in Him. He has provided for our parents,
grandparents, and us out of His love. Love Him. Trust Him.

August 31

Do you not know that in a race all the runners run,
but only one gets the prize? Run in such a way as to
get the prize. Everyone who competes in the games
goes into strict training. They do it to get a crown
that will not last, but we do it to get a crown that will
last forever.

—1 Corinthians 9:24–25

What do you want people to say about you? How do you want to be
remembered? Are you doing what you should to build the reputation
you want? Are you working toward it each day?

It doesn't matter who we are, we will be remembered for
something. Whether we move away, or we pass on. Someone or many
people will remember us for something or many things. By and large
we make the decision of what they remember.

We are running a race. Unfortunately, most of us don't realize it.
Our race is to achieve the goal that was set for us by God. When we run
the race He put before us to win, we decide that others will remember
the good we did, said, and our good attitude toward life.

I pray we all decide to have a good attitude, do good things, and
say good things. Let's all run the good race God laid out before us.
Follow His lead.

September

September 1

The sting of death is sin, and the power of sin is the
law. But thanks be to God! He gives us the victory
through our Lord Jesus Christ.

—1 Corinthians 15:56–57

What choices will you make today? Will you weigh the consequences
of those choices? Do you realize each choice results in either a good or
bad outcome? Will you think through the potential outcomes before
you make that choice?

This world will tell us to make choices that make us happy. There
is a tidbit of truth in that advice, but the happiness or joy we seek
comes from God. So simply making choices that makes us happy for
a moment or a day are not the choices that bring everlasting joy.

Satan wants us to believe the half-truths purported by the world.
He wants us to fall into the trap. God wants us to choose Him in all
choices—follow the example of Jesus. When we make the choice to
allow God and Jesus' teachings guide all our choices, we find true joy
and happiness.

I pray we all choose to follow Jesus, making choices based on His
guidance. He will not lead you astray. Choose the victory that comes
through Jesus.

September 2

Finally, all of you, be like-minded, be sympathetic,
love one another, be compassionate and humble. Do
not repay evil with evil or insult with insult. On the
contrary, repay evil with blessing, because to this you
were called so that you may inherit a blessing.
—1 Peter 3:8–12

Are you pursuing God? Are you wholeheartedly pursuing His will,
His purpose for your life? Are you willing to give up yourself for Him?
Are you? Will you pursue His goodness, His righteousness? Will you?

The world doesn't like it when told their actions are evil. Most of
us don't either. We don't like to be told that our speech is hateful. We
don't like to be told our actions are disrespectful. We don't want to
hear we are being selfish. We think we are better than everyone else.
We think we deserve it.

God calls us to be humble before Him and to be servants of all.
That means we have to turn away from the evil of this world, the
examples we see everywhere we turn, and follow His teachings. The
more we become like Jesus, the more joyful we become.

I pray we all decide to turn away from this evil world and pursue
being like Jesus. It is only this pursuit that can bring true joy, peace,
and wholeness. Pursue His righteousness.

September 3

Timothy, my son, I am giving you this command in keeping with the prophecies once made about you, so that by recalling them you may fight the battle well, holding on to faith and a good conscience, which some have rejected and so have suffered shipwreck with regard to the faith.

—1 Timothy 1:18–19

Are you holding onto your faith? Do you ask God to strengthen it every day? Do you reflect on your day and see how God worked in your life today? Do you really want your faith to increase, to experience the true joy He promised?

We often stumble and feel like failures or our world is crashing in around us. Satan loves those times and feeds our anxiety, depression, and lonely feelings. When we wallow in these feelings, we begin to feel overwhelmed. We may even feel like giving up.

Rather than dwell on these feelings, look up and take hold of God's promises. Know that He is always with us, always protecting us. Do something simple, simply ask God to protect you and to give you comfort. He won't disappoint.

I pray we all hold onto our faith. I pray we all trust God to do what He has promised. Sure, it may be tough at times, but He is always there. Keep your faith.

September 4

May he strengthen your hearts so that you will be
blameless and holy in the presence of our God and
Father when our Lord Jesus comes with all his holy
ones.

—1 Thessalonians 3:13

Are you a welcoming person? Do you welcome God into your life,
into your heart? Are you willing to stand in His presence and ask Him
to take control? Will you allow Him to make the changes in you He
desires to make?

God has a wonderful plan for us. He knows the trials we need to
go through to change us into the person He wants us to be. He knows
the blessings that will have a major impact on us. He knows where He
wants us to go, who He wants us to become.

We simply need to welcome Him into our hearts and follow His
guidance. Are we willing to do that? Sometimes we are and sometimes
we are not. If we will allow Him to make changes in our lives, we will
be surprised by the amazing life we will live. We will experience life
in a whole new way.

I pray we all are willing to stand in God's presence and allow Him
to take control. Submit to His guidance and experience an abundant
life. God is good all the time.

September 5

All this took place to fulfill what the Lord had said
through the prophet: "The virgin will conceive and
give birth to a son, and they will call him Immanuel"
(which means "God with us").

— Matthew 1:22–23

Do you believe God is with you? Do your actions show others you
believe it? Do you understand what it means to have God with you at
all times? Are you living as though you believe it?

We get wrapped up in this world, trying to do it all ourselves. We
may ask for help from others, but we often don't ask for help from God.
We realize a little success and that drives us toward further goals. Yet
we don't often give God the credit nor do we ask for His guidance.

God is with us all the time. We are to trust in Him, ask Him for
guidance, listen intently for His wisdom, and follow it. When we rely
on His wisdom, His guidance, we succeed beyond our wildest dreams.
No, we may not become millionaires or celebrities, but we will realize
the success He has in store for us.

I pray we all trust God and seek His wisdom and guidance. I pray
we all know that He is with us at all times. Rely on God. He is always
there.

September 6

"Come," he said. Then Peter got down out of the
boat, walked on the water and came toward Jesus.
— Matthew 14:29

Are you trusting in God today? Are you trusting in Him every day?
Are you willing to step out in faith and follow where He leads? Are you
willing to give up your old self to be who He wants you to be?

We hold on to who we think we are or perhaps who we think we
want to be. It may be that our vision of who we are or who we want to
be is true. Too often we have a false understanding of ourselves. We
don't see the beautiful life God has in store for us.

God has not promised it will always be a rose garden. What He
has promised is He will never leave us. He has a wonderful plan for us.
We often find the poorest among us are the most blessed with faith.
We also find those who trust in God are the happiest people we know.

I pray we all trust in God, step out in our faith. Trust that He has
a wonderful plan for you. He has promised an abundant life. Trust
in Him.

September 7

"But seek first his kingdom and his righteousness,
and all these things will be given to you as well."
— Matthew 6:33

Are you seeking God? Are you seeking Him before anything else? Or are you looking to Him as a magic genie, simply asking Him to grant your every wish? Will you seek Him first and trust in His love for you?

So many of us often want God to grant our wishes. We think because He loves us, He will give us everything we want. We want riches in this world. We want a perfect partner and perfect relationship. We want, we want, we want.

When we stop putting our earthly wants ahead of our desire to know and trust God, then we are truly blessed. We may or may not find earthly riches. We will absolutely find peace, grace, understanding, wisdom, contentment, joy, and so many other blessings. There will be so many we will believe we are richest person in the world. And, we are.

I pray we all seek God first, with our whole heart. I pray each of us will experience the blessings God will shower on us when we do. Know you are loved by Him and trust Him.

September 8

For the message of the cross is foolishness to those
who are perishing, but to us who are being saved it is
the power of God. For it is written:
"I will destroy the wisdom of the wise;
the intelligence of the intelligent I will frustrate."
—1 Corinthians 1:18–19

Are you crazy? Are you crazy for God? Are you crazy for Jesus Christ? Are you willing to be as crazy for Jesus as you are for movie, TV, or sports stars? Are you willing to boast about Jesus like you do about them?

We see the wisdom and the stardom of this world pass away. We know this inherently, because we see it all the time. Can you name any one of the Oscar winners from 10 or 15 years ago? Probably not without doing some research.

Jesus has been the standard for roughly 2,000 years. Let's speak of Him as the star of yesterday, today, and tomorrow. Let's be crazy over His love for us. Let's trust Him with all our being. Let's follow Him to the point of being fanatical (in a good way). Let's show others just how awesome He is.

I pray we all come to the conclusion that we need to be crazy about Jesus and do all we can to emulate Him, follow Him, be His representative on this earth. Be Jesus' ambassador.

September 9

Praise be to the LORD,
for he has heard my cry for mercy.
The LORD is my strength and my shield;
my heart trusts in him, and he helps me.
My heart leaps for joy,
and with my song I praise him.

— Psalm 28:6–7

Praise the Lord! How often do you praise God? Everyday? Multiple times a day? Or perhaps rarely? Is it because you recognize His blessings or fail to do so? Are you aware He is always with you?

We can be easily distracted by our jobs, a car that cuts us off, a task that needs done, a lesson that needs completed or prepared, and so many other things. We get distracted with the immediate and lose sight of the big picture.

God is with us through all those immediate tasks and He has a longer-range plan for us. We need to step back, see the bigger picture, and recognize how God is working in our lives. He protects, provides for us, and educates us.

I pray we all praise God for what he has and is doing in our lives. He certainly deserves it. Praise God. Praise Him always.

September 10

When Jesus spoke again to the people, he said, "I am
the light of the world. Whoever follows me will never
walk in darkness, but will have the light of life."
— John 8:12

Do you see the light? Are you in the light? Are you following the light?
Are you living in the light? Are you aware of the light or continuing to
walk in the darkness? The light is available to all of us.

This world can be a dark place. People fall into traps laid out by
Satan and evil people. People can be so blinded by the darkness they
don't even know there is light nor want to seek the light. This happens
within our heads and our hearts.

There is a light that has broken the darkness forever. He is
waiting for us to choose Him. Once we've taken the initial step and
experienced His light, we desire it even more. When we are in His
light, we have no fear of darkness anymore.

I pray we all seek the light of Jesus, surrendering to His light
forever more. I pray we all experience the wonder of walking in His
light. Choose light over darkness.

September 11

And whatever you do, whether in word or deed, do it all in the name of the Lord Jesus, giving thanks to God the Father through him.

— Colossians 3:17

What are you thankful for? Family? Friends? Co-workers? Bosses? Teachers? Pastors? We often say we are thankful for these people, but are we really thankful?

We often treat people badly; yelling, demeaning, being disrespectful, antagonizing, and generally being selfishly hateful. Why? We listen too much to the world around us, rather than listening to God's Word.

Jesus taught us to be thankful through His example and His words. The Apostle Paul taught us to be thankful for all that God has blessed us with. When we have a heart of thankfulness, the selfishness and hatefulness leave us. Anger and fear leave us as well.

I pray we all decide to be thankful in our hearts. I pray we all take on and live the teachings of Jesus. Let's all be thankful and enjoy an abundant life.

September 12

This is how we know that we live in him and he in us: He has given us of his Spirit. And we have seen and testify that the Father has sent his Son to be the Savior of the world.

—1 John 4:13–14

Do you proclaim Jesus as Savior? Do you claim Him as your Lord and Savior? Do you sing praises to Him? Do you share Him with others? Do others see Him in you? We are called to share Jesus, to proclaim Him as Savior.

The world proclaims many people as their savior's. They believe so-so will save the company, save the school, save the country. Unfortunately, they have put their faith in someone who is fallible and who will fail them.

Jesus is our perfect Savior. He will not fail—He has already triumphed. Jesus is the only One who can save us from all our troubles, all our fears, all our anxieties, and all our failures. He is the Savior of the World.

I pray we all acknowledge and fully believe that Jesus is our Savior. I pray we all turn our whole hearts over to Him. Sing His praises. Proclaim Him to the world. Jesus, Savior of the World.

Marty Pressey

September 13

We have come to share in Christ, if indeed we hold
our original conviction firmly to the very end.

— Hebrews 3:14

Are you guilty? Are you convicted? Do you believe with all your heart that Jesus is the Son of God? Is He your Lord and Savior? Are you willing to stand convicted when others accuse you of this? Even if it costs you everything?

We see people's beliefs change with the wind today. They follow whatever today's fad is until tomorrow comes with a new one. It doesn't matter if it's clothing, entertainment, complaining about the boss, or any number of other things.

Jesus calls us to believe in Him, to follow Him, and to stop worrying about this world. He didn't say we were to stop living in this world, but to understand that it will pass away and a permanent home for us is waiting. One that will not pass away.

I pray we all come to realize just how little this world really means and how much Jesus means. I pray we all are willing to stand convicted of being His followers in all we do. Be convicted in Christ.

September 14

So in Christ Jesus you are all children of God through
faith, for all of you who were baptized into Christ
have clothed yourselves with Christ.

— Galatians 3:26–27

What are you thankful for? Are you thankful for family, friends, a
job, an education? Are you thankful to be a child of God? We should
all be thankful to call God our Father and for the sacrifice made by
Jesus for each of us.

The world too often tells us to be thankful for material things. It
wants us to be thankful for relationships, until they become a struggle,
then we toss them away. The world says we are to be thankful for what
we have or achieve.

God tells us to be thankful for who we are, His children. It is quite
different to be thankful for who you are, who you belong to, than to
be thankful for stuff. When we are thankful for being chosen by God
to be His children, all else falls into place.

I pray we all choose to be thankful for being His, being loved by
Him, and for being who He created us to be. Be thankful for who
you are.

September 15

In the beginning was the Word, and the Word was
with God, and the Word was God. He was with God
in the beginning. Through him all things were made;
without him nothing was made that has been made.
— John 1:1–3

Do you know that Jesus is God? Do you really realize that He is one
with the Father and the Spirit? Do you fully understand Jesus is
eternal, that He existed before time? Do you know this world and all
that was created was made through Him?

Many Christians recognize Jesus' birth, life, death, and
resurrection. Many will recite and follow His teachings. Many will
call Him Messiah or Christ or Savior. Many will go to church and
worship God, praying in Jesus' name.

We need to understand that Jesus is God. There are several
analogies or allegories provided in Scripture to help us understand
God and the relationship among the Father, Son, and Spirit. However,
they do not take away from the fact that all three are God.

I pray we all come to fully realize Jesus is God. The world was
created through Him. He is to be worshiped and revered above all.
Be in awe of Jesus.

September 16

Every day they continued to meet together in the temple courts. They broke bread in their homes and ate together with glad and sincere hearts, praising God and enjoying the favor of all the people. And the Lord added to their number daily those who were being saved.

— Acts 2:46–47

Do you celebrate life every day? Do you wake up grateful for another day? Do you look forward to spending the day with God? Are you joyous and confident in what God will do in your life?

We often get wrapped up in the minutiae of daily life and don't stop to think about what God has done in our lives. We don't celebrate the many blessings we receive. We focus too much on the negative.

We can be joyous every day. We can celebrate our blessings from God every day. When we are grateful and celebrate our many blessings, our day is much better. When we meet with other Christians and praise God, we are more joyous. Why not choose to celebrate every day?

I pray we all enjoy our lives through the many blessings we receive from God. I pray that as we appreciate them, our joy increases. Be with other Christians and celebrate life, giving praise to God.

Marty Pressey

September 17

The Spirit you received does not make you slaves,
so that you live in fear again; rather, the Spirit you
received brought about your adoption to sonship.
And by him we cry, "Abba, Father."

— Romans 8:15

What do you fear? Why do you fear? Should you fear? Why do so many in this world today fear so many different things?

It seems this world is fraught with fear. There is a medical term and diagnosis for fear of just about anything. There is even a fear of flowers. Now, what can a flower do to any of us? Why should we fear them? That's not to say that we should not be educated about those that may be poisonous.

We are told we have no real reason to fear. Sure, we should be aware of dangers, but to be truly fearful is not in our spiritual DNA. When we wholly love and trust God, there is nothing to fear, not even death. We are His children and He will take care of us.

I pray we all eliminate our fears through our love and trust in God. He can and will remove your fears, if you turn them over to Him. Trust God. Know He is there. Know He cares.

September 18

The night before Herod was to bring him to trial, Peter was sleeping between two soldiers, bound with two chains, and sentries stood guard at the entrance. Suddenly an angel of the Lord appeared and a light shone in the cell. He struck Peter on the side and woke him up. "Quick, get up!" he said, and the chains fell off Peter's wrists.

— Acts 12:6–7

Are you bound by chains? Perhaps not physical chains, but mental or emotional chains. Do you live bound up in traditions or thoughts or behaviors that are not healthy for you? Do you know that Jesus will break those chains and set you free?

We often live in a self-made prison. We hold onto grudges. We continue in bad behaviors. We allow ourselves to be deceived with worldly wealth. We allow others to have an emotional hold over us. We stay in this prison, much like criminals who prefer to stay in prison rather than be set free.

Jesus has promised to set us free. Not only that, but He has promised to be with us every step of our lives—helping us to live in that freedom. He will break the chains that bind us and show us the wonderful life God has planned for us. Our part in this is to trust Him and allow Him to break those chains.

I pray we all decide to trust Jesus, allow Him to break our chains. I pray we all decide to live free, rather than be bound by worldly chains. Trust Him. Live free.

Marty Pressey

September 19

In the beginning was the Word, and the Word
was with God, and the Word was God...The Word
became flesh and made his dwelling among us. We
have seen his glory, the glory of the one and only Son,
who came from the Father, full of grace and truth.

—John 1:1, 14

Do you hear God's voice? Are you following His Word? Do you
know the Word of God? Do you believe in His Word? Do you accept
Him as your Savior? Will you ask Him to speak to you, to fill you, to
rescue you?

There is One Word of God and that is Jesus Christ. He is the One
who can save each one of us. He created the world and all that has been
created. He has promised to be with us through all our ups and downs.
The Word of God has always been and always will be.

When we follow Him and trust Him in whatever situation we find
ourselves, He is there with us. We need to listen to hear His whisper,
His guidance. His grace is sufficient and overwhelming when we truly
trust Him. We are amazed when we open our eyes and see Him.

I pray we all trust the Word of God. He will cover us in His grace
and truth. See His glory. Trust Him to provide.

September 20

Moved by the Spirit, he went into the temple courts.
When the parents brought in the child Jesus to do for
him what the custom of the Law required, Simeon
took him in his arms and praised God, saying:
"Sovereign Lord, as you have promised,
you may now dismiss your servant in peace.
For my eyes have seen your salvation,
which you have prepared in the sight of all nations:
a light for revelation to the Gentiles,
and the glory of your people Israel."

— Luke 2:27–32

Do you recognize Jesus for who He is? Have you accepted Him as your Savior? Are you following Him as He has commanded? Do you realize why He came into this world? Will you call Him King?

Jesus came into this world as the Son of God. He came to be our Savior, to provide a way for us to be reconciled with God. He came to be our role model for living the life God has planned for us. He came to be King of kings.

When we recognize Jesus is King of the world, above any other king or president or governor, we will praise Him, revere His life, and revere His words—His teachings. We will follow Him wholeheartedly. We will seek Him and live our lives so others will see Him in us.

I pray we all recognize Jesus as our King, our Savior. I pray we all live our lives as a reflection of Him. Listen to His words. Follow His teachings. Follow His example. Be a reflection of Him.

Marty Pressey

September 21

Rejoice always, pray continually, give thanks in all circumstances; for this is God's will for you in Christ Jesus.

—1 Thessalonians 5:16–18

How thankful are you? Do you regularly give thanks to God for the blessings in your life? Are you thankful for each day? Do you give thanks for the simple things? Do you give God the credit for your successes?

This world will tell us to toot our own horn. It will encourage us to say, "look how great I am." The world wants us to put our self on a pedestal. It also wants to knock us off that pedestal and often does.

When we give thanks to God for all we are and all we have, we don't need to be on that pedestal. When we live a life of thankfulness, we see God at work. We were made to praise God for every blessing we receive. Even something as small as the drink of water we have.

I pray we all live with thankful hearts and rid ourselves of the negative thoughts we have. I pray we give thanks to God for each moment of our lives. Be thankful. Praise God. Live a thankful life.

September 22

Instead, speaking the truth in love, we will grow to become in every respect the mature body of him who is the head, that is, Christ.

— Ephesians 4:15

Do you speak the truth? Are you sure it's the truth? Do you know there is only one truth? Do you know the truth? Are you willing to give up your false ideas to understand the truth?

We hear people speak truth that hurts others. They will reason that it's the truth and not care if it hurts. Yet we can speak truth in a loving way that lessens the pain and may actually have a positive impact on the other person, rather than negative.

We are to speak the truth and that truth is God's Word. Yet, if we use it in hateful ways, we are no better than Satan. The truth is to be spoken in loving and mentoring language. It is to encourage, lift up, and create a positive change in someone.

I pray we all will speak the truth in a loving manner. I pray we all lean on the Holy Spirit to guide us in our words. Speak truth. Love others. Be an encourager. Be a positive influence.

September 23

In fact, this is love for God: to keep his commands.
And his commands are not burdensome, for everyone
born of God overcomes the world. This is the victory
that has overcome the world, even our faith. Who is it
that overcomes the world? Only the one who believes
that Jesus is the Son of God.

—1 John 5:3–5

Do you like to win? Are you competitive? Do you like to celebrate
your victories? Would you like to live in that celebration all the time?
Do you know you can and should celebrate the biggest victory of all?

The world counts and celebrates small victories. Sometimes it's
just getting through a tough day. It could be as big as winning the
Super Bowl. It may be passing that tough final exam. The world will
also celebrate the victory that comes through revenge.

We are called to the ultimate victory. We are called to live in the
victory and to celebrate it every day. Too often we miss the celebration,
caught up in unimportant and petty trifles of this life that will soon
pass away. If we belong to Jesus, we have a continual and everlasting
victory to celebrate.

I pray we all come to realize the victory we have through Jesus.
I pray we all celebrate that victory every day. Let the joy of victory
change your life. Live a life of victory.

September 24

For you know that it was not with perishable things
such as silver or gold that you were redeemed from
the empty way of life handed down to you from your
ancestors, but with the precious blood of Christ, a
lamb without blemish or defect.

—1 Peter 1:18–19

Have you strayed from God? Have you turned back to your old life? Or perhaps Satan is tempting you with worldly ways. Are you mistreating others because of your feelings, rather than loving them like Jesus?

We often fall into traps set by Satan. We fall back into old ways. We allow hurt feelings to become anger. We decide we are judge and jury of others. We sometimes believe our way is the only way and everyone else is wrong.

When we act worldly, that is when we need to turn to Jesus the most. We need to realize that Jesus came to not only save us, but to change us. We need to recommit to Him each and every day. We need to ask Him to guide us during every moment. We need to allow Him to fill our hearts and guide our thoughts and actions.

I pray we all recommit our hearts to God today and every day. I pray we allow Him to fill us with His Spirit and guide us. Forget the world. Be filled with God. Be Jesus to others.

Marty Pressey

September 25

"Then the King will say to those on his right,
'Come, you who are blessed by my Father; take your
inheritance, the kingdom prepared for you since the
creation of the world. For I was hungry and you gave
me something to eat, I was thirsty and you gave me
something to drink, I was a stranger and you invited
me in, I needed clothes and you clothed me, I was
sick and you looked after me, I was in prison and you
came to visit me.'"

— Matthew 25:34–36

Do you give of yourself? Are you willing to give up something for
yourself in order to give to others? Will you deny your own comfort
to give to someone in need? Or are you selfish, self-centered, worried
only about what you want?

Too often we worry about our wants when there are so many in
need. Many, if not the vast majority, of us have no needs, we have only
wants. Yet we also see many in need in our communities, our country,
and our world.

We are told that when we meet the needs of someone else, we are
serving Jesus. When we are willing to give up something we want to
meet the need of another person, we are serving a brother or sister.
Will we give to someone in need or continue to be selfish?

I pray we all find a way to meet the needs of one person today. I
pray we all make it our lifestyle to help others when we see the need.
Be Jesus to others. Serve Jesus by serving others.

September 26

And Mary said:
"My soul glorifies the Lord
and my spirit rejoices in God my Savior,
for he has been mindful
of the humble state of his servant.
From now on all generations will call me blessed,
for the Mighty One has done great things for me—
holy is his name."

— Luke 1:46–49

What are you celebrating? Who do you celebrate? Have you forgotten the joy of celebrating someone else's victory? Have you lost the feeling of overcoming an obstacle? Don't you remember you are saved?

Jesus came into this world to give us joy, peace, and victory. We have no reason to fear, no reason to doubt, no reason to be angry. We have a victory that was freely given to us. Perhaps that is why we don't celebrate. We don't want to accept it but earn it.

We are to celebrate the joyous birth, death, and resurrection of Jesus our Savior. He provides us with a victory no one else can. His coming into the world to be an example for us was God living among His created. He conquered Satan for us in the form of a human.

I pray we all celebrate Jesus and the victory He has provided to us. Accept the victory freely. Rejoice in the victory. Praise God for the victory!

September 27

Then they brought him a demon-possessed man who was blind and mute, and Jesus healed him, so that he could both talk and see. All the people were astonished and said, "Could this be the Son of David?"

— Matthew 12:22–23

What amazes you? Is it celebrities? Movie stars? TV stars? Sports stars? Politicians? Parents? Teachers? Mentors? Why is it that we will hold some of these people in such awe and yet not Jesus?

We celebrate Jesus on special holidays. At Christmas, we celebrate His birth. At Easter, we celebrate His death and resurrection. When do we celebrate His life? Shouldn't we celebrate His life every day? How would that change our lives?

Jesus was born, died, and rose again. He taught lessons and provided a wonderful example for us. Through Him all things were created. In Him we all live. We should celebrate and live our lives in awe of Him and His wonderful saving grace.

I pray we all live in Jesus every day, celebrating His life and our salvation. Yes, celebrate His birth, His death, and His resurrection. Celebrate Jesus always.

September 28

Do not love the world or anything in the world. If anyone loves the world, love for the Father is not in them. For everything in the world—the lust of the flesh, the lust of the eyes, and the pride of life—comes not from the Father but from the world. The world and its desires pass away, but whoever does the will of God lives forever.

—1 John 2:15–17

Are you willing to take the next step? Are you willing to take the most important step? Will you decide to follow Jesus with your whole heart? Are you willing to risk this world's temporary treasures and pleasures for an eternity of joy?

We are called to commit our hearts to Jesus. When our hearts are fully committed to Him, we reflect Him in all we do. Jesus comes into our lives not to make small changes in our behavior, but to totally transform us. When we dedicate our whole heart, we become the new person God created us to be.

There is never a better time to commit our hearts to Jesus than today; each and every day. Jesus has given His life to cover our sin, yes, but He also rose to life again to give us eternal hope. Ultimately, it's our choice to give Him our heart or not. Do we dare take the risk?

I pray we all live in His hope, live in His Spirit, live full of Jesus. He will not disappoint in this life nor in all eternity. Hand your heart over to Him.

Marty Pressey

September 29

Do not be anxious about anything, but in every situation, by prayer and petition, with thanksgiving, present your requests to God. And the peace of God, which transcends all understanding, will guard your hearts and your minds in Christ Jesus.

— Philippians 4:6–7

Do you pray? Are your prayers always asking for things for yourself? Do you ever thank God for what you have? Do you pray for others? Do you pray for what's best for them or for what's best for you?

Many people will say they pray, but what they often mean is they are asking God for things in their lives, as if He is a genie. Often people will say they are praying for others, but what they mean is they are praying for the other person to change to their expectations.

Jesus has told us to pray in accordance to His will. Sometimes we need to pray others change, but change into who God wants them to be, not what we want. We aren't all the same nor can we all be the same. God has an individual purpose for each of us.

I pray we all learn to pray for ourselves and others as Jesus would have us pray. If you don't know what you should pray for, ask God to show you what to pray for. That's praying in accordance with His will. Pray like Jesus.

September 30

You, then, why do you judge your brother or sister?
Or why do you treat them with contempt? For we will
all stand before God's judgment seat. It is written:
"'As surely as I live,' says the Lord,
'every knee will bow before me;
every tongue will acknowledge God.'"
So then, each of us will give an account of ourselves
to God.

— Romans 14:10–12

Are you accountable? Do you hold yourself accountable? Or do you depend on others to hold you accountable? Do you listen to others when they are trying to hold you accountable? Do you not realize we are all held accountable by God?

This world proposes we can do whatever we want. The world couldn't be more wrong. Sure, we can do what we want, but bad decisions result in bad consequences. And, ultimately, we are all held accountable for our actions and our words.

Jesus came to be our shining example. He came to be our Savior. Yet He did not come to allow us to do whatever we want without consequences. God will still hold us accountable. One day we will have to answer to God. Is it a day we look forward to with joy or trepidation?

I pray we all come to realize we are held accountable. I pray we all decide to hold ourselves accountable, not to our standard, but to God's. When we hold ourselves accountable, our lives become more joyful. Be like Jesus.

October

October 1

Give us today our daily bread.

— Matthew 6:11

What is it you need today? Have you asked God to give it to you? Have you noticed that He gives you what you need every day? We all have needs and God provides for those. Do we truly recognize it?

God is the great provider. He provides for all our needs each and every day. Sometimes our needs are all He provides, and we feel let down. We want so much more. Our wants may even become desires or cravings.

Our basic needs are food, water, clothing, shelter, and love. God provides those for us through a variety of means. Perhaps by providing us with a job that allows us to afford them. It may be through a homeless shelter. No matter how He provides it, it is provided with His love.

I pray we all recognize that God provides for our needs. I pray we all appreciate the day God has given us. Too often we take it for granted. See God today. Be thankful for His blessings.

October 2

Do not repay anyone evil for evil. Be careful to do
what is right in the eyes of everyone. If it is possible, as
far as it depends on you, live at peace with everyone.
— Romans 12:17–18

Do you take responsibility? Do you take responsibility for your actions? For your words? It's not as simple as stating, "I take responsibility." You are also responsible for the good or bad consequences of your words or actions.

We often want to blame our situations on others. We don't want to take responsibility for ourselves. But far too often, it's our own actions or words that put us in the situation we are in. We've made a choice. We've decided to take an action. We've decided to say something.

We are taught by the Apostle Paul to live at peace with everyone to the degree we can control it. That means we are to be the ones who make the right choices concerning our actions and our words. We are responsible for them, whether we want to be or not.

I pray we all recognize our responsibility. I pray we all decide to make better choices. It is when we listen for God's guidance through His Word and follow it that our lives become better. Heed God's Word.

October 3

In fact, this is love for God: to keep his commands.
And his commands are not burdensome, for everyone
born of God overcomes the world. This is the victory
that has overcome the world, even our faith.

—1 John 5:3–4

Do you feel defeated? Does the world get you down? Do you feel as though everyone is against you? Do certain situations completely take over your thoughts and cause depression? There is a way out of it.

We have a lot of pressures in our life. Often, we feel all alone. Or we feel no one else understands. Those thoughts couldn't be further from the truth. As Solomon wrote, "there is nothing new under the sun" (Ecclesiastes 1:9).

Our problem is we don't want to be vulnerable with someone else, even God. We need to not only pray, but trust God. He will lead us to the right people to confide in. He will lead us to the help we need. He will show us that our troubles are really not nearly as bad as Satan would have us believe.

I pray we all turn to God and trust Him. I pray we all increase in faith. I pray each one of us will take the next step on the path God has laid out for us. Have faith of a mustard seed.

October 4

Each one should test their own actions. Then
they can take pride in themselves alone, without
comparing themselves to someone else, for each one
should carry their own load.

— Galatians 6:4–5

How do you take responsibility for yourself? Do you take a good, hard look in the mirror and see yourself for who you really are? Do you recognize your faults? Are you willing to make the changes needed to be who you are meant to be?

There are times in our lives when we get down on ourselves and don't know how to get up. There are times when we don't recognize we are heading down the wrong path. There are times when we don't even care.

Each one of us should step back and look at our actions, our words, and our current situation from time-to-time. We should evaluate ourselves, where we're at in life, what our past has been, what we want our future to be. No, not fantasy, but something achievable. Not general, such as "be a better person." Be specific, such as "I will treat _____ with love and compassion."

I pray we all reflect on ourselves, our current situation, our past, and what we desire our future to be. I pray we all commit to follow Jesus and become who He wants us to be. Become a true follower of Jesus, be a disciple.

Marty Pressey

October 5

Suddenly a furious storm came up on the lake, so that the waves swept over the boat. But Jesus was sleeping. The disciples went and woke him, saying, "Lord, save us! We're going to drown!"

He replied, "You of little faith, why are you so afraid?" Then he got up and rebuked the winds and the waves, and it was completely calm.

— Matthew 8:24–26

How do you face storms? What is your reaction? Do you stay calm? Or do you panic and completely lose control? Do you reach out for help? Or do you just struggle your way through it?

We have a way to get through storms without having a panic attack. We have help readily available. Too often we just panic and don't stop to reach out. We forget, all too easily, that God is in control, even in the storm.

A contributing factor to our panic is we think it's all about us. To some degree we are correct. Yet not in the way we think. God is in control and He is working on us to make us who He wants us to be. When we decide to rely on Him, we will no longer panic in the storm.

I pray we all decide to lean on God, understand He is in control. I pray we all find the peace and calm in putting the storm in God's hands. Trust God.

October 6

Let the morning bring me word of your unfailing
love, for I have put my trust in you.
Show me the way I should go, for to you I entrust
my life.

— Psalm 143:8

How do you face each day? What is your attitude when you wake? Are
you joyful that God has given you another day? Or are you in a bad
mood because you have to work, go to school, or have some other task
ahead of you? Why let the tasks or others define you?

Too often we let the tasks ahead of us define our mood or attitude.
Too often we allow others to alter our outlook on life in a negative
way. Too often we are a prisoner of our own negative thoughts. God
has set us free.

When we accept God's freedom and live in it, we free ourselves
from the negativity of this world. Jesus told us that no one can take
it away from us. It's always there for our choosing. We are to live in
God's freedom and the best way to do that is to start each morning
recognizing His great love for us and trusting in Him.

I pray we each choose the freedom God has provided. I pray we
wake each morning appreciating another day of God's blessing. Be
positive in God's love. Be thankful for His gift. Trust in Him.

Marty Pressey

October 7

David said to Abigail, "Praise be to the LORD, the God of Israel, who has sent you today to meet me. May you be blessed for your good judgment and for keeping me from bloodshed this day and from avenging myself with my own hands. Otherwise, as surely as the LORD, the God of Israel, lives, who has kept me from harming you, if you had not come quickly to meet me, not one male belonging to Nabal would have been left alive by daybreak."

—1 Samuel 25:32–34

Do you listen to the advice of others? Do you recognize good advice when you hear it? Are you willing to change your plans? Will you follow God's plan or continue down the path you have already decided?

We hear lots of advice in this world. There is advice for planning our future, for planning for retirement, for losing weight, for climbing the corporate ladder, for making new friends, for marriage, and on and on. It's all human advice.

God also gives us advice. He does so through His Word. He also gives us advice through others. We may hear the advice, know in our heart it is good, and then be posed with the decision to adhere to it or not. When we adhere to God's advice, our lives are changed for the better.

I pray we all listen for and adhere to God's advice. Be keen to discern whether it is coming from God or if it is human advice. Listen for God. Follow His Word.

October 8

Repent, then, and turn to God, so that your sins may
be wiped out, that times of refreshing may come from
the Lord.

— Acts 3:19

Are you comfortable with where you are? Will you continue to live in
your misery? Do you not want to live a life of joy? Are you unwilling
to make a change? Have you not opened your eyes and assessed your
current state?

Too often we are willing to continue to live in the misery, the
cesspool we have been in for so long. We have grown comfortable
with the pain. It has become familiar to us. We decide to live in its
familiarity rather than step out of it.

God has promised us joy. He has promised us an abundant life.
No, that doesn't mean riches and fame. It means we don't have to
live in the drudgery of life. It means we can experience His joy, often
called heaven on earth. All we have to do is decide to step out of the
cesspool and into God's waiting arms.

I pray we all decide to take God at His Word. Claim His promises
for your life. Decide to take that step of faith and trust in Him. Be bold.
Trust God. Claim His promises.

October 9

"Come to me, all you who are weary and burdened,
and I will give you rest."

— Matthew 11:28

Have you grown weary? Are you just worn out? Have you had enough?
Are you ready to give up? Have you hit the end of the line?

Many of us will answer "yes" to one or more of those questions
at some point in our lives. It's one thing to be physically tired from
exertion. It's something totally different to be mentally, emotionally,
and spiritually drained.

There is one source that can refill us completely. His name is
Jesus. He has promised to refill us every single day. We do have a
choice. We can reject His offer, or we can take Him up on it. All we
need to do is ask Him to fill us and believe that He will.

I pray each of us decides to go to Jesus and ask Him to fill us. He
will give you rest and fill you with a Spirit that overflows. Go to Him.
Be filled. Find rest.

October 10

Therefore, since we are surrounded by such a great cloud of witnesses, let us throw off everything that hinders and the sin that so easily entangles. And let us run with perseverance the race marked out for us, fixing our eyes on Jesus, the pioneer and perfecter of faith. For the joy set before him he endured the cross, scorning its shame, and sat down at the right hand of the throne of God.

— Hebrews 12:1–2

Who is your hero? Who is it that you look at with awe? Is it a parent? A grandparent? An uncle or aunt? Perhaps it is a movie star, singer, or sports figure? Too often we place other human beings on a pedestal.

Sure, there a people we can and should admire. They've done some wonderful things. There are people who are great leaders, philanthropists, achievers, and caregivers. There are people that we love to be around. But should we worship them?

Jesus is far more than any human hero. He has provided us with more than we could ever ask for. Our humanness fails to comprehend the immensity of what He has done for us. Perhaps that is why we trivialize it. Instead, we should be striving to become more like Him.

I pray we all decide to look to Jesus as our example, as our goal, and not grow weary of working toward becoming more like Him. He is our perfecter of faith. He is our Savior. He is our encouragement. Be like Jesus.

October 11

Do not conform to the pattern of this world, but be transformed by the renewing of your mind. Then you will be able to test and approve what God's will is—his good, pleasing and perfect will.

— Romans 12:2

Are you stuck? Do you feel like you're just going through the same ole grind over and over again? Perhaps every day feels like ground hog day.

There are many books that will give us all kinds of advice to "spice up" our life. Change our hair color. Go on an exciting vacation. Buy our self a new dress or suit. All of these will cost us money and provide temporary excitement.

Our days seem boring or monotonous because our minds our stale. Our minds need to be active; they need to be learning. Isn't it enjoyable when you learn something new? Don't you feel like it was a good day? Read God's Word, learn something knew about Him that will make your life better.

I pray we all continue to learn more about God and grow in our relationship with Him. I pray we all seek His guidance. Our lives will be better for it. We will find excitement. Activate your brain. Seek God.

October 12

The Son is the image of the invisible God, the firstborn over all creation. For in him all things were created: things in heaven and on earth, visible and invisible, whether thrones or powers or rulers or authorities; all things have been created through him and for him.

— Colossians 1:15–16

How are you doing today? Did you awake with a good outlook for the day? Did you awake with the dread of what was before you? What was your decision on the type of day you would have?

Too often we let this world get us down. It may be some struggle we have or a difficult task awaiting us. We often focus on the negative. We forget there is always a positive. We forget the power of God inside us.

Jesus told us He would send a Helper to us. We have the Helper living in us in the Holy Spirit. The Creator of all things is with us. Imagine the power to create this world and all the stars in the sky. We have the ability to reach out to that power.

I pray we all decide to have a good day. I pray we all reach out to God today. Know that the Creator is there for you. Know that He has a plan for you. Let your troubles pass to Him.

October 13

"I have told you these things, so that in me you may have peace. In this world you will have trouble. But take heart! I have overcome the world."

— John 16:33

Do you feel overwhelmed? Do you have too many tasks to complete? Are you fearful of something or someone? Do you feel as though you are climbing a mountain? Do you feel all alone in your struggle?

We get wrapped up in our day-to-day lives. Our focus narrows to a single moment. We can't seem to see beyond today. We see some people that don't seem to have that problem. In all likelihood, they do. They either know they have God on their side, or they are just oblivious.

We who are in Christ have God on our side. We can live with the comfort that Jesus has overcome this world. Knowing that, we can look at what it is we fear, the mountain ahead, or anything else that is overwhelming us and know that Jesus has already defeated it for us.

I pray we all come to know the peace, comfort, and joy of knowing that Jesus has overcome this world. Turn it all over to Him. Let Him guide you through it. Let Him give you strength. You, too, will overcome this world.

October 14

When you were dead in your sins and in the uncircumcision of your flesh, God made you alive with Christ. He forgave us all our sins, having canceled the charge of our legal indebtedness, which stood against us and condemned us; he has taken it away, nailing it to the cross.

— Colossians 2:13–14

Do you pay back your debts? Do you take repaying a loan seriously? How do you handle it when someone does something really amazing for you when you most need it?

Some of us will make extra payments to pay a loan off early. Some of us will go out of our way to do something nice for someone who did something nice for us. Some of us will track our debt to the penny.

Yet we won't do what we should do to honor the debt we owe Jesus. We decide to put it off. We decide we can only give part of it. We may even ignore it in hopes it will go away. What does He want? He wants our whole hearts. He wants our commitment to Him.

I pray we all commit our whole heart to Him. I pray we take seriously our commitment to follow Him, to do as He did, to reflect Him. Recommit yourself to Him today and every day.

Marty Pressey

October 15

For everything that was written in the past was written to teach us, so that through the endurance taught in the Scriptures and the encouragement they provide we might have hope.

May the God who gives endurance and encouragement give you the same attitude of mind toward each other that Christ Jesus had, so that with one mind and one voice you may glorify the God and Father of our Lord Jesus Christ.

— Romans 15:4-6

How do see the people you come across every day? Do you see them as children of God? Do you truly see them? Or do you just see an object? Do you try to understand the other person or only care about yourself?

We all have our own troubles, our own issues. We are all tempted to focus only on ourselves. We know our struggles intimately. We know our hidden failures. We often feel unworthy.

It is only when we focus on Jesus that we can move forward. It is when we see the trouble another person is going through and help them that our troubles start to disappear. When we help others, our joy increases, our troubles dissipate.

I pray we all try to truly see others and focus less on ourselves. Help someone today. Provide an encouraging word. Lend a hand. Focus on Jesus. See how He wants you to move forward.

October 16

Keep your lives free from the love of money and be
content with what you have, because God has said,
"Never will I leave you;
never will I forsake you."
So we say with confidence,
"The Lord is my helper; I will not be afraid.
What can mere mortals do to me?"

— Hebrews 13:5–6

What are you afraid of today? Do you fear for your job? Are you in fear
of losing a relationship? Are you afraid of bringing up a tough topic
to a friend or family member? We all face some type of fear nearly
every day.

The world wants us to live in fear. Actually, Satan wants us to live
in fear. Why? So we can be controlled. If we are afraid of losing our
job, we'll do just about anything to keep it. If we are afraid of losing a
relationship, we'll become a slave to the other person.

Jesus came to set us free from those fears. We are to live in the
freedom of knowing that He is always with us. He has freed us from
slavery. Yes, living in fear is slavery. God has promised He will never
leave us all alone and Jesus has set us free.

I pray we all live in the freedom of Jesus. I pray we all overcome
our fears through our trust in Jesus. I pray we all accept our release
from slavery.

Marty Pressey

October 17

I know what it is to be in need, and I know what it
is to have plenty. I have learned the secret of being
content in any and every situation, whether well fed
or hungry, whether living in plenty or in want.

— Philippians 4:12

Are you content? Or are you urgently struggling for something more?
Are you striving to get something that seems to be out of reach? Are
you anxious for something new? Will you continue your frustration?

We often chase after things we think we want or need. Sometimes
we are correct, yet the timing isn't right. We also fail to be satisfied
with who we are. We want to be the star, the one getting attention, the
one with all the accolades. That's not wrong in itself, but that may not
be who God made us to be.

God put each of us on this earth to fulfill a piece of His plan. We
need to understand where we fit in and be content with that. When
we do, we find the everlasting joy He promised. We need to trust He
knows what He is doing.

I pray we all find our proper place as God has planned. I pray
we find the contentment Paul did. Trust God. He has put you where
you are.

October 18

Therefore we are always confident and know that as long as we are at home in the body we are away from the Lord. For we live by faith, not by sight. We are confident, I say, and would prefer to be away from the body and at home with the Lord. So we make it our goal to please him, whether we are at home in the body or away from it.

—2 Corinthians 5:6–9

Where is your home? Do you live in the here and now? Do you live by the law of the land? Are you living from meal-to-meal, day-to-day? Or are you living in the law of the Spirit? Are you living in God's Kingdom?

Many people are really living moment-to-moment, even if they are planning for the future. They live and react to the immediate. This type of living is of the world. It allows the world to dictate how we react, how we make decisions.

When we live by the Spirit, we don't have the same reactions. We react according to God's plan. We live on a different plane. We see things as being minuscule in comparison to what God has in store for us. The spilled milk is of no consequence when we are confident there is an endless quantity waiting for us.

I pray we all come to live by God's plan, rather than the worlds. I pray we all change our way of thinking with the renewing of our minds. Trust God. Live in Him. Be at home in Him.

October 19

And whatever you do, whether in word or deed, do
it all in the name of the Lord Jesus, giving thanks to
God the Father through him.

— Colossians 3:17

Are you willing to give all you have? For what are you willing to give
it? For you children? For your spouse? For your friends? Are you
willing to give everything for the joy, peace, and love that only God
can give you?

The world often calls us to noble causes. It demands we give up
something to be part of something bigger. Sometimes we find the
cause to be of enough interest to do so. Sometimes it's of no interest
to us at all.

God doesn't call us to give up something, but everything. He calls
us to give up our selfish desires, our evil ways, our self-righteousness.
He doesn't necessarily call us to give up our professions. Jesus
commended the soldier for great faith. We are to give up our inner
selves to be His follower.

I pray we all give our full selves to Jesus. Give Him yourself at all
times, every moment of every day. When we do, we find the peace,
love, and joy that He promised. Be His true follower.

October 20

"This is my command: Love each other."

— John 15:17

Do you have questions? Do you wonder why it seems you're making no progress? Does it feel like every time you take a step forward, something happens, and you fall back into those old, bad habits again? Do you sometimes feel like giving up?

We have many struggles in this life. We form bad habits, then find it's hard to break them. Experts tell us it takes 30 days of doing something consistently to build a new habit and replace and old one. That takes discipline, caring, support, and love.

God loves us, even with our bad habits. That doesn't mean He wants to leave us like that. He will continually work on us, mostly through other people. He provides people in our lives to give us encouragement, kick us in the butt, provide support, and to love us.

I pray we all realize that God loves us and is working to make us into His vision for us. I pray we all listen, truly listen, to those God puts in our lives. I pray we accept His love and return our love to Him by loving others.

October 21

But now you must also rid yourselves of all such things as these: anger, rage, malice, slander, and filthy language from your lips.

— Colossians 3:8

Are you angry? Why are you angry? Do you know? Are you sure you know why you are angry? Are you willing to go to the root cause of your anger? Will you look at the situation objectively and what led up to it?

Too many in this world are angry. Nearly all of us don't know why. We want to blame someone else for it. We won't dig to the bottom of it to understand that it is our own doing that has caused the anger. And many will quickly deny what I just said, proving my point.

Our anger in nearly all cases comes from our own failure. We are the ones who put ourselves in that situation. Our past behavior has caused someone to treat us in a way that makes us angry. Our failure to follow Jesus' teaching has created our failure. Our choice.

I pray we all determine to make better choices, changing our behavior, setting ourselves up for success. I pray we all lean on Jesus to do this. He will make the changes, if we let Him. Make the right choice today.

October 22

Who shall separate us from the love of Christ? Shall trouble or hardship or persecution or famine or nakedness or danger or sword? ... No, in all these things we are more than conquerors through him who loved us. For I am convinced that neither death nor life, neither angels nor demons, neither the present nor the future, nor any powers, neither height nor depth, nor anything else in all creation, will be able to separate us from the love of God that is in Christ Jesus our Lord.

— Romans 8:35, 37–39

When will you find love? Maybe you've already found it. Is it true love? Is it a never-ending love? Do you even want a love that never ends? Have you been searching for love? Will you know love if it stares you in the face?

The world looks at love as an emotion and often fleeting. It comes and goes like the wind. It's OK to love someone today and hate them tomorrow. The world has no idea what true love is.

God has shown us and continues to show us what true love is. Those who are fully dedicated to Christ know it and show it to those around them. Are any perfect? No, only Christ is perfect. Yet we can know the true love God has for us in Jesus Christ. But we must choose to accept His love.

I pray we all find and accept the love of Christ in our lives. It will transform us, if we allow it. Be filled with love today. Show that love to others.

October 23

"No one lights a lamp and hides it in a clay jar or puts
it under a bed. Instead, they put it on a stand, so that
those who come in can see the light."

— Luke 8:16

Are you being a light today? Will you make someone's day brighter?
Are you willing to put someone before yourself? Will you shine love,
grace, and mercy on someone today?

This world is full of darkness. It seems nearly everyone we run
into is full of selfishness, self-pride, do what I want, I'm the most
important person. Few will serve someone else ahead of themselves.

Yet Jesus calls us to be a servant to all. It is through our service
in love that we shine His light into this world. We become a beacon
of light and wonder to those we come in contact with. We show the
world Jesus living in us when we put others first.

I pray we all become beacons of light in our service to others. I
pray we show the world Jesus in our actions. Be the light. Be Jesus to
someone today.

October 24

Each of you should use whatever gift you have
received to serve others, as faithful stewards of God's
grace in its various forms.

—1 Peter 4:10

Who are you helping today? Who are you encouraging today? Who
are you lifting up today? Who are you building up today? Who are you
being a positive example for today?

Too often we melt into the world and follow the lead of those
around us, even when we know we shouldn't. That may mean that we
don't do the right thing, don't say the right thing, don't help others.
Why are we unwilling to be the light in this world?

Jesus has called us to be the light. We see several instances where
the apostles taught the early Christians to lift each other up, to
encourage each other, to help each other. This may be in monetary
form, lending a helping hand, praying for someone, or offering an
encouraging word.

I pray we all decide to be a person of positive attitude and an
encourager of others. I pray we all lift up each other in prayer. I pray
we all decide to put others ahead of ourselves. Be the light.

October 25

"You call me 'Teacher' and 'Lord,' and rightly so, for that is what I am. Now that I, your Lord and Teacher, have washed your feet, you also should wash one another's feet. I have set you an example that you should do as I have done for you. Very truly I tell you, no servant is greater than his master, nor is a messenger greater than the one who sent him. Now that you know these things, you will be blessed if you do them."

—John 13:13–17

Do you think you are better than you are? Do you think more highly of yourself than you should? Are you showing the attitude that you are above others in your words or your actions?

Many of us will say that we do not think we are better than others, yet our actions and words betray us. Should we think lowly of ourselves and live our lives depressed? No! We should live looking up to Jesus and striving to be more like Him.

Jesus is our perfect example. Will we ever achieve being perfect like Him? No! But that shouldn't stop us from trying. How do we try? We give ourselves up, turning our lives over to Jesus and welcoming His Spirit in us. We allow Him to take control of our lives.

I pray we all strive to be like Jesus. I pray we all allow Him to take control. I pray we all follow His example. Do not think you are better than others. Be a servant of all.

October 26

"Come, follow me," Jesus said, "and I will send you out to fish for people." At once they left their nets and followed him.

— Matthew 4:19–20

How well are you doing God's work today? How quickly did you follow? Did you also quickly start falling behind? Did you slow down? Did you stop to take a break? Will you decide to do His work again and stick with it?

Jesus has called us to bring people into His Body, the Church. He has called us to spread His Word. He has called us to be His shining light. Jesus calls us every day to be His follower and to bring others into the fold.

We often think that means being a preacher. Well, that is one way, but that's not what most of us will be. Most of us will bring people in by being the very best we can possibly be, by striving to imitate Jesus, by being the shining light to those we encounter. That is how we do our fishing.

I pray we all make the decision to follow Jesus as closely as we possibly can. I pray we all decide to imitate Him and bring others to Him. I pray we all decide to go fishing.

Marty Pressey

October 27

"Come to me, all you who are weary and burdened, and I will give you rest. Take my yoke upon you and learn from me, for I am gentle and humble in heart, and you will find rest for your souls. For my yoke is easy and my burden is light."

— Matthew 11:28–30

Are you leaning on Jesus today? Have you gone to Him to help you through your struggle? Are you willing to lay your problems at His feet and allow Him to take them from you? Are you willing to walk toward Him, rather than walking away from Him?

We are told by Jesus that this world has enough trouble of its own (Matthew 6:34). We can see with our own eyes and through our own experiences that His Word is true. Yet we won't trust His Word when He says He will take on our burdens for us.

We often will state that we can do anything with Jesus on our side. Yet we don't live that way. We quickly give up. We are to be bold in Jesus name. We are to be unafraid because He is with us. We are to be so much more than we allow ourselves to be.

I pray we all decide to walk toward Jesus, laying down our burdens at His feet. I pray we allow Him to take them on and become the bold person He wants us to be. Take that step today.

October 28

He says, "Be still, and know that I am God;
I will be exalted among the nations,
I will be exalted in the earth."

— Psalm 46:10

Do you hear God? Are you being quiet enough to hear Him? Are you taking time to listen? Will you set aside the noisiness of this world to seek His voice? Despite what many people think, God does still speak to us.

This world is a noisy place. There's the rush to get work done. We have places to go. We have wants that demand we spend time on them. We bombard ourselves with TV, talking, and thinking about what we are seeing and hearing.

God wants us to spend some quiet time with Him. We need to spend quiet time with Him. It is in the quiet that He speaks to us. This is when we learn to not only listen for His voice, but to put our cares and troubles in His hands.

I pray we all will set aside some time to be quiet with God. I pray we all seek Him in prayer, both speaking to Him and listening to Him. Be still and know that He is God.

Marty Pressey

October 29

"Now I commit you to God and to the word of
his grace, which can build you up and give you an
inheritance among all those who are sanctified."
— Acts 20:32

Have you committed to God? Are you committed to following
Jesus? Will you dedicate all you do for Him? Or are you expecting an
immediate removal of all that you deem to be unpleasant from your
life and if that doesn't happen you give up?

So many people in this world will only commit until it gets
tough or things don't go quite their way, then they give up. They
have the attitude of expecting something immediately in return for
their commitment. If they don't get what they want, they quit their
commitment.

We are called to commit to God all that we are with everything we
have. We are called to trust Him who will bless us in ways we would
never think of. Does that mean we always get what we want? No. It
means we will receive something far better and it will be what we need
or what God wants for us.

I pray we all commit ourselves to God, to following Jesus. He
is our perfect example. He is the one who will lead us to the full
realization of His plan. Stick with it.

October 30

All this took place to fulfill what the Lord had said through the prophet: "The virgin will conceive and give birth to a son, and they will call him Immanuel" (which means "God with us").

— Matthew 1:22–23

Do you fully comprehend that God is with you at *all* times? Do you remember that He is with you when things are going well? Do you remember to lean on Him when the going is tough? Do you think about Him being with you when you say and do ugly things?

The world wants us to believe we can do what feels right to us. We are inundated with the phrase "you deserve it." Too often we listen to the lies of the world. We only deserve death for the sin we have committed.

However, God has blessed us with His presence, with His salvation, with His grace, with His blessings. Yet we live life as though we don't appreciate them. If we all lived a thankful life, remembering that God is *always* with us, the world would be a totally different place.

I pray we all remember God is with us. He will never leave us. I pray we lean on Him when we need to and trust Him always. Be thankful. Praise God. Live the life He desires for you.

October 31

"He himself bore our sins" in his body on the cross, so
that we might die to sins and live for righteousness;
"by his wounds you have been healed." For "you were
like sheep going astray," but now you have returned
to the Shepherd and Overseer of your souls.

—1 Peter 2:24–25

Do you feel broken at times? Do you feel as though no one understands?
Do you go through times of depression and anxiety? Are you willing
to be healed?

The world will slowly, or perhaps quickly, bring us down. It can
happen in the snap of our fingers. Or it can be a slow erosion of our
inner peace. Unfortunately, the world will just trample on us and leave
us lying in our misery.

Jesus has already healed us, if we will accept His healing. When
we are well grounded in Him, the brokenness is healed, the depression
is less severe or goes away entirely. When we know He is with us, truly
know, our anxiety becomes irrelevant.

I pray we all decide to hold onto Jesus, come to know Him, and
depend on Him. I pray we all come to be healed and enjoy inner peace.
Know Him. Trust Him.

November

November 1

So then, brothers and sisters, stand firm and hold
fast to the teachings we passed on to you, whether
by word of mouth or by letter. May our Lord Jesus
Christ himself and God our Father, who loved us and
by his grace gave us eternal encouragement and good
hope, encourage your hearts and strengthen you in
every good deed and word.

—2 Thessalonians 2:15–17

Do you feel like you are barely holding on sometimes? Perhaps you
are having relationship problems. Maybe it's a tough day or week at
work. It could be that you are struggling financially. We all go through
rough spells.

It's during these rough times that the world will continue to kick
us, continue to say that we are worthless, or taunt us. Many will push
us away, wanting nothing to do with us. That is this world we live in.

However, there is always One who welcomes us with open arms.
Jesus is willing to give us comfort, strength, courage, and His love.
He will be there for us in many different ways. Sometimes it's in other
people. Sometimes it's in the magic of nature. Sometimes it's simply
in those quiet times of prayer and thought.

I pray we all determine we will hold on to Jesus, no matter what.
I pray we will see Him at work in our lives, even the bad times. Trust
Him. He is there for you always.

November 2

Do not conform to the pattern of this world, but be transformed by the renewing of your mind. Then you will be able to test and approve what God's will is—his good, pleasing and perfect will.

— Romans 12:2

How much do you appreciate what has been done for you? Do you show your appreciation? Do you do what you should? Are you willing to make the right decisions, take the right actions, accept the positive change in yourself?

If we are thinking worldly, we are thinking about what others have done for us. There's nothing wrong with that. Yet did we also think about what God has done for us? What Jesus did on the cross for us?

Each of us should remember that Jesus didn't simply go to the cross and give His life for us. He gave up living in Heaven for over 30 years to walk this earth. He gave up being in the presence of the Father, the angels, the perfect place. Jesus forfeited heaven for earth for a period of time in order to be our Savior.

I pray we all show our appreciation and love of God through our actions and words. I pray we all continue to mature in our Christian walk, becoming more like Christ. Decide today. Be like Jesus.

November 3

The angel said to the women, "Do not be afraid, for I know that you are looking for Jesus, who was crucified. He is not here; he has risen, just as he said. Come and see the place where he lay. Then go quickly and tell his disciples: 'He has risen from the dead and is going ahead of you into Galilee. There you will see him.' Now I have told you."

— Matthew 28:5–7

Do you believe Jesus lives today? Do you believe He overcame death? Do you believe with your whole heart? Will you submit to His Lordship? Will you follow Him?

The world thinks it is foolish to believe someone can be raised from the dead. People of the world have believed that for centuries. Yet it is the power of God overcoming death that is the foundation of our belief.

If we choose to follow Jesus and believe He overcame death, shouldn't we devote our lives to Him? We are called to turn everything over to Him. Yes, everything. All our thoughts, all our actions, all our words, all our belongings, all of our being. We come to understand we have nothing that doesn't belong to God.

I pray we all turn everything over to Jesus. I pray we give up who we are to be the image of Christ. Believe Jesus died and rose. Believe it to your very core. Be His disciple.

November 4

Keep on loving one another as brothers and sisters.
Do not forget to show hospitality to strangers, for
by so doing some people have shown hospitality to
angels without knowing it.

— Hebrews 13:1–2

Have you ever thought that you might be ministering to an angel? Perhaps the homeless person you are feeding? Would you be surprised if the stranger who bumped into your shopping cart was an angel?

We often ignore those we don't know. Or we make fun of them. Perhaps we look down on them for the way they are dressed. Sometimes we will feel sorry for them but do nothing.

We are told we are to love all people. That doesn't mean we have to like their actions. But it seems especially important to treat people we don't know well. We never know, it could just be angel walking this earth to see how we will react, how well we love others.

Remember that Abraham entertained angels who brought the message that he would have a son in his old age (Genesis 18:1-15). Keep your faith in God and be kind to others. God is always watching.

Marty Pressey

November 5

Grace and peace to you from God our Father and the
Lord Jesus Christ, who gave himself for our sins to
rescue us from the present evil age, according to the
will of our God and Father, to whom be glory for ever
and ever. Amen.

— Galatians 1:3–5

Do you sometimes feel like you are a total disaster? Are you struggling
with issues that you don't see a way out of? Do you wonder if you will
ever get your life together? Are you willing to seek help from the One
who can pull you out of the drudgery of this world?

There is no doubt this world is broken and needs healing. We see
so much sickness, sinfulness, and brokenness we have become blind
to it. The world has come to accept it as normal.

We are called to a better place. We are called to rise above the fray.
We are called to rely on Jesus as our guide, our leader, our Savior. He
can pull us out of the ditch and put us on the high road. Will we ask
Him and trust Him?

I pray we all ask Jesus to be our guide and that we will listen to
Him and follow His lead. I pray we all turn every moment of our lives
over to Him. Rise above. Trust Jesus.

November 6

The thief comes only to steal and kill and destroy;
I have come that they may have life, and have it to
the full.

—John 10:10

Do you live life out of scarcity or abundance? Are you pursuing more things, more money, more relationships? Or, are you content and have confidence that God will provide? Are you sure you know where you stand?

When we live out of scarcity, we desire more and more and more. We never get enough. We continue our pursuit endlessly. We hold on to what we have, because we are afraid of losing it or sharing it. Why? We don't think we have enough. We live in scarcity.

When we live in abundance, we are confident that God will provide. We are willing to share and give to others. We will look for ways to share the abundance God has blessed us with. We have no fear of not having enough. We trust that God will provide.

I pray we all live in abundance. I pray we let go of our scarcity attitudes. I pray we give of our blessings, knowing God will continue to provide. Trust God. He will provide.

Marty Pressey

November 7

So you are no longer a slave, but God's child; and
since you are his child, God has made you also an
heir.

— Galatians 4:7

Do you forget who you are? Do you fall back into old ways, old traps?
Have you started down the straight path only to fall back into old
habits? Do you need to be reminded of who you are?

This world will tug us back into old habits, bad habits, trying to
keep its hold on us. The busyness of work, maintaining a household,
keeping up with schoolwork, and any number of other things.

God wants us to know that we belong to Him. Take comfort and
be at peace that He is in control and we are His children. Be reminded
that He cares for us and loves us more than we can imagine.

I pray each of us are reminded that God loves us. Remember Jesus
died for you out of love. Be well. Be comforted. Be content in His love.

November 8

Ascribe to the Lord the glory due his name; worship
the Lord in the splendor of his holiness.

— Psalm 29:2

Do you understand and recognize the holiness of God? Do you
realize that He is righteous? Are you willing to follow His commands,
guidance, direction, and example? God is the Holy One.

The world wants us to forget about God. Satan wants us to ignore
God, to believe we can do what we want, and God won't care. That is
why he is called the great deceiver. This world would have us follow
after it, rather than follow God.

God does know that we are human and that we will fall short
of His holiness. However, He doesn't want us to stop trying and He
wants us to recognize Him for who He is. God will never leave us,
unless we choose to follow the world rather than follow Him.

I pray we all decide to follow God. I pray we all recognize His
awesome holiness. I pray that each of us continues to pursue His ways,
never giving up. See His holiness. Trust in God.

November 9

Jesus called them together and said, "You know that the rulers of the Gentiles lord it over them, and their high officials exercise authority over them. Not so with you. Instead, whoever wants to become great among you must be your servant, and whoever wants to be first must be your slave—just as the Son of Man did not come to be served, but to serve, and to give his life as a ransom for many."

— Matthew 20:25–28

Are you willing to give your life for Jesus? Really? Are you willing to live for Him? Really? Are you willing to give everything you have for Him? Are you willing to be a servant to all? I dare say the vast majority of us are not.

The world often looks down on servants. For many years, it looked down on public servants such as the military, police, and rescue workers. It still looks down on many servant positions. How do many in the world look at waitresses and waiters?

Jesus has called us to be servants. Servants to Him, servants to others. That means we must give up our pride, our "I'm better than you" mentality. It means we must be willing to share or give away our belongings. It means giving up ourselves.

I pray we all decide to serve one another, especially our families and fellow Christians. I pray we set aside our differences and pride to become humble servants of the King. Be a servant. Be a disciple. Be a follower of Jesus.

November 10

Jesus said to them, "The kings of the Gentiles lord it over them; and those who exercise authority over them call themselves Benefactors. But you are not to be like that. Instead, the greatest among you should be like the youngest, and the one who rules like the one who serves.

— Luke 22:25–26

How do you support others? Do you help out when you see someone in need? Do you support them in their activities? Are you willing to put others needs or wants ahead of your own? Will you serve and support?

So many in this world are selfish, only looking out for themselves. They believe the lies they hear, that they deserve to have it all. We, too, often listen to the lies of the world and only look out for ourselves.

We are called to serve others. When we do, we find satisfaction and worth far beyond what we will ever find being selfish. Unfortunately, we don't believe it until we experience it. We need to take the chance and go experience servanthood.

I pray we all support our brothers and sisters in Christ. I pray we decide to serve others and experience the joy of it. Be a servant. Be a follower of Christ. Experience true joy.

November 11

"Come to me, all you who are weary and burdened, and I will give you rest. Take my yoke upon you and learn from me, for I am gentle and humble in heart, and you will find rest for your souls. For my yoke is easy and my burden is light."

— Matthew 11:28–30

Are you weary? Are you carrying a heavy load? Do you feel overwhelmed? Are you trying to do it all by yourself? Are you willing to ask for help? Will you accept it if it is offered?

We often think we have to do it all ourselves. Or we don't trust someone else to do it. Perhaps we are unwilling to let go of a worry. Maybe we prefer to live in the comfort of our quagmire, rather than living free.

Jesus is always there to lift our burdens from our shoulders. It doesn't matter if it is emotional, spiritual, or physical. He is there to pull us through. All we need to do is let go and let Him take it from us. That's not always easy.

I pray we all look to Jesus to lift the weight of this world off our shoulders. I pray we all allow Him to take our burdens. Trust Jesus. Give it to Him.

November 12

When anxiety was great within me, your consolation brought me joy.

— Psalm 94:19

Do you have the joy of Jesus in you? Do you feel His presence at all times? Do you turn over your worries to Him? Will you allow Him to give you the joy you seek?

This world will take away our joy in a heartbeat. It will steal our very breath. All we have to do is forget that God is in control and all is doomed. Or, at least, it is in our own minds.

On the other hand, if we remember that God is in control, we continue in His joy. He fills us with His Spirit. He provides peace, calm, and joy, even in our most anxious moments.

I pray we all allow Jesus to fill us with joy. It's not all happiness, but it will always be joy. Trust in Him. Turn it all over to Him. Live a life of joy.

November 13

And whatever you do, whether in word or deed, do
it all in the name of the Lord Jesus, giving thanks to
God the Father through him.

— Colossians 3:17

What are you doing for God today? Are you doing anything for Him?
Shouldn't you be doing everything for Him? Hasn't He given you
everything you have? No? Yes? Aren't sure?

We are constantly told we have earned what we have. We are
bombarded with the message that we deserve this or that. The
overwhelming mentality of the day is that we are owed everything.

Yet, none of us are able to give ourselves talent or knowledge or
wisdom or any other special abilities. Those are all given to us by God.
He provides us with even more than that, which means all that we do
should be for Him. That would simply be showing Him our gratitude.

I pray we all realize that who we are and what we have is a gift
from God. I pray we all do everything we do today for Him, including
both actions and words. Show gratitude to God. Give Him the glory.

November 14

"Come, follow me," Jesus said, "and I will send you out to fish for people." At once they left their nets and followed him.

— Matthew 4:19–20

What are you doing to bring others to Jesus? Is your life a positive example? Is it a life that others will want to imitate? Are you living so that others want to know what you have and how they can get it?

Whether we believe it or not, this world is hungry for God. Unfortunately, it doesn't know it. All of us have a desire for something better. A common joke is, "I don't know what I want, but I'll know it when I see it."

God is what all of us desire. Only He can satisfy our true desire. We need to not only recognize this but live our lives such that others see it and want it too. When we become examples of Jesus, we become fishers of people. We've put the lure in the water.

I pray we all decide to live our lives imitating Jesus. I pray we all pursue our desire, which is God. He is there. He will fill us. Trust in Him.

November 15

So then, just as you received Christ Jesus as Lord, continue to live your lives in him, rooted and built up in him, strengthened in the faith as you were taught, and overflowing with thankfulness.

— Colossians 2:6–7

Do you feel like you are failing? Do you feel as though you are overcome by events? Do you think you will never get beyond this tough spot you are in? Are you willing to turn to the One who can help?

We all get into some tough spots and have some rough times we go through. We all have heartaches, hurdles to overcome, promotions that don't happen, broken relationships, or even the death of a loved one. These all threaten to overwhelm us.

God is always there. He continues to work on us. He holds our hand as we go through these tough times like a Dad holds the seat of the bicycle while teaching his child to ride. He is training us to be stronger, be more confident in Him and in ourselves.

I pray we all continue our walk with God, trusting Him to give us the strength we need for each day. He is always there. Trust Him. He won't let you down.

November 16

The apostles said to the Lord, "Increase our faith!"
He replied, "If you have faith as small as a mustard
seed, you can say to this mulberry tree, 'Be uprooted
and planted in the sea,' and it will obey you."
— Luke 17:5–6

Do you feel as though your faith is failing? Do you sometimes have doubts? Is your faith strong right now? Do you ever think about your faith? Are you looking to increase your faith?

Too often we are not aware of our faith. We just kind of take it for granted. We go to church. We sing songs. We pray sometimes. We listen to sermons by televangelists or on the radio. We may even read our Bible occasionally. Yet we don't really think about our faith.

We should be aware of our faith and continue to ask God to increase it. We should rely on our faith, banking on God to do according to His promises and His plan. It is our faith that will allow us to step out into new opportunities. It is our faith that will keep us going.

I pray we all think about our faith and continue to grow in it. God will increase our faith if we will only ask for it with our hearts. Trust God. Increase in your faith.

Marty Pressey

November 17

"Do not judge, or you too will be judged. For in the same way you judge others, you will be judged, and with the measure you use, it will be measured to you."
— Matthew 7:1–2

Do you like to judge other people? Do you like it when other people judge you? How often are you judging others and don't even realize it? What can you do about either of these cases?

I would venture to say that none of us like it when we are judged negatively by others. Yet we judge others negatively and think nothing of it. "They deserve it," we say. Do we deserve it? Especially, when we are judging others?

We are called to lift others up, not tear them down. We are not the judge of others and warned very sternly against doing it. There are consequences to judging others. Very bad ones. Too often we don't know the whole story and judge based on glimpses.

I pray we all stop judging and instead start lifting up. I pray we all look at others as Jesus does. Lift each other up. Lift all people up. Make a positive difference in this world. Do as Jesus would do.

November 18

May the God of hope fill you with all joy and peace as
you trust in him, so that you may overflow with hope
by the power of the Holy Spirit.

— Romans 15:13

Do you trust God? No, I mean really trust Him. Are you willing to
step out and do something He has called you to do, even when you
can't see a way for it to work out? Are your willing to trust Him with
all your fears? Are you willing to trust Him with all your worries?

We all know this world has its fill of dangers. We know this world
would have us worry about being prettier, more popular, being with
the "in crowd." We are inundated with reasons to worry, fear, and fret
over this world.

Yet God has asked us to trust Him. We are to hold onto our faith
in Him and His plan. We are to step out, regardless of fear, and do
what He has called us to do. All we need to do is trust in Him. Sounds
simple. Yet it is hard for many of us to do.

I pray we all trust God with all our heart. I pray we listen to His
call, to His still, small voice. Listen and trust God.

November 19

In the beginning was the Word, and the Word
was with God, and the Word was God...The Word
became flesh and made his dwelling among us. We
have seen his glory, the glory of the one and only Son,
who came from the Father, full of grace and truth.
　　　　　　　　　　　　　　　　— John 1:1, 14

Do you ever think about the fact that Jesus was there at the beginning?
Do you realize that all things were created through Him? Do you stop
to ponder Him being both your Creator and Savior? Do you fully
grasp this?

We hear the lessons and teachings of Jesus being our Savior and
that He is. We hear how God created the world, all the animals, and
humans in the beginning and He did. Yet we don't often think about
Jesus being the one through Whom *all* was created.

When we look at the opening of the book of John and truly see
what He is saying, we see that all things were created through Him.
We see that not only is Jesus our Savior, He is also our Creator. Yes,
there is the Father, the Son, and the Holy Spirit. Yes, they are all
one God.

I pray we all spend more time in our Bibles, reading and
understanding just how wonderful God is and His Word. I pray we
come to understand more so that we won't be fooled by false teachings.
Spend time in God's Word.

November 20

And so we know and rely on the love God has for us.
God is love. Whoever lives in love lives in God, and
God in them.

—1 John 4:16

Who do you rely on? Do you rely only on yourself? Do you rely on family or friends? Do you rely on those you work with? Perhaps you don't rely on anyone, including yourself. Do you want to have someone you can rely on?

There's no doubt living in this world can be tough. We all have our share of hard times. We all go through rough spells when it seems nothing will ever go right again. It is in these times we need someone we can lean on.

God is always there for us. We are told that Jesus sent His Spirit to live within us. We are told in several Scriptures that God will never leave us. We are to trust that God is always there and that He will help us get through those tough situations.

I pray we all decide to lean on God, to trust Him in all situations. Know that He is with you.

November 21

Jesus performed many other signs in the presence
of his disciples, which are not recorded in this book.
But these are written that you may believe that Jesus
is the Messiah, the Son of God, and that by believing
you may have life in his name.

— John 20:30–31

Do you believe? What do you believe? Do you believe in material
things? Do you believe in people you know? Do you believe that Jesus
is the Son of God, the Messiah, Lord and Savior?

Many people in this world will say they believe in God. They will
say they are "spiritual." Yet their actions show they believe more in
their work, their friends, their family, their things than they do God.

We are to believe in Jesus. We are to believe that He is the Son of
God. We are to believe that He is the Messiah. As His followers, we
are to act as He expects us and according to our belief that He is our
Lord and Savior.

I pray we all believe Jesus is our Lord. I pray our actions show our
belief. Believe in Jesus. Follow Him. Show Him to others. Experience
life in Him.

November 22

Now you are the body of Christ, and each one of you
is a part of it.

—1 Corinthians 12:27

Are you a part of the body? The body of Christ? Or are you apart from the body? Do you make it a point each day to realize you are a part of the body of Christ? Will you begin today?

This world will tempt us to join many organizations and some of them are very good. Those organizations will often try to sell themselves as a body or brotherhood. Yet there is only one body that can provide us with eternal life and joy in this life.

The body of Christ is the one body to provide us life. Sure, there are wounded pieces of the body, just as each of us may wound a part of our bodies. Yet each wound will heal in Jesus' hands. We are to be those hands and arms to help heal those wounds.

I pray each us will consciously be part of Christ's body today. I pray we will make that commitment each day. Be a part of the body. Ask Jesus to show you the way.

November 23

There are different kinds of gifts, but the same Spirit distributes them. There are different kinds of service, but the same Lord. There are different kinds of working, but in all of them and in everyone it is the same God at work.

—1 Corinthians 12:4–6

Do you feel it? Do you feel God working in your life? Do you see Him working in the lives of the people around you? No? Are you not looking? Yes? Good for you!

The world will tell us there are coincidences in our lives. It will tell us the good things are a result of our hard work and the bad things are a result of our choices. To some degree that is true.

As Christians, we know God is at work in our lives. When we open our eyes, we see His providence, we see His handiwork. When we pray in all earnestness, we see God answer our prayers even if not the way we would prefer.

I pray we all see God moving in our lives and those around us. I pray we all open our eyes to see His handiwork. See with new eyes. See through Jesus' eyes. See God working.

November 24

Jesus replied: "'Love the Lord your God with all your heart and with all your soul and with all your mind.' This is the first and greatest commandment. And the second is like it: 'Love your neighbor as yourself.' All the Law and the Prophets hang on these two commandments."

— Matthew 22:37–40

Are you on fire? Are you on fire for Jesus? Does He have your whole heart? Or are you on fire for something or someone else? Have you fallen for Satan's temptations...again?

We all give in to temptations sometimes. Does that make it right? No. Yet we are not to willingly go out and sin, just because we know God will forgive us. The world will bamboozle us into cheating, lying, stealing, and despair.

We have a Savior in Jesus Christ who will rescue us, if we will turn our hearts over to Him. It's hard to believe. Yet it is true. Jesus will pull us out of the muck and mire of this life. All we need to do is turn our hearts over to Him.

I pray we all turn our hearts over to Jesus. From personal experience, I know He can heal us and lift us up. Trust Him. Give Him your heart. All of it.

November 25

But when the kindness and love of God our Savior
appeared, he saved us, not because of righteous things
we had done, but because of his mercy. He saved us
through the washing of rebirth and renewal by the
Holy Spirit, whom he poured out on us generously
through Jesus Christ our Savior, so that, having been
justified by his grace, we might become heirs having
the hope of eternal life.

— Titus 3:4–7

Do you realize that God loves you and is always with you? Do you
grasp the fact that God's Holy Spirit is living within you? Do you
realize that means He is always there, always available, always ready
to help you?

There are times in this world that we feel all alone. There are
times when we wonder where God is. Satan likes to pounce on those
opportunities to pull us away from God. Our small doubts become
huge fears.

Don't give into Satan, instead trust in God. Know that God is
always there. If needed, repeat it over and over and over until we
believe it. It's not always easy, but it does get easier the more often we
do it. God won't leave us alone.

I pray we all come to realize that God loves us so much that He
will never leave us. I pray we all learn to trust Him. Know His love.
Turn to Him always. He is always there.

November 26

"Therefore I tell you, whatever you ask for in prayer,
believe that you have received it, and it will be yours."
— Mark 11:24

Where do you go? Where do you go for refuge? Where do you go to seek safety? Where do you go for healing? Where do you go to find acceptance and grace? Do you know where you can get all of this?

We often find ourselves troubled or in trouble, hurting, or fearful. We may be in pain; emotional, physical, or spiritual. We may be worried about ourselves or others. We find ourselves in all types of difficult situations.

There is a place where we can find the peace, grace, strength, and courage to keep going. A place where we can experience joy. We must submit to Jesus, pray in His holy name, and truly believe He will deliver us.

I pray we all decide to trust Jesus and pray for His grace. We all need it. It's a matter of recognizing our need and trusting Him to provide. Submit to Jesus. Trust Him. Pray for your needs.

Marty Pressey

November 27

In him was life, and that life was the light of all mankind. The light shines in the darkness, and the darkness has not overcome it.

— John 1:4–5

Are you a beacon for others to follow? Are you a light for others to see? Do you light the way so others will follow the right path? Are you allowing Jesus to shine through you? The light chases the darkness away.

We can see more darkness in this world than we care to see. Darkness in people's lives. Darkness in entertainment. Darkness in actions taken against others. Darkness just about everywhere we look.

Yet we are called to be a light by the Light of the World, Jesus. When we allow Him to fill us, we can do nothing but shine. His light will not just wipe away our darkness but can wipe out the darkness in this world.

I pray we all decide to be filled by Jesus and be the light to those around us. It's not just a positive attitude, but an attitude of Jesus. Be filled. Shine for others.

November 28

Because of the service by which you have proved yourselves, others will praise God for the obedience that accompanies your confession of the gospel of Christ, and for your generosity in sharing with them and with everyone else.

—2 Corinthians 9:13

Where are you leading those who follow you? Are you willing to lead them to God? Are you willing to share your faith in Jesus with others? Do you realize that you only have one life to be the shining example to others?

We often feel as though no one is paying attention to us. We may believe we are not a leader at all. The world puts so many options out there for us to follow and we may fall into that trap. We call them idols or stars or celebrities.

We are called to be a leader. Sometimes it's in very small ways. It can be as simple as being nice, smiling, or providing a hug. Of course, it can also be taking on larger tasks and leading a group on a mission. Despite how we may feel, none of us go unnoticed.

I pray we all lead in the small or large ways that God has put in front of us. I pray we follow Him and lead others to Him. Ask God for guidance. Follow His lead. Lead others to Jesus.

Marty Pressey

November 29

Then I heard what sounded like a great multitude,
like the roar of rushing waters and like loud peals of
thunder, shouting:
  "Hallelujah! For our Lord God Almighty reigns.
Let us rejoice and be glad and give him glory! For the
wedding of the Lamb has come, and his bride has
made herself ready. Fine linen, bright and clean, was
given her to wear."

— Revelation 19:6–8

Do you sing praises to God? Do you lift Him up in your thoughts, in your prayers, in your conversations? Is He an important part of your life? Or do you not realize He is? Are you willing to worship Him?

This world will try to make anything it can market be the most important thing in our life. So much so that even something as simple as hand soap will be touted as needing to be prominent in our lives. All this is done to drown out the One who should be most important.

We too often forget that all we have is given to us by God. We think we've earned it. We think we deserve it. We forget that the very talent we have to earn a living comes from God. He provides it all. Shouldn't we give Him praise for providing all that we need?

I pray we all praise God and give Him the thanks and glory He deserves for providing everything we have. Most important, He has provided eternal life. Recognize what He has done for you. Praise Him. Give Him the glory.

November 30

This is how we know who the children of God are
and who the children of the devil are: Anyone who
does not do what is right is not God's child, nor is
anyone who does not love their brother and sister.

—1 John 3:10

Do you know you are a child of God? Do you know what is expected of a child of God? Are you willing to be a child of God? Will you make the choice to do what is right, to follow Jesus?

We are too often led astray by the trappings of this world. We see others doing something and think we would like to as well. We see what others have and we want it, too. Our fleshly body has its own desires.

Yet we are called to be children of God, to do what is right in God's eyes, not our own. God has a much better plan for His children than we can comprehend. It's much like a parent in this world who desires better for their own children. Too often, the child doesn't understand.

I pray we all trust in God's plan and do what is right in His eyes. I pray we all turn our lives over to Him and His plan. God knows what's best for each of us. Trust Him. Follow Jesus. Do what is right.

December

December 1

Jesus answered, "Everyone who drinks this water
will be thirsty again, but whoever drinks the water I
give them will never thirst. Indeed, the water I give
them will become in them a spring of water welling
up to eternal life."

— John 4:13–14

Do you know that you were made for eternity? Do you know you were
made to walk with God? Do you understand that God has invited you
to be with Him forever? Are you willing to step out in faith?

We know the story of Adam and Eve. We know they were created
to be eternal, to walk with God in the garden, to talk with Him face-
to-face. Yet they succumbed to Satan's temptation to eat the forbidden
fruit. Death followed.

Now, we all will die one day, unless Christ returns first. However,
the invitation to walk with God forever is still there. We only need
to accept Jesus Christ as our Lord and Savior. Of course, part of that
acceptance is also doing as He has told us.

I pray we all decide to accept Jesus as Lord and Savior. I pray we
all worship Him and submit to His calling. Drink the living waters.
Live life abundantly.

December 2

And I pray that you, being rooted and established in love, may have power, together with all the Lord's holy people, to grasp how wide and long and high and deep is the love of Christ, and to know this love that surpasses knowledge—that you may be filled to the measure of all the fullness of God.

— Ephesians 3:17–19

Are you willing to be empty? Will you empty yourself of your selfishness? Will you become empty of yourself so you can be filled with God's Holy Spirit? Are you willing to be changed into the person God desires?

We see people constantly trying to change themselves. Perhaps it's through weight loss or gain, hair styles, professional study, or any number of other ways. We also see those people fail more times than they succeed.

When we are willing to empty ourselves of ourselves and allow God to fill us, we change, and it endures. It can be scary giving up our self, but it is so rewarding. We must be willing to see our selfishness and ask God to fill us with His unselfishness.

I pray we all empty ourselves and allow God to fill us with His Holy Spirit. I pray we all experience the wonder of becoming a new person. Empty yourself. Be filled by God.

Marty Pressey

December 3

And you also were included in Christ when you heard the message of truth, the gospel of your salvation. When you believed, you were marked in him with a seal, the promised Holy Spirit, who is a deposit guaranteeing our inheritance until the redemption of those who are God's possession—to the praise of his glory.

— Ephesians 1:13–14

Do you praise Jesus' name? Do you really praise Him, or do you simply give a nod and praise earthly things instead? Will you make a conscious decision to praise Him every day until it becomes automatic and simply who you are?

We praise people for their accomplishments. We believe that some of them are truly amazing. We look at what they do and are astonished that a person could do that. We put human accomplishments in front of God.

We are to praise God and His Son Jesus. When we think about what He accomplished, shouldn't we be amazed, thankful, and humbled? He has saved us from eternal punishment. He has granted us eternity with Him, including today!

I pray we all make the decision to praise Jesus' name and what He has done for us. He has accomplished something far greater than any human could ever comprehend. Praise Jesus. Praise God. Give Him the glory.

December 4

Therefore, since we are surrounded by such a great cloud of witnesses, let us throw off everything that hinders and the sin that so easily entangles. And let us run with perseverance the race marked out for us, fixing our eyes on Jesus, the pioneer and perfecter of faith. For the joy set before him he endured the cross, scorning its shame, and sat down at the right hand of the throne of God.

— Hebrews 12:1–2

Who is your hero? Is your hero someone you really know or someone you have only seen on occasion and whom you have put on a pedestal? Who should your hero be? Do you know?

We have hero's in our lives. Sometimes our heroes are our Mom's or Dad's. Sometimes they are movie or TV stars. Sometimes they are sports stars. We may even have people we work with or other relatives that are our heroes.

We should make Jesus our true hero. He is the only truly perfect person to walk this earth. All the rest of us have our faults and failures. Jesus is who we should worship, put on a pedestal and continually look up to.

I pray we all make Jesus our hero. I pray we all strive to be more like Him every day. I pray we make our world around us better because we put Jesus first. Keep your eyes on Jesus. Focus on His example.

December 5

Every day they continued to meet together in the
temple courts. They broke bread in their homes and
ate together with glad and sincere hearts, praising
God and enjoying the favor of all the people. And
the Lord added to their number daily those who were
being saved.

— Acts 2:46–47

Are you a lone ranger Christian? Do you think you can do it by
yourself? Do you think you don't need anyone else to help you? Are
you foolish enough to try?

This world blasts us with so many mixed signals, we will
continually be mixed up if we listen to them. "You're strong and don't
need anyone." "You deserve whatever it is you want." "You're sick and
need help." "You need to work for your goals."

On the other hand, God is consistent. One of the necessities is
to meet with other Christians. Some will say they don't like religion.
That's okay. Not every church is the same. Churches are made up of
people. Therefore, each church has its own personality. Find one that
fits you.

I pray we all determine to meet with other Christians regularly.
Each of us needs it. I know personally how meeting with others can
pull you through tough times.

December 6

Therefore God exalted him to the highest place
and gave him the name that is above every name,
that at the name of Jesus every knee should bow,
in heaven and on earth and under the earth,
and every tongue acknowledge that Jesus Christ is
Lord,
to the glory of God the Father.

— Philippians 2:9–11

Are you humble? Have you humbled yourself before others? Before God? Have you submitted to His will for your life? If you haven't, will you do so today? Even if only for one day? Are you willing to accept what's best for you?

We are stubborn people much of the time. We want our way and we don't care what it cost. It may cost us our relationship with our family. It may cost us a friendship. It may cost us our very lives. We don't care, even if we don't admit it.

God has a much better plan for us. If we will set aside our desires and seek His, our lives flourish. When we submit to Him, we soar to new heights. No, this does not mean we get rich. It does mean our mental, emotional, and spiritual health improves beyond our wildest dreams.

I pray we decide to pursue God's will for our lives. I pray we all submit to Him. Live a better life. Live your best life. Be God's. Humble yourself before Him.

Marty Pressey

December 7

"Come to me, all you who are weary and burdened, and I will give you rest. Take my yoke upon you and learn from me, for I am gentle and humble in heart, and you will find rest for your souls. For my yoke is easy and my burden is light."

— Matthew 11:28–30

Are you running to Jesus? Are you laying down your worries, concerns, frustrations, and your joys at His feet? Do you seek Him every day? Will you submit to Him and His will for your life?

Too often we try to handle everything on our own in our human way. We don't seek wise guidance. We struggle our way through the situation in anguish, frustration, and bull headedness.

Jesus has told us to hand it over to Him and take on His load. He will carry our load for us. When we trust in Him, turn our entire lives over to Him, He is trustworthy and will give us the rest we desire.

I pray we all run to Jesus on a daily basis. I pray we lay our lives at His feet. I pray we put our full trust in Him. Believe Jesus. Give Him your load. Take your rest in Him.

December 8

"The virgin will conceive and give birth to a son, and they will call him Immanuel" (which means "God with us").

— Matthew 1:23

Do you know that God is with you? No, do you really know?! Or do you acknowledge it intellectually, but not with your heart, with your whole being? Are you afraid He is with you?

We often wonder through our lives from day-to-day in a fog. Sometimes we don't know where we're at or where we're going. Perhaps we aren't sure what we are doing. Maybe we simply get to a point of not caring.

In times like these, we need to remember that God is with us. He is always there, no matter what the situation, no matter what our mindset is. God is continually taking care of us, even when we think He isn't.

I pray we all remember that God is always there. I pray each of us will trust in Him our deepest desires and our worst fears. Know that God is with you. Trust in Him.

Marty Pressey

December 9

Do you not know that your bodies are temples of the Holy Spirit, who is in you, whom you have received from God? You are not your own; you were bought at a price. Therefore honor God with your bodies.
—1 Corinthians 6:19–20

Are you taking care of God's temple? Do you know where God's temple is? Do you think it is a building across town? Do you think it has a steeple and rows of pews? Do you not know that your body is God's temple?

We hear of all types of weight loss and exercise programs in this world today. We see in the media what is being proposed as healthy and beautiful. Yet the world is wrong as it so often is.

Our bodies are the Holy Temple of God. He lives in us in the form of His Holy Spirit. We are to take care of God's temple. Does that mean we need to be fitness fanatics? No! It does mean we should eat healthy and take care of our bodies. If we don't, how can we expect to do God's work?

I pray we each decide to be physically healthier. The earlier in life we do this, the better off we will be when we get older, and the better we are prepared to do God's work. Eat right. Exercise. Take care of God's Holy Temple.

December 10

So then, those who suffer according to God's will
should commit themselves to their faithful Creator
and continue to do good.

—1 Peter 4:19

Is today the day? Will you commit yourself to Jesus today? Are you willing to follow Him in everything you do? Will you allow Him to rule every aspect of your life? Do you really, really desire to live a better life? Or do you only want to do so if you don't have to change?

We see all types of transformation books and processes out there. They provide us with steps and checklists and a wide variety of thoughts. Do this and our lives will change. Do that and we will prosper.

There is only one true way to change and make it stick...commit ourselves to Jesus. Oh, it's not easy. Yes, it takes work on our part. We must commit ourselves to following Jesus' teachings and actions every single day. Why? Satan is working every day to keep us from Jesus.

I pray each of us commit ourselves today to Jesus. I pray it shows in our words, actions, thoughts, prayers, work, school, and every aspect of our lives. Commit to the true Healer. Commit to the true Therapist. Commit to the true Guide. Commit to the true Savior.

December 11

I sought the LORD, and he answered me;
he delivered me from all my fears.

— Psalm 34:4

Do you have hidden fears? Are they buried deep? Will they forever go unspoken? Are you willing to give them up? Will you turn them over to the only One who can take them away?

We all have at least one fear we just can't give up. Some of our fears we will grow out of as we grow into adults. Other fears hang on well into our adult lives. We may even have a fear or a few that we will keep until we die.

There is a way for us to relieve ourselves of our fears. We can turn them over to God and ask Him to remove them. Sure, we need to believe He can. We also need to be willing to give them up. It may take time for us to get to that point. But when we do, God will take our fear away.

I pray we all decide to give up our fears. I pray we all turn them over to God. Go through the process. Trust God. Let go of your fears.

December 12

You, however, are not in the realm of the flesh but are in the realm of the Spirit, if indeed the Spirit of God lives in you.

— Romans 8:9

Are you living by the Spirit? Or are you living in the flesh? Will you allow the Spirit to lead your life? Or do you only want what you want? Will you commit to a better life? Or will you continue in a life filled with doubt?

We see people every day, often friends and family members, who pursue only their wants. Sometimes they don't even know what they want beyond today. We also do this and often don't even realize we are.

There is a better life waiting for us. If we will allow God's Spirit to guide us, we can live the best life. Rather than allowing ourselves to be upset because something didn't go our way, we should be looking for the Spirit to lead us to something better.

I pray we all decide to allow the Spirit to lead us. I pray each of us will live by the Spirit each day. Submit yourselves to Him and be lifted up. Feel His joy. Live the life He has planned for you.

December 13

It is for freedom that Christ has set us free. Stand firm, then, and do not let yourselves be burdened again by a yoke of slavery.

— Galatians 5:1

How are you doing at living free? Are you living free of slavery to the modern world? Have you broken the chains of earthly desires? Or are you like so many in this world who long for more, more, more?

Too often we are slaves and we don't even realize it. We are slaves to TV shows. We are slaves to fashion. We are slaves to our sports teams. We are slaves to our jobs. We are slaves to whatever we can think of.

Yet we are called to be free and to be slaves to God. Isn't it interesting that being a slave to God sets us free? Jesus came to set us free from sin, including the sin of worshiping idols of this world that we make more important in our lives than God.

I pray we all choose to be free. I pray we all decide to be a slave to God only. Enjoy the freedom Jesus came to give you. Trust Him. Follow Him. Accept freedom.

December 14

Preach the word; be prepared in season and out of season; correct, rebuke and encourage—with great patience and careful instruction. For the time will come when people will not put up with sound doctrine. Instead, to suit their own desires, they will gather around them a great number of teachers to say what their itching ears want to hear.

—2 Timothy 4:2–3

Are you prepared? Are you helping to prepare others? Are you ready for Jesus to come again? Are you sure? Does your life show it? Does your life speak of Christ? Do you tell others of the joy you have in Christ?

During this season of Advent, we participate in the waiting for Jesus. During the very early first century and for centuries before that, the Jews anxiously awaited the Messiah. They also worshiped God in preparation for His deliverance.

We, too, wait for Jesus. We celebrate His original coming into this world, but also wait for His return. We often forget that He gave us a command to spread the news about Him. We are to share His wonderful saving grace with others. Yet we often don't associate preparing with waiting.

I pray we all realize we have a responsibility to prepare for Christ's coming again while we wait. Waiting does not mean inaction. It means we still have time to bring others to know Jesus. Prepare the way for Him.

December 15

The whole earth is filled with awe at your wonders;
where morning dawns, where evening fades,
you call forth songs of joy.

— Psalm 65:8

Are you in awe of God? Do you sometimes stand in complete wonder at His creation? Have you taken time from your busy day to notice, to appreciate it? Have you marveled at how complex you, His creation, are?

This world will rob us of our wonder, if we let it. There are people who will attempt to explain everything, rather than simply be in awe at what God created. Science continues to try to explain, yet only further points to a wondrous Creator.

God has wonderfully created us, the earth we live on, and the stars we see in the sky. He continues to create in ways that we don't understand. Our God is awesome!

I pray we all take time each day to appreciate what God has created. See the wonder in it all. See His awesome power. Thank God for creating you! Be in awe.

December 16

LORD my God, I called to you for help,
and you healed me.

— Psalm 30:2

How many walls have you built? How many hurts do you harbor? Do you still maintain a list of all your failures? Do you let these hold you back from living a good life? Are you ready to let them go?

We are often hurt, then build a wall so we can't be hurt that way again. Too often we hold onto those hurts and allow them to become our prison. We know all our failures and let them stop us from trying again.

Jesus has called us to lay them *all* at His feet. We are to set down our burdens, meaning our pains and failures. When we are finally willing to give them up, we can be healed, we can be set free.

I pray we all let go of past hurts and failures. God will heal each one of us. Trust Him to set you free. Allow God to be the great Healer you need.

Marty Pressey

December 17

Don't be deceived, my dear brothers and sisters. Every good and perfect gift is from above, coming down from the Father of the heavenly lights, who does not change like shifting shadows.

—James 1:16–17

What gift has given you the most joy? What have you received that you most appreciated? Do you still have that gift? Do you still relish it? Why did you appreciate it so much?

Many of us will immediately think of a gift we received at Christmas or a birthday. A bicycle or dress or board game or computer may come to mind. It may have been from a parent or other family member. We may be amazed years later, wondering how that person was able to afford that gift.

But do we truly appreciate the gift God gave us? Or has it become blasé for us? Mundane? Easily forgotten? The gift we received from God should amaze us every day. We should be so appreciative of it that we don't want it to be wasted. It should bring us so much joy that we must allow it to reflect in our lives so that we share it.

I pray we all greatly appreciate God's gift and allow it to take over our lives. I pray we share our joy with everyone we meet. Recognize God's gift. Share His gift with others.

December 18

Then he got into the boat and his disciples followed him. Suddenly a furious storm came up on the lake, so that the waves swept over the boat. But Jesus was sleeping. The disciples went and woke him, saying, "Lord, save us! We're going to drown!"

He replied, "You of little faith, why are you so afraid?" Then he got up and rebuked the winds and the waves, and it was completely calm.

— Matthew 8:23–26

Are you overcome by fear? Have you allowed earthly situations to overwhelm you? Is it the unknown that causes you to be afraid? Is it because you realize you are not in control?

We often become fearful in situations where we don't know what the outcome will be. We fret over it. Sometimes we worry ourselves to the point of being sick. We allow fear to ruin our lives.

Yet we don't have to live this way. Jesus has overcome this world. He can quiet our storms. He can relieve us of our fears. The easiest and yet hardest thing we need to do is trust in Him, our Savior.

I pray each of us will decide to trust in Jesus. I pray we each turn over our fears to Him. Lay your fear at Jesus feet. Trust He will take it away. Live a life of freedom.

December 19

But Christ is faithful as the Son over God's house.
And we are his house, if indeed we hold firmly to our
confidence and the hope in which we glory.

— Hebrews 3:6

Do you struggle to keep it together at times? Does it seem as though things are falling apart all around you and there is nothing you can do about it? Do you feel like just giving up? Are you ready to trust the One who can make it all better?

This world can close in on us from multiple angles all at once. We may feel as though everything, and everyone is against us. We may even feel as though there is no way out and we will be crushed by the weight of it all.

There is One who will be with us through it all. There is One who will lift us up from the depths. Jesus is with us at all times, in all situations. We often need to be reminded that He is always there. Hold on to that truth.

I pray we each will remember that Jesus is with us. Remember it in tough times and in good times. Hold on to Him. Trust in Him. You belong to Him.

December 20

On coming to the house, they saw the child with his mother Mary, and they bowed down and worshiped him. Then they opened their treasures and presented him with gifts of gold, frankincense and myrrh. And having been warned in a dream not to go back to Herod, they returned to their country by another route.

— Matthew 2:11–12

Are your gifts appropriate? Or are they superficial? Do they fit you physically, emotionally, and spiritually? Or are they more worldly and soon to fade into a distant memory? We all have one gift that fits us perfectly.

The world looks for presents that fills its wants, the latest fashion, the coolest gadget, and on and on. If worldly people don't get what they want, Christmas is a failure. Such is life in the wealthiest country in the world.

When we accept Jesus as our perfect gift, all other gifts pale in comparison. God works through everyone, not just those who have accepted Him. God worked through the wise men to give the perfect gifts. Gold is fit for a King. Frankincense is fit for a High Priest. Myrrh is to prepare a body for burial in the Jewish custom. Christ is the King of kings, our High Priest, and our Savior who died, was buried, and overcame death.

I pray we all realize that God has already given us the greatest gift but cherish the other gifts we receive as well. God's timing is perfect, and His gift is perfect. Feel blessed today.

Marty Pressey

December 21

Out of his fullness we have all received grace in place
of grace already given. For the law was given through
Moses; grace and truth came through Jesus Christ.
— John 1:16–17

Have you received the grace of Jesus Christ? Do you appreciate the
cost of the grace He is giving you? Jesus was already God, Creator of
all things, and reigned in heaven. He gave it all up for us when He came
into the world through a lowly birth.

The world celebrates Christmas with bright lights, lots of
decorations, an overabundance of spending on gifts, and misses the
point completely. If the person of the world doesn't get the right gift,
they throw childish temper tantrums or determine not to speak to
that person for some period of time or just decide to be in a bad mood
all day.

Jesus came to set us free from the world's behavior. He came to free
us from the selfishness of the world. He came to have a relationship
with us. He came to be our Savior and show us grace that we could
never earn and don't deserve. Our response should be to accept it,
show respect, show appreciation, show His grace to others, love the
way Jesus loves, and be joyful in the perfect gift.

I pray we all accept the wonderful grace freely given to us. Let us
all be gracious and loving throughout our Christmas celebrations.
Let us all remember Jesus and spend a few moments of quiet time
with Him.

December 22

"But God has helped me to this very day; so I stand here and testify to small and great alike. I am saying nothing beyond what the prophets and Moses said would happen—that the Messiah would suffer and, as the first to rise from the dead, would bring the message of light to his own people and to the Gentiles."

— Acts 26:22–23

Where do you rank yourself among others? Is it all about you? Are you always the first thought in your own mind? Do you ever put someone else ahead of you? Do you put yourself ahead of Jesus?

We are inundated each day by the media and commercials that tell us we should put ourselves first. Sure, we need to take care of ourselves. Yet we are being blasted with a message that goes far beyond that...and we don't even realize it.

Jesus taught us over and over again to put others ahead of ourselves. He was our perfect example of how to do that. So, if we are not putting others ahead of ourselves, we are putting ourselves ahead of Jesus.

I pray we all make Jesus our first choice and by doing so put others ahead of us. I pray we all come to realize the power of being second to Jesus. Trust Him. Follow Him.

Marty Pressey

December 23

Who is it that overcomes the world? Only the one
who believes that Jesus is the Son of God.

—1 John 5:5

What will you overcome today? What difficulty stands in front of
you? What fears are you facing? Is there a challenge that you need
to take on? What have you been putting off and need to simply get it
over with?

We all face many challenges in our lives. Sometimes there are
several in a single day. At other times all is going well. Yet it seems
there is always something nagging us in the back of our minds.

Through our faith we can overcome whatever it is in front of us.
Knowing that God is there with us, giving us the strength and courage
to not just get through but to truly succeed is our encouragement.

I pray we all overcome through faith. I pray we all pull from God's
strength. Go overcome. Live in faith. Know in your heart that God is
with you. Trust in Him.

December 24

"'If you can'?" said Jesus. "Everything is possible for one who believes."

Immediately the boy's father exclaimed, "I do believe; help me overcome my unbelief!"

— Mark 9:23–24

Are you lost on your journey today? Do you feel as though you are just wondering through life? Are you looking for something, but don't know what it is? Are you willing to listen to guidance from others?

We all have times of searching in our lives. Those times are longer for some us than for others. We inherently know something is missing, yet we can't quite put our finger on it. It even happens to those of us who believe in Jesus.

To more easily overcome those times of searching, we must increase our belief. Unfortunately, we can't do that on our own. We need to ask for help. We need to reach out to the perfecter of our faith.

I pray we all seek Jesus and ask Him to increase our belief in Him. Ask Him to increase your faith. Reach out to Jesus. Ask Him for your daily needs. He is faithful. Trust Him.

Marty Pressey

December 25

"In the same way, let your light shine before others,
that they may see your good deeds and glorify your
Father in heaven."

— Matthew 5:16

Is your light shining? Are you letting the light of God shine through
you today? Will you allow Him to shine in you and through you to
light up the world around you? Or will you keep it hidden, deep inside?

This world often encourages us to show our feelings, to let them
out. There are numerous TV shows for just that purpose. There are
doctors who make a living from giving that advice.

Yet we are not instructed by God to show our feelings, we are told
to let His light shine though us. When we allow Him to fill us with
His light and then share that, we are doing God's work. He wants the
world to see His glory in us.

I pray each of us allow God's light to shine through us. I pray
we each allow Him to fill us with His light. Be the light to those you
encounter today. Shine like a beacon on a hill.

December 26

"And even the very hairs of your head are all numbered."

— Matthew 10:30

How big is your world? How big is your God? Is He big enough to solve your problem? Is He big enough that you trust Him with everything? Or do you take it on yourself, not allowing God to handle it?

We often take on our troubles without God. We decide we have to fix it ourselves or it won't get fixed. Sometimes we simply think too highly of ourselves. Then we wonder why things don't work out well.

God is so big that He not only knows us, but He knows everything about us, down to the last piece of our DNA. Not only that, but He knows that about each and every animal and plant on this earth. After all, He created it all.

I pray each of us will realize that God knows all there is to know about us. I pray we trust Him in all that we do. God is far bigger than we give Him credit for. Trust Him. He never fails.

Marty Pressey

December 27

And we know that in all things God works for the
good of those who love him, who have been called
according to his purpose.

— Romans 8:28

Do you hear the call? Are you listening for it? Have you perhaps heard
it and are trying to ignore it? Maybe you just want to continue with
your life the way it is with no disruption. Will you heed the call now?

Our lives are so distracted by the multitude of things going on in
this world. Sure, some of them affect us, but the vast majority do not.
In fact, less than 1% of all that is going on just in our own hometowns
will affect us.

The distractions keep us from hearing Jesus calling out to us. He
has a plan for us, yet we go down different paths. No, not everyone
will be called to be a preacher, but everyone is called to something.
Perhaps you are simply to be the shining light in your workplace.

I pray we all heed the call of Jesus. I pray each of us will seek His
plan and follow it. Submit to Him. Follow His plan for your life. He
will not fail you.

December 28

Through Jesus, therefore, let us continually offer to
God a sacrifice of praise—the fruit of lips that openly
profess his name.

— Hebrews 13:15

How do you feel today? Are you well? Do you need healing? Do you
need physical healing? Emotional healing? Spiritual healing? How
will you react if your healing isn't full? What if it never comes at all?

We all seek to be whole. We typically look at that as being
physically whole. More recently, we have begun to look at it as being
emotionally or psychologically whole. Have we forgotten about being
spiritually whole?

When we are spiritually whole, we can still by joyous, even if we
are physically or emotionally lacking. When we rely on God for our
well-being, we live an abundant life. We are spiritual beings and our
spirit is the foundation of who we are. We strengthen our foundation
by praising God.

I pray we all take time to praise God and fill our spirit. God will
fill us to overflowing. He has no limits. Praise God for your many
blessings. Praise Him for your shortfalls. Praise Him in all situations.

December 29

When I said, "My foot is slipping,"
your unfailing love, LORD, supported me.
When anxiety was great within me,
your consolation brought me joy.

— Psalm 94:18-19

Do you realize you are being held? No, not held back or held up, but held in safety. Do you know that God puts His arms around you? Will you trust Him to guide your path? Do you understand that His hands hold on to yours?

Too many of us feel like we are on our own. We feel as though no one cares. We believe everyone is out to get us. We are deceived by Satan's lies. We run scared and don't even know where we are going.

God is always there for us. He is holding on to us, even if we don't realize it. Sure, He allows us to make decisions and get ourselves in trouble, but He's always there. When we trust God, we come to feel Him there with us.

I pray we all realize that God is always with us. I pray we all trust Him in all situations. Feel God in you and with you. Trust He is there. Ban Satan's lies from your mind.

December 30

But God demonstrates his own love for us in this:
While we were still sinners, Christ died for us.

— Romans 5:8

Do you know how much you are loved? Do you grasp how important you are to God? Do you appreciate and return His love for you? Will you remind yourself today that He loves you far more than you can fathom?

We all go through periods in our lives when we feel unloved or abandoned or discarded or unwanted. There are more reasons for us to feel that way than we can count. Yet we don't need to stay in that state for long.

When we feel unloved, we need to remind ourselves that God loves us. He blesses us in so many ways. He doesn't do it for His sake, but for ours. Jesus loves us and died for us. He rose again to give us the ultimate hope.

I pray all recognize and live in the love God has for us. I pray we all love God with our whole heart. He deserves it far more than any person on this earth. Love God. Live in His love.

December 31

But in your hearts revere Christ as Lord. Always be prepared to give an answer to everyone who asks you to give the reason for the hope that you have. But do this with gentleness and respect,

—1 Peter 3:15

Are you prepared? This is a question that is often asked as we approach a new year. The answer is often no, so we make resolutions to do better in the coming year. Unfortunately, many of those resolutions are frivolous or we don't really commit to them. They are only thoughts for the moment and last just a few days.

Our commitment to God, particularly to following Jesus and His teachings, is a commitment worth making and keeping. We are to be prepared to give an answer at a moment's notice. Prepared to state why we have joy and peace, even in times of trial or difficulty or sickness or sorrow. His joy and peace are available to us if we will seek Him.

Our preparation includes getting to know Jesus and His teachings. We can through reading and study. We also need to discuss our thoughts and understanding with others. We typically do this during Bible Study at our church, but we can also do this in our homes. You may even discuss it with your co-workers.

I pray we all decide to be prepared to give an answer for our joy and peace. It may have a significant impact on someone you never expected. Be prepared.

Epilogue

It is my sincere hope that as you have read each devotion throughout the year, you have found it helpful in your daily life. My prayer is that you have seen an improvement in your attitude, your dedication to God, your trust in Him, and your spiritual wellness. I pray you continue to read and study God's Word.

If you are willing, restart this devotional again on January 1 as you start a new year. Or find another devotional you can read throughout the year. Whatever you do, don't stop reading, learning, and growing closer to God. You need Him and He has a plan for you.

Thank you for reading this devotional and I wish you all the best in the coming year.

Printed in the United States
By Bookmasters